graphis posters 85

The International Annual of Poster Art
Das internationale Jahrbuch der Plakatkunst
Le répertoire international de l'art de l'affiche

Edited by: / Herausgegeben von: / Réalisé par:

Walter Herdeg

Graphis Press Corp., Zurich (Switzerland)

GRAPHIS PUBLICATIONS

GRAPHIS, International bi-monthly journal of graphic art and applied art
GRAPHIS ANNUAL, The international annual of advertising and editorial graphics
PHOTOGRAPHIS, The international annual of advertising and editorial photography
GRAPHIS PACKAGING VOL. 4, An international survey of package design
CHILDREN'S BOOK ILLUSTRATION VOL. 3, VOL. 4, An international survey of children's book illustration
GRAPHIS DIAGRAMS, The graphic visualization of abstract data
FILM + TV GRAPHICS 2, An international survey of the art of film animation
ARCHIGRAPHIA, Architectural and environmental graphics
GRAPHIS EPHEMERA, Artists' Self-Promotion

GRAPHIS-PUBLIKATIONEN

GRAPHIS, Die internationale Zweimonatsschrift für Graphik und angewandte Kunst
GRAPHIS ANNUAL, Das internationale Jahrbuch der Werbegraphik und der redaktionellen Graphik
PHOTOGRAPHIS, Das internationale Jahrbuch der Werbephotographie und der redaktionellen Photographie
GRAPHIS PACKUNGEN BAND 4, Internationales Handbuch der Packungsgestaltung
KINDERBUCH-ILLUSTRATION BAND 3, BAND 4, Eine internationale Übersicht über die Kinderbuch-Illustration
GRAPHIS DIAGRAMS, Die graphische Visualisierung abstrakter Gegebenheiten
FILM + TV GRAPHICS 2, Ein internationaler Überblick über die Kunst des Animationsfilms
ARCHIGRAPHIA, Architektur- und Umweltgraphik
GRAPHIS EPHEMERA, Künstler-Eigenwerbung

PUBLICATIONS GRAPHIS

GRAPHIS, La revue bimestrielle internationale d'arts graphiques et d'arts appliqués
GRAPHIS ANNUAL, Le répertoire international de l'art publicitaire et l'art illustratif
PHOTOGRAPHIS, Le répertoire international de la photographie publicitaire et rédactionnelle
GRAPHIS EMBALLAGES VOL. 4, Répertoire international des formes de l'emballage
ILLUSTRATIONS DE LIVRES D'ENFANTS VOL. 3, VOL. 4, Un aperçu international des illustrations de livres d'enfants
GRAPHIS DIAGRAMS, La visualisation graphique de données abstraites
FILM + TV GRAPHICS 2, Un panorama international de l'art du film d'animation
ARCHIGRAPHIA, La création graphique appliquée à l'architecture et à l'environnement
GRAPHIS EPHEMERA, Autopromotion des artistes

Distributors / Auslieferung / Distributeurs:

USA: WATSON-GUPTILL PUBLICATIONS, INC., 1515 Broadway, New York N.Y. 10036 **(ISBN: 0-8230-2135-1)**
CANADA: HURTIG PUBLISHERS, 10560–105 Street, Edmonton, Alberta, T5H 2W7, tel. (403) 426-2469
FRANCE: GRAPHIS DISTRIBUTION, Milon-la-Chapelle, F-78470 St-Rémy-lès-Chevreuse, tél. 052-13-26
ITALIA: INTER-ORBIS, Via Lorenteggio, 31/1, I-20146 Milano, tel. 42 25 7 46
SPAIN: COMERCIAL ATHENEUM, S.A., Consejo de Ciento, 130–136, Barcelona 15, tel. 2231451-3
AMERICA LATINA, AUSTRALIA, JAPAN AND OTHER ASIAN COUNTRIES, AFRICA:
FLEETBOOKS S.A., c/o Feffer & Simons, Inc., 100 Park Avenue, New York, N.Y. 10017, tel. (212) 686-0888

All other countries / Alle anderen Länder / Tout autres pays:

GRAPHIS PRESS CORP., 107 Dufourstrasse, CH-8008 Zurich (Switzerland)

PUBLICATION No. 178 (ISBN 3-85709-385-4)

Contents

Inhalt

Sommaire

Abbreviations	6	Abkürzungen	6	Abréviations	6
Introduction	8	Vorwort	10	Préface	12
Index to Artists	14	Verzeichnis der Künstler	14	Index des artistes	14
Index to Photographers	14	der Photographen	14	Index des photographes	14
Index to Designers	16	der Gestalter	16	Index des maquettistes	16
Index to Art Directors	18	der künstlerischen Leiter	18	Index directeurs artistiques	18
Index to Agencies	20	der Agenturen und Studios	20	Index des agences	20
Index to Advertisers	21	der Auftraggeber	21	Index des clients	21

Advertising Posters

Werbeplakate

Affiches publicitaires

Direct Mail	54	Direktwerbung	54	Aliments	42
Fashion	26	Industrie	36	Industrie	36
Food	42	Lebensmittel	42	Mode	26
Industry	36	Mode	26	Publicité directe	54
Publishers' Publicity	58	Tourismus	74	Publicité d'éditeurs	58
Tourism	74	Verlagswerbung	58	Tourisme	74

Cultural Posters

Kulturelle Plakate

Affiches culturelles

Cultural Events	168	Ausstellungen	148	Evénements culturels	168
Exhibitions	148	Filme	132	Expositions	148
Films	132	Theater	100	Films	132
Theatre	100	Veranstaltungen	168	Théâtre	100

Social Posters

Soziale Plakate

Affiches sociales

Education	196	Ausbildung	196	Affiches éducatives	178
Educative Posters	178	Erzieherische Plakate	178	Affiches politiques	184
Political Posters	184	Politische Plakate	184	Affiches sociales	194
Social Posters	194	Soziale Plakate	194	Education	196

Decorative Posters

Dekorative Plakate

Affiches décoratives

| Decorative Posters | 198 | Dekorative Plakate | 198 | Affiches décoratives | 198 |

Abbreviations   Abkürzungen   Abréviations

Australia	AUS	Australien	AUS	Afrique du Sud	SAF
Austria	AUT	Belgien	BEL	Allemagne (Est)	GDR
Belgium	BEL	Brasilien	BRA	Allemagne (Ouest)	GER
Brazil	BRA	Bulgarien	BUL	Australie	AUS
Bulgaria	BUL	Dänemark	DEN	Autriche	AUT
Canada	CAN	Deutschland (Ost)	GDR	Belgique	BEL
Czechoslovakia	CSR	Deutschland (West)	GER	Brésil	BRA
Denmark	DEN	Finnland	FIN	Bulgarie	BUL
Finland	FIN	Frankreich	FRA	Canada	CAN
France	FRA	Grossbritannien	GBR	Danemark	DEN
Germany (East)	GDR	Hongkong	HKG	Espagne	SPA
Germany (West)	GER	Israel	ISR	Etats-Unis	USA
Great Britain	GBR	Italien	ITA	Finlande	FIN
Hong Kong	HKG	Japan	JPN	France	FRA
Hungary	HUN	Jugoslawien	YUG	Grande-Bretagne	GBR
Israel	ISR	Kanada	CAN	Hongkong	HKG
Italy	ITA	Luxemburg	LUX	Hongrie	HUN
Japan	JPN	Mexiko	MEX	Israël	ISR
Luxemburg	LUX	Niederlande	NLD	Italie	ITA
Mexico	MEX	Norwegen	NOR	Japon	JPN
Netherlands	NLD	Österreich	AUT	Luxembourg	LUX
Norway	NOR	Polen	POL	Mexique	MEX
Poland	POL	Rumänien	RUM	Norvège	NOR
Rumania	RUM	Schweden	SWE	Pays-Bas	NLD
South Africa	SAF	Schweiz	SWI	Pologne	POL
Soviet Union	USR	Sowjetunion	USR	Roumanie	RUM
Spain	SPA	Spanien	SPA	Suède	SWE
Sweden	SWE	Südafrika	SAF	Suisse	SWI
Switzerland	SWI	Tschechoslowakei	CSR	Tchécoslovaquie	CSR
USA	USA	Ungarn	HUN	Union Soviétique	USR
Venezuela	VEN	USA	USA	Venezuela	VEN
Yugoslavia	YUG	Venezuela	VEN	Yougoslavie	YUG

Cover / Umschlag / Couverture: Shigeo Fukuda

Once again this year thousands of posters arrived for us from all parts of the world, and our sincere thanks go to the contributors. Only through their help was it possible to compile this collection of international poster creations. No matter what its purpose, the poster is a challenge for the designer and he must be fully aware of his responsibility towards every aspect of today's environment.

Auch dieses Jahr haben uns wieder Tausende von Plakaten aus aller Welt erreicht, und unser herzlicher Dank gilt allen Einsendern. Nur dank ihrer Hilfe war es möglich, diese Übersicht des internationalen Plakatschaffens zusammenzustellen. Gleich für welchen Zweck bestimmt, ist das Plakat eine Herausforderung an den Gestalter, der seine Arbeit als wirtschaftlichen, kulturellen und sozialen Beitrag an die Gesellschaft verstehen darf und sich dieser Verantwortung bewusst sein muss.

Cette année encore, des milliers d'affiches nous sont parvenues de tous les coins de la Terre. Nos remerciements sincères vont à tous ces artistes sans l'aide desquels ce panorama de l'affichisme international n'aurait pu voir le jour. Quel que soit le but qui lui est assigné, l'affiche est un véritable défi à la créativité de l'artiste appelé à livrer une contribution responsable à la vie sociale, culturelle et économique de son temps.

The distinctive handwriting of the designer of the dust jacket on this current edition of GRAPHIS POSTERS is unmistakable. Born in Tokyo in 1932, an art graduate of the Tokyo National University of Fine Arts and Music, SHIGEO FUKUDA ranks among the world's best and most renowned poster designers. His book, published in 1982, *Posters of Shigeo Fukuda*, lists more than three large-format, closely-printed pages of his awards and exhibitions—too numerous therefore to mention even the most important here.

Die eigenwillige Handschrift des Gestalters des Umschlags der diesjährigen Ausgabe von GRAPHIS POSTERS ist unverkennbar. SHIGEO FUKUDA gehört zu den besten und bekanntesten Plakatgestaltern der Welt. Er wurde 1932 in Tokio geboren; 1956 schloss er sein Kunststudium an der Tokyo National University of Fine Arts and Music ab. In seinem 1982 veröffentlichten Buch, *Posters of Shigeo Fukuda*, füllen die Angaben über Auszeichnungen und Ausstellungen mehr als drei grossformatige, dicht bedruckte Seiten. Es ist deshalb nicht möglich, hier auch nur die wichtigsten aufzuführen.

La couverture de cette édition de GRAPHIS POSTERS porte la marque extrêmement originale de SHIGEO FUKUDA, l'un des meilleurs affichistes du monde, dont la réputation n'est plus à faire. Né à Tōkyō en 1932, il termine ses études d'art à la Tokyo National University of Fine Arts and Music. Dans son livre de 1982, *Posters of Shigeo Fukuda*, les expositions qui lui ont été consacrées et les prix qu'il a remportés remplissent trois pages de texte serré au grand format. On comprendra que nous ne pouvons même pas en citer les plus importantes.

Eckhard Neumann

Preface

ECKHARD NEUMANN was born in 1933 in Königsberg, Prussia, and studied advertising and graphic design in Berlin and Ulm. Although he was at first active in advertising, he began to devote more and more of his time to design and art—in particular to the history and theory of graphic design in the 20th century and the Bauhaus reasoning. He has published a collection of memoirs of one-time Bauhaus teachers, pupils and their contemporaries, *Bauhaus and Bauhaus People* (New York 1970, Berne 1971), a history of new typography, *Functional Graphic Design in the 20s* (New York 1971) and numerous texts on his specialized subjects in the international media. In 1964 he founded the German *Jahrbuch der Werbung* (Annual of Advertising) and still acts as co-editor. He has held the chair of Design and Form Consultancy in Darmstadt since 1975. Eckhard Neumann lives in Frankfurt am Main.

Advertising does not have a good reputation. Worldwide it is regarded as irksome—an unalterable, inevitable evil to be endured rather than welcomed. One has become accustomed to the involuntary confrontation with it because one has to. The information potential of advertising and its economic function are held suspect and the general public sets no yardstick for the design of advertising if one disregards the internal surveys market-research analysts undertake prior to the large campaigns, which allegedly reflect the average citizen's ability to grasp the content and the aesthetics. The poster can also be considered within this context. Having been forced to relinquish its status as supreme advertising medium in the early days—firstly to the advertisement and later on to the TV commercials—the poster is often relegated to being only one section of a whole media package. Advertising concepts are normally not created *for* posters, they are adapted *to* posters. The motif of a colour-magazine advertisement is frequently blown up to the format of a large-size poster. Similarly it is customary practice today to take an old-master or a contemporary work of art and reduce it to the miniature size of a postage-stamp, without taking into consideration that each medium is subject to its own specific conditions of perception and experience.

The poster is in this way robbed of its characteristic effect. Thus seen can posters still be regarded as posters? Franz Mon once declared at a poster exhibition that posters are surfaces which should "leap to the eye". That was at the turn of the century. Today this dynamic impact is still apparent in certain spheres—for example, the posters created for small, highly-specialized groups, or those created for events of "superior" interest, such as art, music, theatre or other idealistic targets— to which, however, politics should not be counted.

In the present-day environment these types of poster attract relatively little attention. They become somewhat submerged under the multitude of optical signals because they are smaller than the dominating consumer-summoning surfaces, more concealed in their placement and their circulation is lower. And yet, for all this, they play a vital role in the forming of the visual environment. Posters are our design indicators, a guiding-light, so to speak. Culture posters (apart from their direct function of informing about certain events and of motivating patrons to the theatre, concert or exhibition) have their own public stage. It is the "entre nous" forum of the poster designers themselves. They establish and direct the style, they indicate the trends and concern themselves with the high demands in design quality and visual communication. Standards of quality in advertising are derived from this style-setting guiding-light source.

GRAPHIS POSTERS is undoubtedly one of these sources in the professional design world. As a compact overview of current poster-design trends it is ubiquitous; uniting poster designers, reciprocating their ideas and inspiring and challenging them to competitive accomplishments. There is, however, one snag to this. It is that ideals produce post-perceptions. They create stylistic effects which, in less amiable conditions could lead to loss of niveau and national identity. This increasing ambiguity, this blurred vision of the original and urbane design-repertoire could again be recognized at the (9th) 10th International Poster Biennale in Warsaw. The schools of Polish, Japanese, American and German poster art cross all boundaries because their characteristic design, their iconography and techniques are consciously or unconsciously adapted. At present the poster world is as colourful and varied as never before. All forms of visual representation and expression appear parallel even when seen on an international level. Illustrative, photographic, concrete, typographic, historic or computer-graphic design solutions manœuvre in vigorous competition. If one seeks the hub of all this, it is, according to the Poster Biennale, that even more illustrative pictorial work is being done at the present time. The use of photography follows this trend insofar that it has overcome the reality of purely factual representation and has developed a manipulated style conveyed by a psychologically-oriented symbolism. This applies especially to the theatre posters. Here the designer attempts to transpose the literary subject into a visual experience, into psychologically reconstructed signs—possibly as a counter-action to the technological revolution? Yet the visionary Lissitzky said sixty years ago that the individualistic element—the artist's "identity stroke" is of no great consequence in modern advertising. There is a reversion to former styles and this is not new. On one hand these are either quoted or simply used in historical fashion, on the other hand one can recognize beginnings in the new-wave movement based on the "new typography" forms and structures of the twenties; a search for modern ways to signalize the designer's responsibility to the environment.

Shaping the environment is no problem to be solved single-handedly and today's designer must not look on himself as an individualist expressing his own ideas—and nothing else. The applied-art ghetto must be perforated to make way for a new attitude in design where the responsibility for all, design competence and creative technique take priority. The advertising by international corporations has already paved the way with some outstanding examples of this attitude. Good visual design is an economic, social and cultural contribution to society. It provides information and communication between man and market, between man and the public and naturally between man and man. It must not be carried out thoughtlessly, but with commitment, conscience and complete professionalism.

If one looks at the recently-created posters presented in this book—posters for commercial advertising and posters for cultural events—and one regards them as polarities, then there remain only very few common elements. Really the only thing they have in common is that they are all printed on paper. Poster formats are even different and the poster circulation varies considerably, and with that the scope of communicative effect. Design is the pragmatic side of culture which encircles us daily. The visual imagery of our commonplace world is but a sum of signs which, with varied impact, influence and affect us. In this pluralistic sign-world the poster, immediately after architecture, is, as before, the most important signal, the "surface which leaps to the eye"—negatively or positively. For the designer the creation of a poster will also be in the future his most challenging task.

Eckhard Neumann

Vorwort

ECKHARD NEUMANN, geboren 1933 in Königsberg/Preussen, studierte Werbung und Graphik-Design in Berlin und Ulm. Zunächst in der Werbung tätig, wandte er sich mehr und mehr dem Design und der Kunst zu, insbesondere der Geschichte der Theorie des Graphik-Design im 20. Jahrhundert und der Bauhaus-Forschung. Er publizierte eine Sammlung von Erinnerungen ehemaliger Bauhaus-Meister und -Schüler sowie ihrer Zeitgenossen, *Bauhaus und Bauhäusler* (New York 1970, Bern 1971), eine Geschichte der Neuen Typographie, *Functional Graphic Design in the 20s* (New York 1971) und zahlreiche Texte zu seinen Schwerpunktthemen in internationalen Medien. 1964 gründete er das deutsche *Jahrbuch der Werbung* und ist seitdem Mitherausgeber. Seit 1975 ist er Designer im Rat für Formgebung in Darmstadt. Er lebt in Frankfurt am Main.

Werbung hat keinen guten Ruf, sie gilt weltweit als etwas Lästiges, wenn auch Unabdingbares, ein Übel, mehr geduldet als begrüsst. An die unfreiwillige, unausweichliche Begegnung hat man sich gewöhnt, weil man muss. Der Informationscharakter der Werbung und seine volkswirtschaftliche Funktion werden mit Misstrauen betrachtet, für die Gestaltung der Werbung gibt es keine öffentlichen Massstäbe, sieht man von den internen Tests grosser Kampagnen durch die Marktforschung ab, die angeblich inhaltliches und ästhetisches Verständnis des Durchschnittsbürgers reflektieren. In diesen Kontext fällt auch das Plakat. Nachdem es seine Rolle als das bedeutendste Medium der Werbung schon seit langer Zeit grösstenteils an die Anzeige und später auch an die TV-Werbung abgeben musste, ist das Plakat oft nur noch ein Teil eines Medienpaketes. Werbekonzeptionen werden meistens nicht für Plakate entwickelt, sie werden auf Plakate umgesetzt. Das Motiv der farbigen Illustrierten-Anzeige wird auf das Format des Grossflächenplakats aufgeblasen. Es ist der gleiche Prozess, mit dem man heute üblicherweise Bilder klassischer oder moderner Kunst auf das Miniformat von Briefmarken reduziert, ohne zu bedenken, dass jedes Medium anderen Bedingungen der Wahrnehmung und der Erlebnisgewohnheiten unterliegt.

Dem Plakat sind somit typische Eigenschaften seiner Wirkung genommen. Sind Plakate so betrachtet noch Plakate? Plakate seien Flächen, die ins Auge springen sollen, hat Franz Mon einmal eine Plakatausstellung überschrieben. Das war einmal um die Jahrhundertwende. Heute gibt es diese Dynamik noch in spezifischen Bereichen, bei Plakaten, die für kleine, hochspezialisierte Zielgruppen entworfen sind oder die für Ereignisse von übergeordnetem Allgemeininteresse, beispielsweise für Kunst, Musik, Theater oder für ideelle Ziele werben, wozu man die Politik freilich nicht zählen darf.

In der Alltagsumwelt unserer Zeit fallen Plakate dieses Typus relativ wenig auf, sie gehen ein wenig in der Vielzahl der optischen Signale unter, weil sie kleiner als die Übermacht der zum Konsum auffordernden Grossflächen sind, versteckter in der Plakatierung und geringer in der Auflage. Und trotzdem kommt ihnen für die Gestaltung der Umwelt eine besondere Bedeutung zu, nämlich die Rolle des Leitbildes. Plakate für Kultur haben neben ihrer unmittelbaren Funktion, Informationen über ein spezielles Ereignis zu liefern und Ausstellungs-, Theater- und Konzertbesucher zu aktivieren, eine eigene Öffentlichkeit, ein Forum «entre nous» – das der Plakatmacher. Sie entscheiden über die stilbildenden Leitbilder, die Trends und sorgen für hohen Anspruch an Design-Qualität und an die visuelle Kommunikation. Daraus werden auch Massstäbe für die Werbung und die Qualität der Gestaltung von Werbung abgeleitet.

Eines dieser Informationssysteme in der design-internen Fachwelt ist zweifelsohne GRAPHIS POSTERS. Als kompakte Übersicht der Trends der gegenwärtigen Plakatwelt, einsehbar praktisch an jedem Ort, verbindet dieses Buch die Plakatmacher untereinander, reflektiert deren Ideen, regt sie an und fordert sie zu einem Leistungswettbewerb heraus. Ein Nachteil kann allerdings damit verbunden sein, denn Vorbilder produzieren Nachempfindungen, schaffen durch die Beispiele stilistische Fakten, die unter anderen Bedingungen zu Verlusten des Qualitätsniveaus und der nationalen Eigenart führen können. Diese wachsende Unschärfe ursprünglicher und urbaner Gestaltungsrepertoires konnte man wieder an der (9.) 10. Internationalen Plakat-Biennale in Warschau erkennen. Die Schule der polnischen, der japanischen, der amerikanischen und der deutschen Plakatkunst überschreitet jede Grenze, weil ihre Gestaltungsmerkmale, ihre Ikonographie und die Technik unbewusst oder bewusst adaptiert werden. Augenblicklich ist die Plakatwelt bunt und vielfältig wie nie zuvor, alle visuellen Darstellungs- und Ausdrucksformen treten parallel auf, auch international gesehen. Illustrative, photographische, konkrete, typographische, historische oder computer-graphische Gestaltungslösungen leben in einem vitalen Wettbewerb. Sucht man hier Schwerpunkte, so lässt die Warschauer Plakat-Biennale erkennen, dass immer noch und immer mehr illustrativ-malerisch gearbeitet wird. Die Anwendung der Photographie folgt dieser Tendenz, indem sie die Realität der reinen Sachdarstellung überwunden und einen manipulierten Stil entwickelt hat, der von einer psychologisch orientierten Symbolik getragen wird. Das gilt im besonderen für Theaterplakate. Hier versuchen die Designer, die literarische Vorlage in visuell erlebbare, psychologisch wirkende Zeichen umzusetzen – vielleicht als Gegenpol zur fortschreitenden Technisierung des Lebens? Dabei hatte doch ein Visionär wie Lissitzky schon vor sechzig Jahren gesagt, das individuelle Element, des Künstlers «eigener Strich», sei für die moderne Reklame total belanglos. Ein Zurückgreifen auf ältere Stilelemente ist nicht neu; einerseits werden sie zitiert oder in historizistischer Manier lediglich benutzt, andererseits kann man in der Bewegung des New Wave Ansätze erkennen, auf der Basis von Formen und Strukturen der «Neuen Typographie» der zwanziger Jahre neue, zeitgemässe Wege zu suchen, die eine Verantwortlichkeit der Designer für die Umwelt signalisieren.

Gestaltung der Umwelt ist kein individuelles Problem, der Designer von heute darf sich nicht als Individualist verstehen, der sich selbst ausdrückt und seine eigene Vorstellung verwirklicht und sonst nichts. Das kunstgewerbliche Getto muss durchbrochen werden, um einer neuen Einstellung zur Gestaltung Platz zu machen, in welcher Verantwortung für alle, gestalterische Kompetenz und Herstellungstechnik primäre Funktionen haben. Die Werbung grosser internationaler Unternehmen hat für diese Haltung bereits viele herausragende Beispiele gegeben. Gute visuelle Gestaltung ist ein wirtschaftlicher, sozialer und kultureller Beitrag an die Gesellschaft, sie dient der Information und Kommunikation zwischen Mensch und Markt, zwischen Mensch und Öffentlichkeit und natürlich auch zwischen den Menschen selbst. Sie darf nicht gedankenlos, sondern soll verantwortungsbewusst und professionell gemacht werden.

Wenn man bei der vorliegenden Sammlung von internationalen Plakaten der jüngsten Zeit, des vergangenen Jahres, Plakate der Wirtschaftswerbung und Plakate für kulturelle Ereignisse als Polaritäten betrachtet, ergeben sich nur wenige Gemeinsamkeiten. Eigentlich nur das Papier, auf dem sie gedruckt sind, ist gleich, nicht einmal das Format, schon gar nicht die Auflage und damit die Reichweite der kommunikativen Wirkung. Design ist die pragmatische Seite der Kultur, die uns täglich umgibt. Die visuellen Erscheinungsformen der Alltagswelt sind eine Summe von Zeichen, die mit unterschiedlicher Eindringlichkeit auf uns wirken und uns beeinflussen. In dieser pluralistischen Zeichenwelt ist das Plakat neben der Architektur nach wie vor das wichtigste Signal, die «Fläche, die ins Auge springt» – negativ oder positiv. Für Designer bleibt die Gestaltung eines Plakates auch in Zukunft die herausforderndste Aufgabe.

Eckhard Neumann

Préface

ECKHARD NEUMANN, né à Königsberg (Prusse) en 1933, a fait ses études de publicité et d'art graphique à Berlin et à Ulm. Ce publicitaire s'est rapidement orienté vers le design et l'art, en particulier vers l'histoire et la théorie de l'art publicitaire du 20ᵉ siècle et du Bauhaus. On lui doit un recueil de souvenirs d'anciens maîtres et élèves du Bauhaus et de leurs contemporains, *Bauhaus and Bauhaus People* (New York 1970, Berne 1971), une histoire de la typographie nouvelle, *Functional Graphic Design in the 20s* (New York 1971) et de nombreux textes sur ces sujets dans les médias internationaux. En 1964, il a fondé l'annuaire de publicité allemand *Jahrbuch der Werbung* et en est le redacteur en chef associé. Depuis 1975, il est en sa qualité de designer membre du Rat für Formgebung, Darmstadt. Il habite Francfort.

La publicité n'a pas bonne presse. Dans le monde entier, on la considère comme quelque chose de fâcheux mais d'inéluctable, un mal nécessaire. Et l'on s'est habitué à la rencontrer partout, puisqu'on ne peut pas faire autrement. Le caractère informateur de la publicité et sa fonction économique sont perçus avec une certaine méfiance. Aucune réglementation publique ne s'applique à sa mise en forme; seuls les sondages propres aux grandes campagnes d'étude de marchés sont censés nous renseigner sur la perception esthétique et thématique du citoyen. C'est dans ce contexte qu'il convient de placer l'affiche. Depuis longtemps, elle a dû céder une grande partie de son rôle de média-clef de la publicité à l'annonce, puis à la publicité télévisée. De nos jours, elle n'est plus qu'un élément parmi d'autres au sein de la promotion multimédias, ce qui fait que les conceptions publicitaires ne sont pas élaborées en fonction de l'affiche, mais transposées sur affiches. C'est ainsi que le thème de l'annonce de magazine couleur est agrandi aux dimensions de l'affiche grand format – un processus analogue à celui qui fait réduire au mini-format du timbre-poste des tableaux de maîtres anciens ou modernes. C'est là faire fi des conditions de perception et des stimulations affectives propres à chaque média.

L'affiche se voit donc dérobée des qualités typiques assurant son impact. Peut-on alors encore parler d'affiche? Franz Mon a jadis placé une exposition d'affiches sous la devise suivante: les affiches sont des surfaces qui doivent sauter aux yeux. C'était au tournant de notre siècle. Cette dynamique subsiste encore dans des secteurs spécifiques, dans des affiches conçues pour des petits groupes-cibles très spécialisés ou destinées à promouvoir des manifestations d'intérêt public – art, musique, théâtre, campagnes d'idées (sans évidemment y inclure l'affiche politique).

Au sein de notre environnement quotidien, les affiches de ce type ne s'imposent guère à l'attention. C'est qu'elles passent quelque peu inaperçues dans le fouillis des signaux optiques issus de l'écrasante majorité des affiches au grand format incitant à la consommation, qui les isolent dans des coins de panneaux et les écrasent par leur tirage. Pourtant, elles revêtent une importance particulière pour l'aménagement de notre environnement, en tant qu'images directrices. En effet, si les affiches culturelles ont une fonction directe, l'information au sujet d'une manifestation déterminée et le recrutement d'un public adéquat pour les expositions, les théâtres et les concerts, elles en ont une autre plus spécifique: celle de constituer un forum professionnel pour les affichistes. C'est elles qui décident des images directrices formatrices de styles, des tendances du développement et qui assurent le transfert de la présence et de la qualité du design et de la communication visuelle. C'est de là que sont également dérivés les critères publicitaires en général et les critères gouvernant la qualité des messages réalisés à des fins publicitaires.

GRAPHIS POSTERS constitue sans aucun doute l'un de ces systèmes d'information au sein du monde professionnel du design. En offrant un condensé des tendances qui s'affirment dans le monde actuel de l'affiche, et en le rendant pratiquement accessible en n'importe quel point du globe, cet ouvrage unit les affichistes, les branche l'un sur l'autre, les stimule et les invite à une émulation de bon aloi. L'opération peut toutefois présenter un inconvénient. En effet, les modèles de réalisation retentissent sur le système cognitif, sont sources d'incitations stylistiques et risquent, dans certaines conditions, de nuire au niveau de la qualité et à la spécificité nationale. C'est ainsi que la (9ᵉ) 10ᵉ Biennale Internationale de l'Affiche de Varsovie a mis à jour le flou croissant des répertoires urbains originaux. Les écoles affichistes polonaise, japonaise, américaine et allemande diffusent par-delà les frontières, par le biais d'une adaptation consciente et inconsciente, leurs conceptions caractéristiques, leur iconographie, leurs techniques. Actuellement le monde de l'affiche se présente dans une diversité de thèmes et de coloris inouïe; il s'y retrouve en parallèle tous les moyens de présentation et d'expression, même au plan international. Des solutions inspirées de l'illustration, de la photographie, du concrétisme, de la typographie, de l'historicisme ou de la création graphique assistée par ordinateur sont en compétition vitale. A bien chercher les points forts, on réalise à travers la Biennale de Varsovie la continuité, voire le développement de l'approche illustrative picturale. La photographie appliquée lui emboîte le pas en surmontant le réel du rendu purement objectif et en élaborant un style manipulé porteur d'un symbolisme d'essence psychologique, notamment dans le domaine des affiches de théâtre. On voit ici les créateurs s'acharner à transposer le modèle littéraire en signes à charge psychologique accessibles à l'expérience visuelle. Peut-être s'agit-il là d'une réaction extrême à la technicisation continue de l'existence? Pourtant, le visionnaire qu'était El Lissitski avait bien affirmé il y a 60 ans que l'élément individuel, le coup de pinceau caractéristique de l'artiste, n'avait aucune importance pour la réclame moderne. Le retour aux éléments stylistiques du passé n'est pas nouveau. D'une part, on ne fait que les citer ou les mettre en œuvre de manière historisante; de l'autre, la New Wave, la Nouvelle Vague représente un effort délibéré pour trouver, sur la base des formes et structures de la Nouvelle Typographie des années 1920, des voies neuves, conformes à l'esprit du temps, signalisant la responsabilité qu'encourt le designer face aux problèmes d'aménagement de l'environnement.

Or, l'aménagement de l'environnement n'est pas un problème individuel. Le designer d'aujourd'hui ne doit pas agir en individualiste désireux de s'exprimer lui-même, de réaliser sa représentation personnelle des choses, un point c'est tout. Le ghetto des arts appliqués doit exploser pour céder la place à une nouvelle conception réalisatrice dont les fonctions essentielles seront la responsabilité à l'égard du plus grand nombre, la compétence en matière de création et la technique de production. La publicité de diverses grandes entreprises internationales fournit d'ores et déjà de nombreux exemples remarquables de cette attitude nouvelle. La réalisation visuelle de qualité constitue un apport économique, social et culturel de poids à la vie en société, au service de l'information et de la communication entre les hommes et les marchés, entre les hommes et la société et naturellement aussi d'homme à homme. C'est pourquoi elle ne doit pas être élaborée n'importe comment, mais seulement par des professionnels responsables.

En discernant dans la production affichiste internationale très récente telle que nous la propose cet ouvrage les deux pôles des affiches consommateurs et des affiches culturelles de l'année passée, on ne relèvera que peu de points communs. Seul le papier qui leur sert de support est identique, pas même le format, et certainement pas le tirage et donc la portée de leur action communicative. Le design est l'aspect pragmatique de la civilisation où nous baignons. Les manifestations visuelles de notre univers quotidien constituent une somme de signes qui agissent sur nous, nous influencent avec plus ou moins d'intensité. Au sein de cet univers pluraliste de signes, l'affiche constitue avec l'architecture aujourd'hui comme dans le passé le signal le plus important, la «surface qui saute aux yeux» – que ce soit au sens négatif ou au sens positif du terme. Pour le designer, la réalisation d'une affiche reste aussi à l'avenir la tâche qui lui en demande le plus.

Index to Artists and Photographers
Verzeichnis der Künstler und Photographen
Index des Artistes et Photographes

ADAMS, WALTER; GER. 47
ADRANNO, FABIO; ITA. 501, 504
ALAPFY, ANDRAS; NLD. 350
ALEKSIEV, CHRISTO; BUL. 347
ALLAN, POUL; DEN. 39, 176
ALTING, LEEN; NLD. 123
ANDERMATT, JÜRG; GER. 142–144
ANGELI, PRIMO; USA. 215
ARNOLDI, PER; DEN. 78
ASH, STUART; CAN. 213
AVEDON, RICHARD; USA. 549, 553, 554
AWAZU, KIYOSHI; JPN. 90, 482

BARABAN, JOE; USA. 395
BARBER, JIM; USA. 137
BARON, MALCOLM; USA. 403
BASS, SAUL; USA. 530
BEAR, BRENT; USA. 538–540
BELL, GARTH; FRA. 165
BERG, ANDRÉ. 92
BERNARDT, JÜRG; SWI. 37
BEZOMBES, ROGER; FRA. 19
BILLOUT, GUY; USA. 171
BINTCHEV, VALENTINO; BUL. 332
BÖHLE, STEFAN; GER. 512
BORTOLI, JOLE; ITA. 503
BOUCHER, JOHN; USA. 74
BRADE, HELMUT; GDR. 379
BROWN, MICHAEL DAVID; USA. 528
BRUCE, NICHOLA; GBR. 352, 353
BRÜHWILER, PAUL; SWI. 340–346
BRÜLLMANN, DAVE; SWI. 302
BUCAN, BORIS; YUG. 297
BUNDI, STEPHAN; SWI. 282–284, 485, 486
BURI, CLAUDE. 32
BURRI, RENÉ; SWI. 397, 400
BUSCH, LONNIE; USA. 452, 454
BYSTED, PETER; DEN. 207

CAILOR/RESNICK; USA. 136
CAMPBELL, DAVID; USA. 59
CASADO, JOHN; USA. 212
CHRISTENSEN, PAUL; USA. 40
CHWAST, SEYMOUR; USA. 445
CIESLEWICZ, ROMAN; FRA. 372, 413, 497, 548
CLAVERIE, JEAN; FRA. 375
COBER, ALAN E.; USA. 309
COCCHI, LAURENT; SWI. 154
COCHRAN, BOBBYE; USA. 462, 463
COIGNY, CHRISTIAN; SWI. 28
COLLENTINE, BRIAN; USA. 43, 168
COLLIER, JOHN; USA. 182
CONGE, BOB; USA. 187
CONRAD, MARY; USA. 381
COOPER, HEATHER; CAN. 441
COULSON, MIKE; GBR. 352, 353
COURATIN, PATRICK; FRA. 107
CRAIG, JOHN; USA. 472, 473
CRAINE, JON; USA. 517
CRAMP, CHARLES; GBR. 114
CRANE, IRA; USA. 193
CROSS, JAMES; USA. 529
CUSACK, MARIE-LOUISE; CAN. 179

DAVIS, PAUL; USA. 276. 339, 500
DEAHL, DAVID; USA. 87
DE BARI, FREDDY; VEN. 410
DE HARAK, RUDOLPH; USA. 214
DELESSERT, ETIENNE; SWI. 127, 458, 459
DELTOUR, PHILIPPE; BEL. 490
DE QUERVAIN, DANIEL; SWI. 305
DEVONALD, NEIL; GBR. 60, 61

DEZITTER, HENRY; USA. 138
DIETRICH, ALF; SWI. 53, 162
DOLCINI, MASSIMO; ITA. 408, 503, 505–507
DOMON, KEN; JPN. 448
DRZEWINSKI, GRAZYNA; POL. 351
DRZEWINSKI, LESZEK; POL. 351
DUBLIN, RICK; USA. 180

EBERT, DIETRICH; GER. 129
ECKERSLEY, TOM; GBR. 382, 383, 550–552
EGGMANN, HERMANN; SWI. 396
ENDO, SUSUMU; JPN. 56
ERBEN, TINO; AUT. 134, 135
ERNI, HANS; SWI. 447
ERNI, JÜRG; SWI. 71
EROL, JAKUB; POL. 358
EVANS, BARRY; GBR. 149, 153

FALKNER, ERICH; AUT. 199
FARAGO, ISTVAN; HUN. 322
FÄSCH, JÜRG; SWI. 21
FASOLINO, TERESA; USA. 52
FERRIER, WALTER; SAF. 14, 15
FIORENTINO, HELEN; USA. 181
FIORENTINO, LOU; USA. 181
FISHER, JEANNE; USA. 80
FISHER, JEFFREY; USA. 192
FLEJSAR, JOSEF; CSR. 225
FLESHER, VIVIENNE; USA. 99, 100
FLETCHER, ALAN; GBR. 437
FLOHR, JANOS; HUN. 204
FOLON, JEAN MICHEL; FRA. 96, 525
FORBES, COLIN; USA. 211
FORSYTHE, MAX; GBR. 30, 31
FRANÇOIS, ANDRÉ; FRA. 373, 527
FUKUDA, SHIGEO; JPN. 97, 427–430, 542–547
FUNABASHI, ZENJI; JPN. 170, 172
FURIKADO, TOSHIKAZU; JPN. 206
FURMAN, MICHAEL; USA. 72

GEISSBUHLER, STEFF; USA. 270
GELBERG, BOB; USA. 140
GETTIER-STREET, RENEE; USA. 178
GIL, DANIEL; SPA. 120, 401
GIUSTI, ROBERT; USA. 450
GLADWIN, JOHN; GBR. 166
GLASER, MILTON; USA. 189, 460, 461, 526, 541
GMÜR, PAUL; SWI. 155
GOROWSKI, MIECZYSLAW; POL. 236, 237, 324
GOSS, MICHAEL; USA. 478, 479
GOTTSCHALK & ASH; CAN. 213
GRANGER, MICHEL; FRA. 152
GRASHOW, JAMES; USA. 436
GREEN-ARMYTAGE, STEPHEN; USA. 41, 42
GREIMAN, APRIL; USA. 465
GRINDLER, FRIEDER; GER. 257, 301
GRUEN, JOHN; USA. 70
GRÜNIG, URS; SWI. 386
GRÜTTNER, ERHARD; GDR. 314
GUIRÉ VAKA, MICHEL; FRA. 110, 111

HAASE, FRITZ; GER. 414
HALMEN, PET; GER. 295
HANLON, GARY; USA. 510
HAUGHTON, RICHARD; USA. 104
HAYAKAWA, YOSHIO; JPN. 5
HAYS, PHILIP; USA. 523
HEIDENREICH, DIETER; GDR. 355
HENSTRA, FRISO; NLD. 387, 388
HERRON, ALAN; GBR. 261
HICKSON-BENDER; USA. 175
HIESTAND, U., ATELIER; SWI. 77

HIJIKATA, HIROKATSU; JPN. 480, 481
HILLIARD, FRED; USA. 262
HILLMANN, HANS; GER. 128
HIROMURA, MASAAKI; JPN. 333
HISAMATSU, MAKIKO; JPN. 185
HOFFMAN, KRYSTYNA; POL. 323
HUI, RAYMOND; HKG. 121
HÜRRIG, MANFRED, BEL. 245. 278

IANIGRO, ILDE; ITA. 442
IGARASHI, TAKENOBU; JPN. 334, 416, 420

JACKSON, JEFF; CAN. 44
JACOBS, JIM; USA. 196, 335
JAGODIC, STANE; YUG. 329
JAMES, DICK; USA. 141
JÄRMUT, VILLU; USR. 412
JASANSKY, PAVEL; CSR. 122
JEANNERET, CLAUDE; SWI. 17
JETTER, FRANCES; USA. 438
JOHNSON, CHUCK; USA. 51
JOST, HEINZ; SWI. 285, 286
JUNG & JUNG; SWI. 195
JUNKER, ROLAND; GER. 494

KAMEKURA, YUSAKU; JPN. 190, 419, 421
KAMPA, DAVID; USA. 173
KÄRMAS, ENN; USR. 412
KEMENY, GYÖRGY; HUN. 359
KERCHER, SIEGBERT; GER. 54, 55
KIESER, GÜNTHER; GER. 252–256, 306, 405, 411
KOBLER, CYRIL; SWI. 75
KOGOJ, OSCAR; YUG. 73
KOPP, PETER; SWI. 27
KOSTOVIC, CEDOMIR; YUG. 318
KRETZSCHMAR, HUBERT; USA. 101
KRONGARD, STEVE; USA. 516
KURIGAMI, KAZUMI; JPN. 94
KURODA, SEITARO; JPN. 418

LARAINE, GILLES; USA. 103
LEBISCH, GÜNTER O.; AUT. 199
LECLERCQ, JACQUES; FRA. 260
LEFÈVRE, YVES; BEL. 198
LEIDMANN, CHEYCO; GER. 34
LE QUERNEC, ALAIN; FRA. 258, 259, 263, 380
LESNIEWICZ, TERRY; USA. 515
LIDJI, ALAN & LAYNIE; USA. 518
LOOSER, HEINZ; SWI. 184
LUGER, REINHOLD; AUT. 308

MACURA, NIKO; YUG. 394
MAGINNIS, KEN; USA. 381
MAGLEBY, MCRAY; USA. 455–457, 466–468
MAJERA; HÉLÈNE; FRA. 3, 4
MAJEWSKI, LECH; POL. 325, 326, 349
MAK, KAM; USA. 520
MANARCHY, DENNIS; USA. 85
MAPPLETHORPE, ROBERT. 93
MARSH, JAMES; GBR. 66, 67, 98
MARTIN, JOHN; CAN. 443, 444
MASCA; USA. 139
MASSEY, JOHN; USA. 210
MASSIMO, STEFANO; GBR. 115
MATTELSON, MARVIN; USA. 453
MATTHIES, HOLGER; GER. 248–251, 292, 298–300
MCLOUGHLIN, JAMES; USA. 509, 511
MCLOUGHLIN, WAYNE; USA. 451
MCMULLAN, JAMES; USA. 519
MEDINA, FERNANDO; SPA. 317
MEEK, BRUCE. 116–118
MESSINGER, PHILIP; USA. 84

METZNER, SHEILA; USA. 156
MEYER, GARY; USA. 68
MEYERSON, ARTHUR; USA. 395
MIO, KOZO; JPN. 88, 89
MLODOZENIEC, JAN; POL. 228, 361, 371
MLODOZENIEC, PIOTR; POL. 495
MOLLATH, BRAD; USA. 11, 12
MOORE, CHRIS; USA. 119
MÜLLER, ROLF-FELIX; GDR. 242, 244, 290, 363, 378
MURAWSKI, ALEX; USA. 356
MUSSA, PAUL; USA. 533

NAGAI, KAZUMASA; JPN. 158, 431–435
NAVARRE, AL; USA. 515
NOBUYAMA, HIRO; JPN. 46
NOWAK, WITOLD; POL. 409
NYGAARD, FINN; DEN. 205, 264
NYMAN, BJÖRN; FIN. 113

OERTER, FRITZ HENRY; GER. 201
OHASHI, TOSHIYUKI; JPN. 424–426
ONO, MASAKI; JPN. 2
OSBORN, BRUCE; JPN. 1
OSTERWALDER, HANS ULRICH; GER. 513
OTSUBO, KAZUYUKI; JPN. 209
OVERACRE, GARY; USA. 311

PADYS, DIANE; USA. 83
PAGÈS, RAYMOND; FRA. 203
PAGOWSKI, ANDREZEJ; POL. 105, 231–235, 291, 293,
    320, 323, 367
PALLADINO, TONY; USA. 522
PAPE, INGE; GER. 496
PARASCAN, M.; BEL. 278
PENTAGRAM; USA. 211
PERICOLI, TULLIO; ITA. 124, 125
PETERSEN, BILL; USA. 197
PFAFF, CHRIS; AUT. 102
PFÜLLER, VOLKER; GDR. 281
PFUND, ROGER; SWI. 304
PIATTI, CELESTINO; SWI. 35
PICARIA, FRANCIS 398
PINTÉR, FERENC; ITA. 488
PIRTLE, WOODY; USA. 271, 275
PIWONSKI, ANDRZEJ; POL. 319
POPOV; KAMEN; BUL. 498
POST, ANDY; USA. 167
PRECHTL, MICHAEL MATHIAS; GER. 289, 449
PW, INC.; USA. 310

RADOVAN, JENKO; YUG. 268

RAUCH, ANDREA; ITA. 151, 354, 374, 469
RENYI, KATALIN; HUN. 321
RICHEZ, JACQUES; BEL. 287, 288
RISBECK, PHIL, USA. 239
RIZZATO, MARISA; ITA. 357
ROHMAN, JIM; USA. 508
ROLLY, HANSPETER; SWI. 24
ROSENWALD, LAURIE; USA. 45
ROTHBERG, LINDA; USA. 476, 477
RUBIN, MARVIN; USA. 534
RZADKOWSKY, ANDREAS; GER. 230, 246, 247

SADOWSKI, WIKTOR; POL. 266, 267, 269
SAKATA, EIICHIRO; JPN. 95
SALAMOUN, JIRI; CSR. 365
SATO, U.G.; JPN. 48, 49, 422, 423
SAWKA, JAN; USA. 272–274
SCHLEGER, HANS, & ASSOCIATES; GBR. 240
SCHMITZ, DIETER; SWI. 23
SCHNEIDER, URS; SWI. 36
SCHWARK, EVELYN; GER. 303
SCHWARTZ, ORA & ELIYAHV; ISR. 188
SCHWARTZMAN, ARNOLD; USA. 470, 471, 531
SCORSONE, JOE; USA. 464
SENIOR, GEOFF; GBR. 200
SEVERSON, KENT; USA. 82
SHIMODA, KOICHI; JPN. 484
SHINODA, YOSHIHIKO; JPN. 91
SHUEL, BRIAN; GBR. 150
SIERRA, RICHARD; USA. 521
SMITH, ELWOOD; USA. 474, 475
SOKOLOW, BORIS; GER. 312, 315
SOMMESE, LANNY; USA. 265, 440
SORBIE, JOHN J.; USA. 243, 389, 390, 439
SPOHN, JÜRGEN; GER. 80
STAECK, KLAUS; GER. 489, 499
STANTON, KATHY; USA. 64
STAROWIEYSKI, FRANCISZEK; POL.
    217–224, 366
STEINER, ROLAND; SWI. 22
STÖRK, JÖRGEN; GER. 33
STROM, ERNST, GER. 140
STUDIO 33; ITA. 402
SUGA, MASAYA; JPN. 6–10
SWIERZY, WALDEMAR; POL. 369, 370
SZULECKI, TOMASZ; POL. 416

TAMAS BLAER, KLARA; RUM. 330, 331, 368
TANABE, MASAKAZU; JPN. 424–426
TAPPRICH, JÜRGEN; SWI. 18, 160, 161
TARTAKOVER, DAVID T.; ISR. 406

TATTERSFIELD, BRIAN; GBR. 133
TERADA, SHIGERU; JPN. 63
TESTA, ARMANDO; ITA. 376
THOMASSEN, KAJ OTTO, DEN. 483
TOMANEK, JAN; CSR. 348
TOMASZEWSKI, HENRYK; POL. 229, 294
TOMOEDA; YUSAKU; JPN. 174
TOPOR, ROLAND; FRA. 227
TOYOKUNI, NOBUYASU; JPN. 208
TROXLER, NIKLAUS; SWI. 336
TSCHERNY, GEORGE; USA. 126, 446
TSUCHIDA, HIROMI; JPN. 484

VACA, KAREL; CSR. 360, 364
VALERRY, PAUL; GER. 238
VANDERBYL, MICHAEL; USA. 79, 81
VAN DER ELST, ADRIANUS; ITA. 177
VAN DER WYK, GJALT; USA. 537
VAN HAMMERSVELD, JOHN; USA. 532
VARDIMON, YAROM; ISR. 241, 307
VILLEMOT, BERNARD; FRA. 38
VOGELSÄNGER, MANFRED; GER. 157
VON CONTA, MARGRET; GER. 112
VURMA, JIRI; SWI. 57, 163

WALKUSKI, WIESLAW; POL. 327
WASILEWSKI, MIECZYSLAW; POL. 313, 328,
    338, 362
WEIGAND, AXEL; GER. 296
WELLER, DON; USA. 108, 109, 145
WEYER, PIT; LUX. 277, 279, 280
WHITE, CHARLIE; USA. 533
WILDBOLZ, JOST; SWI. 13, 16
WILSON, GAHAN; USA. 377
WINTER, CONNY; GER. 09
WIRTH, KURT; SWI. 385
WOLF, HENRY; USA. 216
WOLL, PAM; USA. 392
WOLYNSKI, WOJCIECH; POL. 226
WOOD, RAY; USA. 186
WOODS, EARL; USA. 65
WUNDERLICH, GERT, GDR. 393

YAMASHITA, YUZO; JPN. 50
YOKOO, TADANORI; JPN. 417
YOKOSUKA, NORIAKI; JPN. 25, 26, 29
YOMOGIDA, YASUHIRO; JPN. 524
YOSHIDA, KATSU; JPN. 131, 132

ZEGGER, FRANS; NLD. 194
ZELGER, ARTHUR; AUT. 183

Index to Designers
Verzeichnis der Gestalter
Index des Maquettistes

ALAPFY, ANDRAS; NLD. 350
ALBERTIN, BRUNO; SWI. 160, 161
ALLAN, POUL; DEN. 39, 176
ALTING, LEEN; NLD. 123
ANGOTTI, TONY; USA. 138
ARNOLDI, PER; DEN. 78
ASAEDA, TAKANORI; JPN. 2
AWAZU, KIYOSHI; JPN. 90, 482

BÄCHLER, O.; SWI. 23
BARTELS, DAVID; USA. 110, 111, 311, 356
BARTSCH & CHARIAU; GER. 377, 445
BAUER, FRED; SWI. 491–493
BECK, RUDOLF; GER. 33
BELL, GARTH; FRA. 165, 166
BEZOMBES, ROGER; FRA. 19
BIERUT, MICHAEL; USA. 11, 12
BING-WAH, HON; HKG. 121
BLACKBURN, BRUCE; USA. 516
BLANCHOUD, JEAN-PIERRE, SWI. 75, 384
BÖHLE, STEFAN; GER. 512
BORCIC, ZELJKO; YUG. 394
BORTOLI, JOLE; ITA. 402, 404, 503
BORTOLOTTI, GIANNI; ITA. 502
BRIGINSHAW, PAUL; GBR. 66, 67
BROWDER, RODGER; USA. 84
BRÜHWILER, PAUL; SWI. 340–346
BRUNSCHWICK, JEAN PAUL; SWI. 28
BUCAN, BORIS; YUG. 297
BUNDI, STEPHAN; SWI. 282–284, 485, 486
BURKHARD NEUMANN; GER. 164

CALLENDER, JEFF; USA. 197
CASTRO, ORLANDO; USA. 335
CHACON, SIGFREDO; VEN. 410
CHERMAYEFF, IVAN; USA. 403
CIESLEWICZ, ROMAN; FRA. 413, 497, 548
CLARK, CHARLIE; USA. 82, 180
CLAVERIE, JEAN; FRA. 375
COCCHI, LAURENT; SWI. 154
COLLENTINE, BRIAN; USA. 43
COLVIN, ALAN; USA. 395
CONGE, BOB; USA. 187
COOKE, KENNETH R.; USA. 103
CRAINE, JON; USA. 517

DAVIS, PAUL; USA. 276, 339, 500
DEAHL, DAVID; USA. 87
DOLCINI, MASSIMO; ITA. 402, 404, 408, 503, 505–507

ECKERSLEY, TOM; GBR. 550–552
EGGERS, SCOTT; USA. 167
EGGMANN, H. M.; SWI. 155
EHRISMANN, ARMIN; SWI. 71
EIBER, RICK; USA. 262
ENDO, SUSUMU; JPN. 56
ERBEN, TINO; AUT. 134, 135
ERNI, HANS; SWI. 447
ERNST, RUEDI; SWI. 195

FANDINO, TONY, GBR. 149, 150, 153
FIORENTINO, LOU; USA. 181, 193
FLEJSAR, JOSEF; CSR. 225
FLETCHER, ALAN; GBR. 437
FLOHR, JANOS; HUN. 204
FORD, BYRNE & ASSOCIATES; USA. 441
FREEDMAN, EDITH; USA. 407
FREUDENREICH, MAREK; POL. 409
FRIEDMAN, JULIUS; USA. 310
FRYKHOLM, STEPHEN; USA. 65
FUKUDA, SHIGEO; JPN. 97, 427–430, 542–547
FURMAN, MICHAEL; USA. 72

GEISSBÜHLER, K. DOMENIC; SWI. 302
GEISSBUHLER, STEFF; USA. 270
GETTIER-STREET, RENEE; USA. 178
GLASER, MILTON; USA. 189, 460, 461, 541
GOBÉ, MARC; FRA. 34
GRANGER, MICHEL; FRA. 152
GREIMAN, APRIL; USA. 465
GRINDLER, FRIEDER; GER. 257, 301
GRÜNIG, URS; SWI. 386

HAASE, FRITZ; GER. 157, 414
HALMEN, PET; GER. 295
HATTORI, SHIGEYUKI; JPN. 185
HAUBMANN, FRITZ; AUT. 32
HAYWARD BLAKE & CO.; USA. 474. 475
HERZOG, ERNST; SWI. 57
HIESTAND, URSULA; SWI. 77
HIRAHARA, AKIHIRO; JPN. 484
HOFER, CHARLIE; SWI. 159
HOLTMANN, HANS J.; SWI. 20
HUMMEL, ROLF; SWI. 27

IANIGRO, ILDE; ITA. 442, 501
IGARASHI, TAKENOBU; JPN. 94, 416, 420
ISRAEL, MARVIN; USA. 549, 553, 554
ITOH, JUTARO; JPN. 484

JACKSON, JEFF; CAN. 44
JACOBS, JIM; USA. 196
JÄRMUT, VILLU; USR. 412
JASANSKY, PAVEL; CSR. 122
JEKER, WERNER; SWI. 397, 400
JETTER, FRANCES; USA. 438
JOHNSON; CHUCK; USA. 51
JOST, HEINZ; SWI. 285, 286, 305
JUNKER, ROLAND; GER. 494

KAKIGI, SAKAE; JPN. 170
KAMEKURA, YUSAKU; JPN. 190, 419, 421, 448
KÄRMAS, ENN; USR. 412
KIER, ELLEN; USA. 99, 100
KIESER, GÜNTHER; GER. 252–256, 306, 405, 411
KINOSHITA, KATSUHIRO; JPN. 5
KNER, ANDREW; USA. 119
KOBASZ, BILL; USA. 519–521
KOGOJ, OSCAR; YUG. 73
KRETZSCHMAR, HUBERT; USA. 101
KRISTOFORI, IRIS; SWI. 399
KROESE, HANS; NLD. 194
KÜLLING, RUEDI; SWI. 163
KUMKE, BILL; USA. 40, 450–454
KUNSTHAUS ZÜRICH; SWI. 398

LECLERCQ, JACQUES; FRA. 260
LEFÈVRE, YVES; BEL. 198
LEONARD, RUTH A.; USA. 202
LE QUERNEC, ALAIN; FRA. 258, 259, 263, 380
LESNIEWICZ, TERRY; USA. 515
LEU, OLAF, DESIGN & PARTNER; GER. 76
LIDJI, ALAN; USA. 518
LJUBICIC; BORISLAV; YUG. 73
LOOSER, HEINZ; SWI. 184
LOVELAND, BARBARA; USA. 64
LUDWIG, GARY; CAN. 443, 444
LUGER, REINHOLD; AUT. 308

MAEDA, MITSUMASA; JPN. 131, 132
MAGIN, WOLF; GER. 147, 148
MAGLEBY, MCRAY; USA. 455–457, 466–468
MAJIMA; TATSUOMI; JPN. 1
MARSH, JAMES; GBR. 98
MARSHALL, RITA; SWI. 127, 458, 459

MARTIN, DAVE; USA. 509–511
MATSUNAGA, SHIN; JPN. 92, 93
MATTHIES, HOLGER; GER. 248–251, 292, 298–300
MAYAHARA, JOHN; USA. 476–479
MENDELL, PIERRE; GER. 58, 106
MENZIES, ALF; GBR. 60, 61
MERLICEK, FRANZ; AUT. 13, 16, 102, 116–118
MICHA, EMIL; USA. 436
MINALE, TATTERSFIELD & PARTNERS; GBR. 133
MIYAMOTO, MITSUAKI; JPN. 6–10
MOCHIZUKI, HIDETAKA; JPN. 172
MOFFET, MARK; USA. 140
MOHR, KLAUS; GER. 337
MÖHR, OSSI; SWI. 399
MOLNAR, KALMAN; CAN. 179
MORAL, MARIANO; SWI. 17
MORTENSEN, GORDON; USA. 59
MÜLLER, PIOTR; SWI. 22

NAGAI, KAZUMASA; JPN. 158, 431–435
NAKADE, TEIJIRO; JPN. 3, 4
NAKAGAWA, TORU; JPN. 206
NAKAMURA, MAKOTO; JPN. 25, 26, 29
NAVARRE, AL; USA. 515

OBERHOLZER, HANSJÖRG; SWI. 195
O'BRIEN, JOHN; USA. 104
OLIVER, DOUGLAS; USA. 514
OSTERWALDER, HANS ULRICH; GER. 513
OTT, NICOLAUS; GER. 316
OVESEY, REGINA; USA. 70

PAGÈS, RAYMOND; FRA. 203
PAGOWSKI, ANDRZEJ; POL. 105
PALLADINO, TONY; USA. 522
PAPE, INGE; GER. 496
PEPE, ANTONIO; ITA. 376
PERICOLI, TULLIO; ITA. 124, 125
PFUND, ROGER; SWI. 130, 304, 384
PIATTI, CELESTINO; SWI. 35
PILVE, PENTTI; FIN. 113
PIRTLE, WOODY; USA. 173, 271, 275, 395
PLANTE, GILLES; FRA. 34
PRECHTL, MICHAEL MATHIAS; GER. 289

RADOVAN, JENKO; YUG. 268
RAUCH, ANDREA; ITA. 151, 354, 469
RAUCH, PETER; USA. 136–138, 141
REISINGER, DAN; ISR. 169
RICHEZ, JACQUES; BEL. 287, 288
RIEBEN, JOHN R.; USA. 535–537
RISBECK, PHIL; USA. 239
RIZZATO, MARISA; ITA. 357, 504
ROBIE, JAMES; USA. 538–540
ROLLY, HANSPETER; SWI. 24
ROSE, PETER; GBR. 114, 115
ROSENWALD, LAURIE; USA. 45
ROSNER, GENE; USA. 197
ROTA, KATHI; USA. 520, 521
ROTH, GEORGE; USA. 472, 473
RZADKOWSKY, ANDREAS; GER. 230, 246, 247

SATO, U.G.; JPN. 48, 49, 422, 423
SAWKA, JAN; USA. 272–274
SCHNEIDER, URS; SWI. 36, 37
SCHWARK, EVELYN; GER. 303
SCHWARTZ, ORA & ELIYAHV; ISR. 188
SCHWARTZMAN, ARNOLD; USA. 470, 471
SCORSONE, JOE; USA. 464
SHIMIZU, MASAMI; JPN. 95
SHINODA, YOSHIHIKO; JPN. 91
SLIKER, ROGER; USA. 74

SOKOLOW, BORIS; GER. 312, 315
SOMMESE, LANNY; USA. 265. 440
SORBIE, JOHN J.; USA. 243, 389, 390, 439
SPOHN, JÜRGEN; GER. 86
STEIN, BERNARD; GER. 316
STEINHILBER, BUDD; USA. 68
STREET, DAVID R.; USA. 178
STROM, ERNST; GER. 146
SUGIMOTO, HIROYA; JPN. 88, 89
SUZUKI, HACHIRO; JPN. 208, 209

TANABE, MASAKAZU; JPN. 424–426
TANAKA, IKKO; JPN. 5
TAPIRO; ITA. 374
TARTAKOVER, DAVID T.; ISR. 406
TERADA, SHIGERU; JPN. 63
THOMASSEN, KAJ OTTO; DEN. 483

TOMANEK, JAN; CSR. 348
TOMOEDA, YUSAKU; JPN. 174
TROXLER, NIKLAUS; SWI. 336
TSCHERNY, GEORGE; USA. 126, 446
TSUCHIYA, NAOHISA; JPN. 418
TYCZKOWSKI, KRZYSZTOF; POL. 227

VANDERBYL, MICHAEL; USA. 79, 81, 191, 391
VAN LEEUWEN, ANDRÊ; NLD. 194
VARDIMON, YAROM; ISR. 241, 307
VILLEMOT, BERNARD; FRA. 38
VOGT, PETER; GER. 47
VON CONTA, MARGRET; GER. 112

WASILEWSKI, MIECZYSLAW; POL. 313, 338
WEEKS, DAN; USA. 508
WEIGAND, AXEL; GER. 296

WEISS, DIDIER; SWI. 17
WEISS, JACK, ASSOC.; USA. 462, 463
WELLER, DON; USA. 108, 109, 145
WHITLEY, JERRY; USA. 139
WINTER, CONNY; GER. 69
WIRTH, KURT; SWI. 385
WOHLER, ROLAND; SWI. 399
WOOD, RAY; USA. 186
WOODWARD, TONY; USA. 538–540
WUNDERLICH, GERT; GDR. 393

YAMASHITA, YUZO; JPN. 50
YOKOO, TADANORI; JPN. 417

ZELGER, ARTHUR; AUT. 183
ZIFF, LLOYD; USA. 156
ZUMBÜHL, PETER; SWI. 21

Index to Art Directors
Verzeichnis der künstlerischen Leiter
Index des Directeurs Artistiques

ADRANNO, FABIO; ITA. 501, 504
ALAPFY, ANDRAS; NLD. 350
ALBERTIN, BRUNO; SWI. 160, 161
ALLAN, POUL; DEN. 39, 176
ANDONOV, IVAN; BUL. 332
ASAEDA, TAKANORI; JPN. 2
AWAZU, KIYOSHI; JPN. 90, 482

BÄCHLER, O.; SWI. 23
BARNES, JEFF A.; USA. 85
BARTELS, DAVID; USA. 40, 110, 111, 311,
   356, 450–454
BELL, GARTH; FRA. 165, 166
BENDER, BOB; USA. 175
BENEDEK, KATALIN; HUN. 204
BIARD, JEAN LOUIS; FRA. 152
BING-WAH, HON; HGK. 121
BITTEL, RENÉ H.; SWI. 18
BLACKBURN, BRUCE; USA. 516
BLANCHOUD, JEAN-PIERRE; SWI. 75
BLUM, CHRIS; USA. 41, 42
BÖHLE, STEFAN; GER. 512
BORCIC, ZELJKO; YUG. 394
BRIGHT, KEITH; USA. 186
BRIGINSHAW, PAUL; GBR. 66, 67
BROWDER, RODGER; USA. 84
BROWN, MICHAEL DAVID; USA. 528
BRÜHWILER, PAUL; SWI. 340–346
BUCAN, BORIS; YUG. 297
BÜHLER, WILLI; SWI. 159
BUNDI, STEPHAN; SWI. 485, 486

CASTRO, ORLANDO; USA. 335
CHERMAYEFF, IVAN; GER. 403
CIESLEWICZ, ROMAN; FRA. 413
CLARK, CHARLIE; USA. 82, 180
CLAVERIE, JEAN; FRA. 375
COIGNY, CHRISTIAN; SWI. 28
COOKE, KENNETH R.; USA. 103
CRAINE, JON; USA. 517
CROOK, CLIVE; GBR. 98
CROSS, JAMES; USA. 210–216, 529
CUSACK, MARIE-LOUISE; CAN. 179
CYBULSKI, BOHDAN; POL. 226

DAVIS, PAUL; USA. 500
DEAHL, DAVID; USA. 87
DENNARD, BOB; USA. 51
DESPOIX, JACQUES; FRA. 96
DEUTSCH, BARRY; USA. 68
DEVILLE, RODOLPHE; SWI. 27
DOLCINI, MASSIMO; ITA. 402, 404, 408, 503, 505–507

EBERT, DIETRICH; GER. 129
EGGERS, SCOTT; USA. 167
EHRISMANN, ARMIN; SWI. 71
EIBER, RICK; USA. 262
ENDO, SUSUMU; JPN. 56
ERBEN, TINO; AUT. 134, 135
ERNI, HANS; SWI. 447

FARAGO, AGNES; HUN. 359
FIORENTINO, LOU; USA. 181, 193
FISHER, DOUG; USA. 175
FLETCHER, ALAN; GBR. 437
FOOTE, DAVE; USA. 309
FREEDMAN, EDITH; USA. 407
FRIEDMAN, JULIUS; USA. 310
FRYKHOLM, STEPHEN; USA. 65
FUKUDA, SHIGEO; JPN. 97, 427–430, 542–547
FÜRER, URS; SWI. 195
FURMAN, MICHAEL; USA. 72

GAFERT, HEINZ; GER. 238
GALCZYNSKI, MIROSLAW; POL. 234
GEISSBÜHLER, K. DOMENIC; SWI. 302
GEISSBUHLER, STEFF; USA. 270
GLASER, MILTON; USA. 52, 189, 460, 461, 541
GLOGOWSKA, MAGDA; POL. 323, 361
GOBÉ, MARC; FRA. 34
GREIMAN, APRIL; USA. 465
GRINDLER, FRIEDER; GER. 257, 301
GRÜNIG, URS; SWI. 386
GRZEGORZEWSKI, JERZY; POL. 227

HAASE, FRITZ; GER. 414
HALMEN, PET; GER. 295
HALPERIN, CINDY; USA. 197
HANUSZKIEWICZ, ADAM; POL. 228
HAUBMANN, FRITZ; AUT. 32
HAYDEN, DARRELL; USA. 530–534
HERZOG, ERNST; SWI. 57
HIESTAND, ERNST; SWI. 399
HIESTAND, URSULA; SWI. 77
HIJIKATA, HIROKATSU; JPN. 480, 481
HILLMANN, HANS; GER. 128
HOLTMANN, HANS, J.; SWI. 20
HORAK, GÖPF; SWI. 53
HÜRRIG, MANFRED; BEL. 245, 278

IANIGRO, ILDE; ITA. 442
IGARASHI, TAKENOBU; JPN. 94, 334, 416, 420
ITOH, JUTARO; JPN. 484
IWANO, AKIRA; JPN. 88, 89

JACOBS, JIM; USA. 196
JAY, JOHN C.; USA. 80
JETTER, FRANCES; USA. 438
JOST, HEINZ; SWI. 285, 286, 305

KAISER, WOLF; GER. 33
KAKIGI, SAKAE; JPN. 170
KAMEKURA, YUSAKU; JPN. 190, 419, 421, 448
KEARNEY, HAL; USA. 462, 463, 472–479
KIER, ELLEN; USA. 99. 100
KIESER, GÜNTHER; GER. 252–256, 306, 405, 411
KITCHEN, ROB; GBR. 30
KLEIN, LARRY; USA. 530–534
KNER, ANDREW; USA. 119, 436
KOBASZ, BILL; USA. 520, 521
KOHARA, ROY; USA. 104
KOSTOVIC, CEDOMIR; YUG. 318
KRETZSCHMAR, HUBERT; USA. 101
KÜLLING, RUEDI; SWI. 163
KÜMPER, L. F.; GER. 201

LEBISCH, GÜNTER O.; AUT. 199
LECLERCQ, JACQUES; FRA. 260
LEICK, CARL; USA. 145
LEONARD, RUTH A.; USA. 202
LE QUERNEC, ALAIN; FRA. 258, 259, 263, 380
LESNIEWICZ, TERRY; USA. 515
LIDJI, ALAN; USA. 518
LLOYD, JOHN; GBR. 261
LOFTHOUSE, ALAN; GBR. 200
LOOSER, HEINZ; SWI. 184
LOVELAND, BARBARA; USA. 64
LUCCHETTA/BACCIOCCHI/PORTINARI; ITA. 177
LUDWIG, GARY; CAN. 443, 444

MAEDA, MITSUMASA; JPN. 131, 132
MAGLEBY, MCRAY; USA. 455–457, 466–468
MAHARRY, ROBERT; USA. 187
MAJIMA, TATSUOMI; JPN. 1
MARABELLI, FRANCO; ITA. 45

MARCZEWSKI, ANDRZEJ; POL. 231
MARSHALL, RITA; SWI. 127, 458, 459
MARTIN, DAVE; USA. 509–511
MATSUNAGA, SHIN; JPN. 92, 93
MATTHIES, HOLGER; GER. 248–251, 292, 298–300
MAYAHARA, JOHN; USA. 462, 463, 472–479
MCDOUGALL, ALAN; GBR. 524–527
MEDINA; FERNANDO; SPA. 317
MENDELL, PIERRE; GER. 58, 106
MENZIES, ALF; GBR. 60, 61
MERLICEK, FRANZ; AUT. 13, 16, 102, 116–118
MICHA, EMIL; USA. 436
MIECZYNSKA, ANNA; POL. 369
MOCHIZUKI, HIDETAKA; JPN. 172
MOFFET, MARK; USA. 140
MORII, HIDEHIKO; JPN. 185
MORTENSEN, GORDON; USA. 59
MÜLLER, PIOTR; SWI. 22

NAGAI, KAZUMASA; JPN. 158, 431–435
NAGATOMO, KEISUKE; JPN. 418
NAKADE, TEIJIRO; JPN. 3, 4
NAKAGAWA, KENZO; JPN. 46
NAKAGAWA, TORU; JPN. 206
NAKAMURA, MAKOTO; JPN. 25, 26, 29
NAKASHIMA, YOSHIFUMI; JPN. 6–10
NAVARRE, AL; USA. 515
NODINE, RICHARD; USA. 43, 168
NORTHOVER, JIM; GBR. 261

PACHÉS, VINCENT; FRA. 548
PAISER, DAN; USA. 178
PALLADINO, TONY; USA. 522
PFEFFER, ERWIN; GER. 157
PFUND, ROGER; SWI. 304
PILVE, PENTTI; FIN. 113
PINTÉR, FERENC; ITA. 488
PIRTLE, WOODY; USA. 173, 271, 275, 395
POL, SANTIAGO; VEN. 410
POPIOLEK, EWA; POL. 105
POTTER, IAN; GBR. 31, 62

RAAF, ALLAN; SAF. 14, 15
RADOVAN, JENKO; YUG. 268
RAUCH, ANDREA; ITA. 151, 354, 374, 469
RAUCH, PETER; USA. 136–138, 141
REISINGER, DAN; ISR. 169
RHODES, SILAS H.; USA. 519
RICHEZ, JACQUES; BEL. 287, 288
RIEBEN, JOHN R.; USA. 535–537
RISBECK, PHIL; USA. 239
RIZZATO, MARISA; ITA. 357, 501
ROBIE, JAMES; USA. 538–540
ROCHER, JEAN PIERRE; FRA. 19
ROSE, PETER; GBR. 114, 115
RUHRMANN, HEINZ; GER. 230, 246, 247

SALA, ANDRÉ; USA. 83, 107
SANTI, MARIA; ITA. 502
SATO, U. G.; JPN. 48, 49, 422, 423
SAWKA, JAN; USA. 272–274
SCHLEGER, PAT; GBR. 240
SCHNEIDER, URS; SWI. 36, 37
SCHWARK, EVELYN; GER. 303
SCHWARTZ, ORA & ELIYAHV; ISR. 188
SCHWARTZMAN, ARNOLD; USA. 470, 471, 530–532
SCHWEERS, HARALD; GER. 157
SCORSONE; JOE; USA. 464
SHIMIZU, MASAMI; JPN. 95
SHINODA, YOSHIHIKO; JPN. 91
SLIKER, ROGER; USA. 74
SOMMESE, LANNY; USA. 112, 265, 440

SORBIE, JOHN J.; USA. 243,
  389, 390
STAECK. KLAUS: GER. 489, 499
STEPHANIDES, DEAN; USA. 141
SUZUKI, HACHIRO; JPN. 208, 209
SZOLLOSI, PETER; USA. 439
SZPYRA, GRAZYNA MARIA; POL. 370
SZULECKI, TOMASZ; POL. 415

TANAKA, IKKO; JPN. 5, 333
TAPIRO; ITA. 374
TARTAKOVER, DAVID; ISR. 406
TERADA, SHIGERU; JPN. 63
TESTA, ARMANDO; ITA. 376
THOMASSEN, KAJ OTTO; DEN. 483
TOMANEK, JAN; CSR. 348
TORA, SHINICHIRO; USA. 424–426

TROXLER, NIKLAUS; SWI. 336
TSCHARNER, G.; SWI. 155
TSCHERNY, GEORGE; USA. 126, 446
TSCHIERSCHKY, SABINE; GER. 230,
  246, 247, 296

VANDERBYL, MICHAEL; USA. 79, 81, 191, 391
VAN LEEUWEN, ANDRÉ; NLD. 194
VARDIMON, YAROM; ISR. 241, 307
VIGNELLI, MASSIMO; USA. 11, 12
VOGT, PETER; GER. 47
VOM ENDT, ERICH; GER. 296

WALSH, MARY JANE; GBR. 352
WARNER, LINDA; AUS. 192
WEBER, MAX; SWI. 162
WEBSTER, PAUL; GBR. 353

WEEKS, DAN; USA. 508
WEISS, DIDIER; SWI. 17
WELLER, DON; USA. 108, 109
WHITLEY, JERRY; USA. 139
WILDE, RICHARD; USA. 520, 521
WINTER, CONNY; GER. 69
WIRTH, KURT; SWI. 385
WOLL, PAM; USA. 392
WUNDERLICH, GERT; GDR. 393

YAMASHITA, YUZO, JPN. 50
YOKOO, TADANORI; JPN. 417
YOUNG, FRANK; USA. 70

ZIELINSKI, ANDRZEJ; POL. 372
ZIFF, LLOYD; USA. 156
ZUMBÜHL, PETER; SWI. 21

Index to Agencies and Studios
Verzeichnis der Agenturen und Studios
Index des Agences et Studios

ABBOTT MEAD VICKERS/SMS LTD.; GBR. 200
ADVICO AG; SWI. 57, 163
AIR FRANCE/SERVICE PUBLICITÉ; FRA. 203
ALLAN, POUL, STUDIO; DEN. 176
AMMIRATI & PURIS INC.; USA. 136–141
ARTIST VISION COMMUNICATION; GER. 238
ART WORK, DESIGN STUDIO; JPN. 91
AZ INC. ADVERTISING; JPN. 170

BACCIOCCHI. VALTER, STUDIO; ITA. 177
BARNES DESIGN OFFICE; USA. 85
BARTELS & COMPANY; USA. 40, 110, 111, 311, 356,
    450–454
BBWH; SWI. 53
BELL & CO; FRA. 165, 166
BITUME; BEL. 490
BLOOMINGDALE'S; USA. 80
BOLT & NUTS STUDIO; JPN. 46
BON GÉNIE/SERVICE PUBLICITÉ; SWI. 28
BORCIC, STUDIO; YUG. 394
BORTOLOTTI, STUDIO; ITA. 502
BRIGHT & ASSOCIATES; USA. 186
BROWN, MICHAEL DAVID, INC.; USA. 528
BROWN & ROSNER; USA. 197
BUNDI, ATELIER; SWI. 282–284, 485, 486
BYSTED, PETER, STUDIO; DEN. 207

CALIDA AG/WERBEABT.; SWI. 23
CAPITOL RECORDS, INC.; USA. 104
CARABOSSE; SWI. 127
CHERMAYEFF & GEISMAR ASSOC.; USA. 270, 403
COCCHI, LAURENT; SWI. 154
CONGE DESIGN; USA. 187
COOPSTUDIO; ITA. 357, 442, 501, 504
CREATOR OY; FIN. 113
CREEL MORRELL INC.; USA. 381
CROSS ASSOCIATES; USA. 210–216, 529
CSU ART. DEPT.; USA. 239
CUNNINGHAM & WALSH; USA. 518

DANNE & BLACKBURN, INC.; USA. 516
DEMNER & MERLICEK; AUT. 13, 16, 32, 102,
    116–118, 199
DENNARD CREATIVE, INC.; USA. 51
DENTSU INC.; JPN. 1, 2, 206, 208, 209, 420
DESGRIPPES BEAUCHANT GOBÉ; FRA. 34
DESIGN FARM; JPN. 48, 49, 422, 423
DOYLE DANE BERNBACH; SWI. 27
DOYLE DANE BERNBACH, INC.; USA. 509–511

EIBER, RICK, DESIGN; USA. 262

FCO UNIVAS LTD.; GBR. 30, 31, 62
FION, ALAIN; GER. 129
FOOTE, CONE & BELDING; USA. 41, 42
FORD, BYRNE & ASSOCIATES; USA. 441
FUORISCHEMA, STUDIO; ITA. 402, 404, 408, 503,
    505–507
FURMAN, MICHAEL; USA. 72

GEISSBÜHLER, K. DOMENIC; SWI. 302
GGK; SWI. 22
GLASER, MILTON, INC.; USA. 52, 189, 460, 461, 541

GRAPHIC COMMUNICATIONS; USA. 455–457,
    466–468
GRAPHITI; ITA. 151, 354, 374, 469
GRC; GBR. 114, 115
GREIMAN, APRIL; USA. 465
GREYS ADVERTISING; GBR. 66, 67

HAASE & KNELS; GER. 157, 414
HABITAT MOTHERCARE GROUP DESIGN LTD.;
    GBR. 524–527
HESSISCHER RUNDFUNK/ABT. PUBLIZISTIK;
    GER. 255, 256
HIESTAND, U., ATELIER; SWI. 77
HOLTMANN, HANS J.; SWI. 20
HOT ART CO., LTD.; JPN. 172
HOUSE & GARDEN MAGAZINE; USA. 156

IBM; USA. 392, 517
IGARASHI, TAKENOBU, DESIGN; JPN. 94, 334, 416
IMAGES; USA. 310
IMPACT FCB; FRA. 96
INTERNATIONALES DESIGN ZENTRUM; GER. 316
ITOH DESIGN INC.; JPN. 484

JACOBS, JIM, STUDIO, INC.; USA. 196, 335
JAQUET, ATELIER; SWI. 36, 37
J. G & PARTNER; GER. 494

KAJ OTTO GRAFISK DESIGN; DEN. 483
KAW; POL. 415
KEHL, MAX, AG; SWI. 71
KENYON & ECKHARDT SA; SWI. 18
KINGGRAPHIC; HKG. 121
KRETZSCHMAR STUDIO; USA. 101
K-TWO CO. LTD.; JPN. 418
KVH/GGK INTERNATIONAL; NLD. 194

LANDOR ASSOCIATES; USA. 103
LESNIEWICZ/NAVARRE; USA. 515
LEU, OLAF, DESIGN & PARTNER; GER. 76
LLOYD NORTHOVER LTD.; GBR. 261
LOOSER, HEINZ; SWI. 184
LORD, SULLIVAN & YODER; USA. 175
LUFTHANSA/WERBEABT.; GER. 142–144

MACYS GRAPHIC DESIGN; USA. 43, 168
MAGIN, WOLF; GER. 147, 148
MAGYAR HIRDETÖ; HUN. 321
MARTIN WILLIAMS ADVERTISING; USA. 82
MEDINA, FERNANDO, DESIGN; SPA. 317
MENDELL & OBERER; GER. 58, 106
MILLER, DOLPH, & ASSOC., INC.; USA. 84
MOBIUM; USA. 535–537
MOLNAR, KALMAN, LTD.; CAN. 179
MORAVA & OLIVER DESIGN OFFICE; USA. 514
MORTENSEN DESIGN; USA. 59
MUIR CORNELIUS MOORE; USA. 193
MUSCLE FILMS/KRUDDART; GBR. 352, 353

NAKADE, TEIJIRO; JPN. 3, 4
NAKATA PUBLICITY; JPN. 50
NIHON-KOUTSU-JIGYO-SYA; JPN. 185
NIPPON DESIGN CENTER; JPN. 158, 431–435

NORTHERN DESIGN UNIT; GBR. 60, 61

OVESEY & CO.; USA. 70

PENN STATE UNIVERSITY; USA. 407
PENTAGRAM; GBR. 437
PERKINS, DAVID, & ASSOCIATES; USA. 74
PFUND, ROGER; SWI. 304
PIRTLE DESIGN; USA. 173, 271, 275
POL, SANTIAGO; VEN. 410
PORTAL PUBLICATIONS LTD.; USA. 83, 107

REACTOR ART & DESIGN LTD.; CAN. 44
REISINGER, STUDIO; ISR. 169
RICHARDS, SULLIVAN, BROCK & ASSOCIATES
    (RICHARDS GROUP); USA. 167
ROBIE, JAMES, DESIGN; USA. 538–540
ROLLY, HANSPETER; SWI. 24
RYUKO TSUSHIN CO. LTD.; JPN. 95

SALVATO & COE ASSOCIATES; USA. 202
SCHOOL OF VISUAL ARTS PRESS; USA. 519–523
SCHWARTZ, O & E; ISR. 188
SCHWARTZMAN, ARNOLD, PRODUCTIONS INC.;
    USA. 470, 471
SCORSONE, JOE, VISUAL DESIGN; USA. 464
SCOTT, FORESMAN & CO.; USA. 462, 463,
    472–479
SHISEIDO CO., LTD.; JPN. 25, 26, 29
SOMMESE, LANNY, DESIGN; USA. 112,
    265, 440
SORBIE ROCHE; USA. 243, 389, 390, 439
SPENCER/FRANCEY INC.; CAN. 443, 444
SPOHN, JÜRGEN; GER. 86
STEINHILBER DEUTSCH & GARD; USA. 68
STREETWORKS STUDIO; USA. 178

TAYLOR, BROWN & BARNHILL; USA. 395
TCD CORPORATION; JPN. 88, 89
TERADA ILLUSTRATION OFFICE; JPN. 63
TESTA, ARMANDO, S. P. A.; ITA. 376
THOMPSON, J. WALTER; JPN. 6–10, 131, 132
TIMMERMANN; GER. 512
T. I. VISUAL PLANNING; JPN. 174
TROXLER, NIKLAUS, GRAFIK-STUDIO; SWI. 336
TSCHARNER, G., AG; SWI. 155, 491–493
TSCHERNY, GEORGE, INC.; USA. 126, 446

VANDERBYL DESIGN; USA. 79, 81, 191, 391
VIGNELLI ASSOCIATES; USA. 11, 12
VISCOSUISSE/WERBEABT.; SWI. 21
VISUAL COMMUNICATIONS; USA. 181
VOGT, PETER, GRAFIK DESIGN; GER. 47

WEEKS, DAN, DESIGN; USA. 508
WEISS, DIDIER; SWI. 17
WELLER INSTITUTE FOR THE CURE OF DESIGN, INC.;
    USA. 108, 109, 145
WINZERHALDE GRAFIK AG; SWI. 162
WIRZ, ADOLF, AG; SWI. 159, 195

YOUNG & RUBICAM, MK & S; SAF. 14, 15
YOUNG & RUBICAM; SWI. 160, 161

Index to Advertisers and Publishers
Verzeichnis der Auftraggeber und Verleger
Index des Clients et Editeurs

AARHUS THEATER; DEN. 264
ABM; SWI. 77
ADLER JOAILLERS; SWI. 18
AES COMPUTERS; GBR. 66, 67
AIR FRANCE; FRA. 203
ALLAN, POUL; DEN. 176
ALLIANZA EDITORIAL S.A.; SPA. 120
ALTE OPER FRANKFURT/M; GER. 252–254
ALVIN AILEY AMERICAN DANCE THEATRE; USA. 270
AMERICAN DIABETES ASSOCIATION; USA. 509–511
AMERICAN INSTITUTE OF ARCHITECS; USA. 391, 395
AMERICAN LIBRARY ASSOCIATION; USA. 460
AMERICAN TELEPHONE & TELEGRAPH CO.; USA. 528, 535, 536
AMNESTY INTERNATIONAL. 483, 486
ANHEUSER-BUSCH, INC.; USA. 40, 450–454
ANIEP; ITA. 502
ARSTON; POL. 105
ART DIRECTORS CLUB KANSAS CITY; USA. 182
ART DIRECTORS CLUB OF LOS ANGELES; USA. 470
ART DIRECTORS/COPYWRITERS CLUB OF MINNE-SOTA; USA. 180
ART DIRECTORS CLUB GALLERY, NEW YORK; USA. 424–426
ASAHI KASAY CO., LTD.; JPN. 1
ASAHI SHIMBUN PUBLISHING CO.; JPN. 421
ASAKUSA OPERA; JPN. 429, 430
ASSICS INC.; JPN. 63
ASSOCIAZIONE NAZIONALE COOPERATIVE AGRI-COLE; ITA. 501
AUDIO-TECHNICA CORP.; JPN. 56

BADISCHES STAATSTHEATER KARLSRUHE; GER. 257
BALLY AG; SWI. 27
BALLY SOCIÉTÉ; FRA. 19
BARTSCH & CHARIAU, GALERIE; GER. 377, 445
BBC SYMPHONY ORCHESTRA; GBR. 240
BDG BREMEN; GER. 414
BEA BERN AUSSTELLUNGSGESELLSCHAFT; SWI. 385
BEFO SOLCENTER; DEN. 205
BENDINGER, BRUCE; USA. 356
BENSON, ELAINE, GALLERY; USA. 461
BERUFSVERBAND BILDENDER KÜNSTLER; GER. 405
BIBERIST, PAPIERFABRIK; SWI. 71
BIENNALE OF INDUSTRIAL DESIGN, LJUBLJANA; YUG. 394
BIG APPLE CIRCUS; USA. 339
BIURO WYSTAW ARTYSTYCZNYCH; POL. 370
BLOOMINGDALE'S; USA. 80
BMW MUSEUM, GER. 411
BMW OF NORTH AMERICA, INC.; USA. 136–141
BOMPIANI EDITORE; ITA. 125
BOS INTERNATIONAL; YUG. 73
BORG-WARNER; USA. 197
BREGENZER FESTSPIELE; AUT. 308
BRIDGESTONE BICYCLE CO., LTD.; JPN. 131, 132
BRIGHAM YOUNG UNIVERSITY; USA. 455–457, 466–468
BRITISH FILM INSTITUTE; GBR. 352
BRITISH TOURIST AUTHORITY; GBR. 149, 150, 153
BÜHNEN DER STADT GERA; GDR. 244, 290
BULGARIAFILM; BUL. 332, 347
BUND GEGEN ALKOHOL IM STRASSENVERKEHR; GER. 512
BUNKA HOSO; JPN. 334
BUREAU D'EXPOSITIONS ARTISTIQUES, POZNAN; POL. 324

CAFÉ GAMST; DEN. 39
CAFÉ THEATRE LE PARVIS; FRA. 259
CALIDA AG; SWI. 23
C.A.N.T.V.; VEN. 410

CAPEZIO BALLET MAKERS, INC.; USA. 70
CAPITOL RECORDS, INC.; USA. 104
CBS RECORDS; USA. 103
CENTRE NATIONAL D'ART ET DE CULTURE GEORGES POMPIDOU; FRA. 217
CENTRO PER LA SPERIMENTAZIONE TEATRALE DI PONTEDERA; ITA. 354, 469
CFW PUBLICATIONS; HKG. 121
CHEMINS DE FER BELGES (SNCB); BEL. 198
CHEMIN DE FER BIÈRE–APPLES–MORGES; SWI. 154
CHETTA B.; CAN. 44
CHINA SEAS, INC.; USA. 171
CHURCH ORGANIZATION; POL. 495
CIBA GEIGY LTD.; GBR. 30, 31
CIGNA CORPORATION; USA. 441
CIPA EUROPE; FRA. 34
CITY OF FORT COLLINS; USA. 239
COLLEGIUM ACADEMICUM, GENÈVE; SWI. 447
COMITÉ EUROPE-AMÉRIQUE LATINE. 490
COMPSHOP; FRA. 165, 166
COMUNE DI COMACCHIO; ITA. 442
COMUNE DI FANO; ITA. 503
COMUNE DI MODENA; ITA. 404
COMUNE DI PESARO; ITA. 408, 505–507
COMUNE DI URBANIA; ITA. 402
COMUNE DI VENEZIA; ITA. 374
CONCORD WATCH COMPANY SA; SWI. 17
CONDÉ NAST PUBLICATIONS, INC.; USA. 156
CONGRESSO PROVINCIALE COOPERATIVE DI PRO-DUZIONE E LAVORO; ITA. 504
COOP SCHWEIZ, SWI. 22
CREATIVE EDUCATION, INC.; USA. 458, 459
CREDITANSTALT WIEN; AUT. 199
CORATIAN NATIONAL THEATRE, SPLIT; YUG. 297
CROSSE & BLACKWELL. 38
CUBIC METRE FURNTURE LTD.; GBR. 133

DALLAS MORNING NEWS, USA. 335
DALLAS PHOTO LABS., INC.; USA. 110, 111
DANISH FURNITURE MAKERS QUALITY CONTROL; DEN. 78
DAVID GROUP; ISR. 169
DAVIDSON GALLERIES, SEATTLE; USA. 438
DEAHL, DAVID, PHOTOGRAPHY; USA. 87
DEISS SCHUHHAUS; SWI. 24
DEUTSCHER AKADEMISCHER AUSTAUSCHDIENST; GER. 316
DEUTSCHE BÜCHEREI, LEIPZIG; GDR. 393
DEUTSCHER SPARKASSENVERLAG GMBH; GER. 513
DIRECTIONS GALLERY; USA. 389
DOMON, KEN, MUSEUM OF PHOTOGRAPHY; JPN. 448
DUNLOP, SPORTS & LEISURE SHOES DIV.; GBR. 60, 61

EASTCOAST JEANS; AUS. 192
ESR GRAPHICS, INC.; USA. 181
EVANGELISCHES FORUM BERLIN; GER. 496
EWING-ROBINSON, INC.; USA. 528

FELTRINELLI EDITORE; ITA. 124
FILM POLSKI; POL. 222, 234, 320, 323, 349, 351, 358, 367, 409
FILM SUPERSAXO; SWI. 127
FIORUCCI S.P.A.; ITA. 45
FOREVER TOYS; USA. 112
FORMA THREE, LTD.; USA. 85
FREMDENVERKEHRSAMT MÜNCHEN; GER. 146
FREMDENVERKEHRSVERBAND INNSBRUCK; AUT. 183
FRIEDENSKUNDGEBUNG BERN; SWI. 485
FUKUTAKE PUBLISHING CO., LTD.; JPN. 92, 93
FUNDACION J. MIRO; SPA. 317

GALERIA STODOLA; POL. 372
GALERIA TEATRU NOWEGO, WARSAW; POL. 369
GALERIE GERSTENBERG, BONN; GER. 249
GALERIE KUNSTSAMMLUNG COTTBUS; GDR. 378, 379
GALLERY OLIVE; JPN. 422, 423
GALLIMARD/CRILY; FRA. 375
GIFU GRAPHIC DESIGNERS CLUB; JPN. 91
GOETHE HOUSE NEW YORK; USA. 446
GOODWILL INDUSTRIES; USA. 518
GRACE, W.R., & CO.; USA. 126
GRAFIA, ASSOC. OF GRAPHIC DESIGNERS; FIN. 113
GRALEN GALLERY; USA. 108, 109
GRAND UNION CO.; USA. 52
GREATER NEW YORK CONFERENCE ON SOVIET JEWRY; USA. 500
GRENSHAW, ANDREW, LTD.; USA. 549, 553, 554
GRIEDER LES BOUTIQUES; SWI. 28
GROSS, BOB; GBR. 437
GUNLOCKE COMPANY; USA. 465

HAARMANN & REIMER GMBH; GER. 201
HABITAT DESIGNS LTD.; GBR. 524–527
HAIFA CITY; ISR. 188
HAMIDASHI-GEKIJO; JPN. 418
HAROLD CLURMAN THEATRE, NEW YORK; USA. 272–274
HARRY'S; GER. 58
HELVETAS; SWI. 491, 493
HESSISCHER RUNDFUNK; GER. 255, 256
HEWLETT-PACKARD AG; SWI. 195
HICKORY BUSINESS FURNITURE; USA. 79
HIDEJO KANZAKI; JPN. 419
HIJIKATA, HIROKATSU; JPN. 480, 481
HIROSHIMA INTERNATIONAL CULTURAL FOUNDA-TION; INC.; JPN. 482
HIROSHIMA PEACE MEMORIAL MUSEUM; JPN. 484
HOCH YBRIG AG; SWI. 184
HOLLAND AMERICA LINE USA INC.; USA. 186
HOUSE OF MONATIC; SAF. 14, 15
HOUSTON INTERNATIONAL FILM FESTIVAL; USA. 381
HUMOR GRAPHIC; ITA. 376

IBM ÖSTERREICH; AUT. 102
IBM CORP.; USA. 193, 392, 516, 517
INSTYTUTO FRYDERYKA CHOPINA; POL. 415
INTERNATIONAL FESTIVAL OF CONTEMPORARY MUSIC, WARSAW; POL. 294
INTERNATIONAL WOOL SECRETARIAT; JPN. 6–10
ISETAN MUSEUM; JPN. 427, 428, 542–547
ISRAEL SINFONIETTA, BEER-SHEVA; ISR. 307

JACOB, TEO, OFFICE; SWI. 130
JAGDA JAPAN GRAPHIC DESIGNERS ASSOC.; JPN. 402
JAPANESE NATIONAL RAILWAY; JPN. 208, 209
JAZZ PIANISTS FESTIVAL, KALISZ; POL. 293
JAZZ IN WILLISAU; SWI. 336
JURAKU CO. LTD.; JPN. 90
JUTLAND BANK A/S; DEN. 207

KANAGAWA PREFECTURAL OFFICE; JPN. 416
KAW; POL. 487
KENCHIKU-SHA, SHOTEN; JPN. 94
KNOLL INTERNATIONAL; GER. 33
KODAK SA; SWI. 57
KODAK PHOTOGRAPHIC GALLERY, LONDON; GBR. 383
KULTURAMT DER STADT ERLANGEN; GER. 380
KULTURBEHÖRDE HAMBURG; GER. 250
KUNSTGEWERBEMUSEUM ZÜRICH; SWI. 396
KUNSTHAUS ZÜRICH; SWI. 397, 398, 400

KURIER AG; AUT. 116–118
KYUSHU GRAPHIC DESIGN ASSOC.; JPN. 174

LADY MANHATTAN TEXTILGESELLSCHAFT; AUT. 13
LAMY GMBH; GER. 47
LEINER; AUT. 32
LE POINT; FRA. 96
LEVI'S; USA. 41, 42
LIBRAIRIE POLONAISE, PARIS; FRA. 413
LOS ANGELES OLYMPIC ORGANIZING COMMITTEE;
    USA. 471, 529–534, 538–540
LOUISVILLE ORCHESTRA; USA. 310
LUCK, J. V., RESEARCH SOCIETY; USA. 514
LUFTHANSA; GER. 142–144
LYRIC OPERA OF CHICAGO; USA. 295

MACYS; USA. 43, 168
MAISON DE LA CULTURE, AMIENS; FRA. 260
MARIANI GALLERY; USA. 390
MARKTEX; GER. 76
MARTIN WILLIAMS ADVERTISING; USA. 82
MASTER EAGLE GALLERY; USA. 387, 388
MATSUYA DEPT. STORE; JPN. 2
MCDONALD, RONALD, HOUSE OF NORTHWEST OHIO;
    USA. 515
MDC PRINTS LTD.; GBR. 550–552
MEDICOR; HUN. 204
MIGROS GENOSSENSCHAFTS-BUND; SWI. 53, 162
MIKAWAWAN-KOKUTEI-KOUEN-CONFERENCE;
    JPN. 185
MILLER, HERMAN, INC.; USA. 64, 65
MINDSET CORP.; USA. 81
MINISTERIO DE CULTURA; SPA. 401
MOBIL CORPORATION; USA. 403
MOBIUM PRESS; USA. 537
MOKEP; HUN. 321, 322, 350, 359
MOLNAR, KALMAN, LTD.; CAN. 179
MONTERE-GALERIE, BERN; SWI. 386
MÜNCHNER VOLKSTHEATER; GER. 289
MUSÉE D'ART ET D'HISTOIRE, GENÈVE; SWI. 384
MUSEUM OF MODERN ART, TOYAMA; JPN. 431–434
MÜSSING, WILHELM, GMBH; GER. 69

NANKAI ELECTRIC RAILWAY CO., LTD.; JPN. 88, 89
NATIONAL SEMICONDUCTOR; USA. 59
NATIONALTHEATER PRAG; CSR. 225
NEELS; NLD. 123
NEUE ZÜRCHER ZEITUNG; SWI. 159
NEVAMAR CORP.; USA. 175
NEW MELSA; JPN. 3, 4
NEW YORK SHAKESPEARE FESTIVAL; USA. 276
NEW YORK STATE DEPARTMENT OF COMMERCE;
    USA. 189
NEW YORK TIMES; USA. 99, 100, 119, 436
NIKE INTERNATIONAL; USA. 62
NIPPON KEIZAI SHIMBUN-SHA; JPN. 420, 435
NOMOS BOLOGNA; ITA. 357
NORDMENDE VERTRIEBS GMBH & CO. KG; GER. 157
NOUVEAU THEATRE DE POCHE, GENÈVE; SWI. 304
NOUVELLES IMAGES; FRA. 373

OBSERVER MAGAZINE; GBR. 98
OHIO PRINTING CO.; USA. 202
ONKYO CORPORATION; JPN. 190
OPER FRANKFURT/M; GER. 306
OPERNHAUS ZÜRICH; SWI. 302
ORGANIZATION OF AD-CREATIVE CORP.; JPN. 170

OWENS-ILLINOIS; USA. 508

PALACE PICTURES; GBR. 353
PENN STATE UNIVERSITY; USA. 265, 407
PERKINS SHEAR; USA. 439
PIZZA INN; USA. 51
PORTAL PUBLICATIONS LTD.; USA. 83, 107
POZNANSKA ESTRADA; POL. 366
PRÄSIDIALABTEILUNG DER STADT ZÜRICH; SWI. 340
PROGRESS FILM-VERLEIH; GDR. 281, 355
PRO HELVETIA; SWI. 341–346
PROPAGANCNI TVORBA; CSR. 122
PROSCENIUM INC.; USA. 514
PROVINCIA DI FIRENZE; ITA. 151
PTT; SWI. 160, 161

Q.P.CORPORATION LTD.; JPN. 50

RHEINISCHES LANDESMUSEUM, BONN; GER. 224
RINASCENTE, LA; ITA. 177
RISISTENZA INTERNAZIONALE; ITA. 488
RIVIERA REMONT, WARSAW; POL. 338
ROCHESTER CHAMBER OF COMMERCE; USA. 187
ROLLING STONES RECORDS; USA. 101
ROMANIA FILM; RUM. 330, 331, 368
ROUSE COMPANY; USA. 167
ROWOHLT VERLAG; GER. 128
ROYAL ACADEMY OF ARTS; GBR. 382
ROYAL SHAKESPEARE COMPANY; GBR. 261

SAN FRANCISCO MUSEUM OF MODERN ART;
    USA. 391
SANTA CRUZ IMPORTS; USA. 11, 12
SCHILLER THEATER BERLIN; GER. 248, 251, 292
SCHLOSS-SPIELE SPIEZ; SWI. 282
SCHNEIDERS BEKLEIDUNG; AUT. 16
SCHOOL OF VISUAL ARTS; USA. 519–523
SCHWEIZ. BANKIERVEREINIGUNG; SWI. 163
SCHWEPPES SWITZERLAND; SWI. 36, 37
SCOTT, FORESMAN & CO.; USA. 462, 463, 472–479
SEATTLE REPERTORY THEATRE; USA. 262
SECTION N; AUT. 134, 135
SEIBU DEPARTMENT STORES LTD.; JPN. 5, 333
SEIYU STORES, LTD.; JPN. 172
SENKO SHA; JPN. 97
SEPTEMVRI, EDITION; BUL. 498
SHA-KEN CO., LTD.; JPN. 46
SHAKESPEARE FESTIVAL OF DALLAS; USA. 271, 275
SHISEIDO CO., LTD.; JPN. 25, 26, 29
SHREVEPORT ADVERTISING FEDERATION; USA. 84
SIMPSON PAPER CO.; USA. 210–216
SPECTRUM CYCLES; USA. 72
SPOHN, JÜRGEN; GER. 86
STAATSTHEATER KASSEL; GER. 303
STADT BONN; GER. 449
STADT KIEL; GER. 399
STÄDTISCHE BÜHNEN MÜNSTER; GER. 221
STÄDTISCHE THEATER KARL-MARX-STADT;
    GDR. 242
STADTTHEATER BERN; SWI. 285, 286, 305
STADTTHEATER LÜNEBURG; GER. 298, 299
STAECK, EDITION; GER. 489, 499
STAT CAT; USA. 196
STATE COLLEGE JUNIOR WOMANS CLUB; USA. 440
STEELCASE; USA. 74
STICHTING SPAARBANK'S GRAVENHAGE; NLD. 194
STRATFORD FESTIVAL; CAN. 443, 444

SÜDWESTFUNK BADEN-BADEN; GER. 494
SUMMER CAFÉ THEATRE; USA. 243
SYSKA & HENNESSY; USA. 191

TDF CELJE; YUG. 329
TEATR DRAMATYCZNY; POL. 223, 235, 291
TEATR JARACZA, LODZ; POL. 220, 233
TEATR KOCHANOWSKIEGO, OPOLE; POL. 218
TEATR MALY, WARSAW; POL. 288
TEATR NOWY, WARSAW; POL. 226, 229
TEATR OCHOTY, ZUMOSC; POL. 232
TEATR POLSKI, POZNAN; POL. 371
TEATR ROSMAITOSCI, WARSAW; POL. 231
TEATR STUDIO, WARSAW; POL. 227
TEATR TARNOWSKI; POL. 236, 237
TEATR WIELKI, WARSAW; POL. 266, 267, 269
TECNO; SWI. 75
TEL AVIV MUSEUM; ISR. 406
THEATER HAUS IM PARK, BERGEDORF; GER. 300
THEATER-KOLLEKTIV BERN; SWI. 283, 284
THEATER DER STADT ESSEN; GER. 230, 246, 247, 296
THEATER IM PALAST, BERLIN; GDR. 314
THEATRE DES CASEMATES; LUX. 277
THEATRE DE FOLLE PENSÉE; FRA. 258, 263
THEATRE LJUBLJANA & CELJE; YUG. 268
THEATRE NATIONAL DE BELGIQUE; BEL. 245; 278
THEATRE OUVERT; LUX. 279, 280
THEATRE DE VILLENEUVE D'ASCQ; FRA. 287, 288
THEATRE OF YOUNGS, SARAJEVO; YUG. 318
TIMES NEWSPAPERS; GBR. 114, 115
TOEI FILM COMPANY; JPN. 417
TOYAMA PREFECTURE; JPN. 158
TYLER SCHOOL OF ART; USA. 464

UNESCO; JPN. 420
UPF; CSR. 348, 360, 364, 365
U.S.I.C.A.; USA. 178
US POSTAL SERVICE; USA. 309

VBZ; SWI. 155
VEREINIGUNG LENKONZERT, LENINGRAD;
    USR. 312, 315
VERKEHRSVEREIN MANNHEIM; GER. 147, 148
VIDEON; GER. 106
VILLE DE MONTREUIL; FRA. 497, 548
VILLE DE ROANNE; FRA. 152
VIOLETTE KOSMETIK-INSTITUT; SWI. 20
VISCOSUISSE AG; SWI. 21
VISICORP; USA. 68
VOICE, STUDIO; JPN. 95
VOLVO CONCESSIONAIRES LTD.; GBR. 200

WALLGRABEN-THEATER, FREIBURG/BRSG.;
    GER. 238
WAXDECK, LEONHARD J.; USA. 311
WELTI-FURRER AG; SWI. 35
WESTDEUTSCHER RUNDFUNK; GER. 337
WESTERN AIRLINES; USA. 145
WÜRTT. STAATSTHEATER STUTTGART; GER. 301
WYNNE, SHANNON; USA. 173

YAMAHA MOTOR CO., LTD.; JPN. 206
YELLO SPORT; GER. 129
YOSHIKUBO SAKE BREWERY CO.; JPN. 48, 49

ZANDERS FEINPAPIERE AG; GER. 54, 55, 164
ZRF; POL. 313, 319, 325–328, 361, 362

■ Entry instructions may be requested by anyone interested in submitting samples of exceptional graphics or photography for possible inclusion in our annuals. No fees involved. Closing dates for entries:
GRAPHIS ANNUAL (advertising and editorial art and design): 31 January
PHOTOGRAPHIS (advertising and editorial photography): 30 June
GRAPHIS POSTERS (an annual of poster art): 30 June
Write to: Graphis Press Corp., Dufourstrasse 107, 8008 Zurich, Switzerland

■ Einsendebedingungen können von jedermann angefordert werden, der uns Beispiele hervorragender Photographie oder Graphik zur Auswahl für unsere Jahrbücher unterbreiten möchte. Es werden keine Gebühren erhoben. Einsendetermine:
GRAPHIS ANNUAL (Werbe- und redaktionelle Graphik): 31. Januar
PHOTOGRAPHIS (Werbe- und redaktionelle Photographie): 30. Juni
GRAPHIS POSTERS (ein Jahrbuch der Plakatkunst): 30. Juni
Adresse: Graphis Verlag AG, Dufourstrasse 107, 8008 Zürich, Schweiz

■ Tout intéressé à la soumission de travaux photographiques et graphiques recevra les informations nécessaires sur demande. Sans charge de participation. Dates limites:
GRAPHIS ANNUAL (art graphique publicitaire et rédactionnel): 31 janvier
PHOTOGRAPHIS (photographie publicitaire et rédactionnelle): 30 juin
GRAPHIS POSTERS (annuaire sur l'art de l'affiche): 30 juin
S'adresser à: Editions Graphis SA, Dufourstrasse 107, 8008 Zurich, Suisse

Editor and Art Director: Walter Herdeg
Assistant Editor: Joan Lüssi
Project Managers: Romy Herzog, Heinke Jenssen
Designers: Marino Bianchera, Martin Byland
Art Assistants: Peter Wittwer, Walter Zuber

1

Advertising Posters

Werbeplakate

Affiches publicitaires

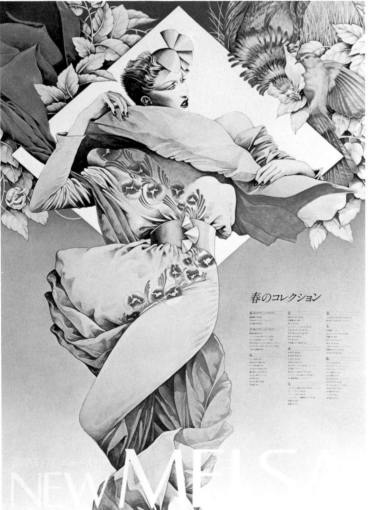

ARTIST / KÜNSTLER / ARTISTE:

1 Bruce Osborn
2 Masaki Ono
3, 4 Hélène Majera
5 Yoshio Hayakawa

DESIGNER / GESTALTER / MAQUETTISTE:

1 Tatsuomi Majima
2 Takanori Asaeda
3, 4 Teijiro Nakade
5 Ikko Tanaka/Katsuhiro Kinoshita

ART DIRECTOR / DIRECTEUR ARTISTIQUE:

1 Tatsuomi Majima
2 Takanori Asaeda
3, 4 Teijiro Nakade
5 Ikko Tanaka

AGENCY / AGENTUR / AGENCE – STUDIO:

1, 2 Dentsu Inc.
3, 4 Teijiro Nakade

1 Poster in various blue tones to advertise the *Lammus* brand of clothing. (JPN)
2 Example from a series of posters for the tenth anniversary of the Japanese department stores *Matsuya*, shown here to advertise their fashions for the ballet. Large Japanese characters in pale green. (JPN)
3, 4 From a four-seasons poster series for the Japanese department stores *New Melsa*; here shown for spring and winter fashions. Fig. 3 is mainly in white, pale blue and pink with black-and-white lettering; Fig. 4 is in black and white and pastel shades with embossed, gold-coloured lettering. (JPN)
5 Poster for the fashion department of the Japanese store *Seibu*. (JPN)

1 Werbeplakat in verschiedenen Blautönen für Bekleidung der Marke *Lammus*. (JPN)
2 Beispiel aus einer Serie von Plakaten zum zehnjährigen Bestehen des japanischen Kaufhauses *Matsuya*, hier als Werbung für Ballettmode. Grosse japanische Schriftzeichen in Hellgrün. (JPN)
3, 4 Aus einer Plakatserie des japanischen Kaufhauses *New Melsa* über die vier Jahreszeiten, hier für Frühlings- und Wintermode. Abb. 3: Weiss, Hellblau und Pink überwiegen; Schriften in Weiss und Schwarz; Abb. 4: Schwarz, Weiss und Pastelltöne, goldfarbene Schrift. (JPN)
5 Werbeplakat für die Modeabteilung des japanischen Kaufhauses *Seibu*. (JPN)

1 Affiche publicitaire en différents bleus pour les vêtements de marque *Lammus*. (JPN)
2 Exemple d'affiche dans une série pour le 10e anniversaire des grands magasins japonais *Matsuya*, ici pour les tenues de ballet. Caractères japonais au grand format, reproduits en vert clair. (JPN)
3, 4 Affiches tirées d'une série réalisée pour les grands magasins japonais *New Melsa* sur le thème des quatre saisons, ici pour les modes de printemps et d'hiver. Fig. 3: blanc, bleu clair, rose prédominants; textes en blanc et noir; fig. 4: noir, blanc, tons pastel, texte or. (JPN)
5 Affiche publicitaire d'une campagne pour le département Mode du grand magasin japonais *Seibu*. (JPN)

Fashion/Mode

ウールって、新しいと思う。

NEW WOOL 100%

6

Fashion/Mode

6–10 Examples from a series of posters for clothing made from 100% pure new wool. The aim of the International Wool Secretariat's advertising campaign is to bring to the fore the fact that famous Japanese fashion designers also work with 100% woollen fabrics. In all the posters the faces of the models are missing to focus attention exclusively on the clothing. Fig. 8 shows a table-tennis player in a coloured pullover. Fig. 9 shows clothing in pale, natural tones with darker pattern. The puppy echoes the colours of the pullover. In Fig. 10 a baseball player is portrayed in an anthracite-grey suit and an off-white pullover with dark pattern. (JPN)

ARTIST / KÜNSTLER / ARTISTE:
6–10 Masaya Suga

DESIGNER / GESTALTER / MAQUETTISTE:
6–10 Mitsuaki Miyamoto

ART DIRECTOR / DIRECTEUR ARTISTIQUE:
6–10 Yoshifumi Nakashima

AGENCY / AGENTUR / AGENCE – STUDIO:
6–10 J. Walter Thompson

ウールって、新しいと思う。

NEW WOOL 100%

8

デザイン：
島田順子

ウールって、新しいと思う。

NEW WOOL 100%

7

6–10 Beispiele aus einer Serie von Plakaten für Bekleidung aus 100% Wolle. Ziel der vom internationalen Wollsekretariat lancierten Kampagne ist es, auf die Tatsache aufmerksam zu machen, dass berühmte japanische Mode-Designer ebenfalls mit 100% Wolle arbeiten. Bei allen Plakaten fehlen die Gesichter der Modelle, um das Augenmerk ausschliesslich auf die Bekleidung zu lenken. Abb. 8: Tischtennisspielerin in mehrfarbig gestreiftem Pullover. Abb. 9: Bekleidung in hellen Naturtönen mit dunklerem Muster. Der Welpe entspricht in den Farben denjenigen des Pullovers. Abb. 10: Baseballspieler in anthrazitfarbenem Anzug und naturweissem Pullover mit dunklen Punkten. (JPN)

6–10 Exemples d'affiches dans une série promotionnelle pour les lainages. Cette campagne lancée par le Secrétariat International de la Laine veut attirer l'attention sur le fait que les grands couturiers japonais utilisent eux aussi de la pure laine vierge. Les têtes des mannequins sont supprimées pour que l'attention se concentre uniquement sur les vêtements. Fig. 8: joueuse de ping-pong au pull rayé multicolore. Fig. 9: vêtements aux tons naturels clairs; les dessins sont plus sombres. Le chiot a le poil de même couleur que le pull. Dans la fig. 10 un joueur de base-ball est photographié en costume anthracite et au pull-over blanc naturel à petits pois sombres. (JPN)

ウールって、新しいと思う。

NEW WOOL 100%

9

ウールって、新しいと思う。

NEW WOOL 100%

10

Santa Cruz

Fall 1983

11

Fashion/Mode

Carducci. Al momento magico. Per l'uomo e la donna. Molto elegante.

14 15

12

13

ARTIST / KÜNSTLER / ARTISTE:

11, 12 Brad Mollath
13, 16 Jost Wildbolz
14, 15 Walter Ferrier

DESIGNER / GESTALTER / MAQUETTISTE:

11, 12 Michael Bierut
13, 16 Franz Merlicek

ART DIRECTOR / DIRECTEUR ARTISTIQUE:

11, 12 Massimo Vignelli
13, 16 Franz Merlicek
14, 15 Allan Raaff

AGENCY / AGENTUR / AGENCE – STUDIO:

11, 12 Vignelli Associates
13, 16 Demner & Merlicek
14, 15 Young & Rubicam, MK & S

11, 12 Posters to promote the clothing by *Santa Cruz*. Fig. 11 is for autumn fashion; Fig. 12 is for summer fashion in pink-white and lilac-white. (USA)
13 Poster in muted shades from an advertising campaign for *Lady Manhattan* fashions. The photograph was taken in the corridor of a house overlooking the lake. (AUT)
14, 15 Examples from a series of point-of-sale posters for elegant fashion by *Carducci*. "For the magic moment." The sombre shades and strict lines of the background apply also effectively to the clothes shown. The photographs were taken in Florence. (SAF)
16 Poster in shades of beige and brown from a campaign for fashions by *Schneiders*. (AUT)

11, 12 Werbeplakate für Bekleidung von *Santa Cruz*. Abb. 11: Herbstmode; Abb. 12: Sommermode in Pink-Weiss und Lila-Weiss. (USA)
13 Plakat in gedämpften Farbtönen aus einer Werbekampagne für *Lady-Manhattan*-Mode. Die Aufnahme entstand im Korridor eines Hauses am See. (AUT)
14, 15 Beispiele aus einer Serie von Innenaushang-Plakaten für elegante Damen- und Herrenmode von *Carducci*: «Für den magischen Moment.» Die dunklen Farbtöne des Hintergrunds wirken wie auf die Kleidung abgestimmt. Die Aufnahmen wurden in Florenz realisiert. (SAF)
16 Plakat in Braun-Beige-Tönen aus einer Kampagne für Damen- und Herrenmode von *Schneiders*. Signete und Schriften in Weiss mit Schwarz. (AUT)

11, 12 Affiches publicitaires pour les modes *Santa Cruz*. Fig. 11: modes d'automne; fig. 12: modes d'été en rose-blanc et lilas-blanc. (USA)
13 Affiche aux tons amortis pour une campagne publicitaire en faveur des modes *Lady-Manhattan*. La photo a pour cadre le couloir d'une maison au bord d'un lac. (AUT)
14, 15 Exemples d'affiches intérieures dans une série réalisée pour promouvoir les modes chics de *Carducci* pour dames et messieurs sous le slogan d'«Au moment magique». Les coloris sombres de l'arrière-plan s'harmonisent avec les vêtements. Photos prises à Florence. (SAF)
16 Affiche aux tons beige-brun dans une campagne en faveur des modes masculines et féminines *Schneiders*. Emblèmes et textes blancs, avec du noir. Slogan: «Points de mire.» (AUT)

16

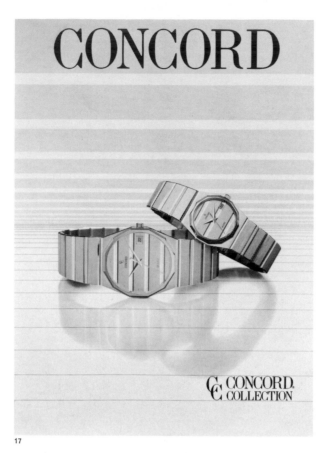

17

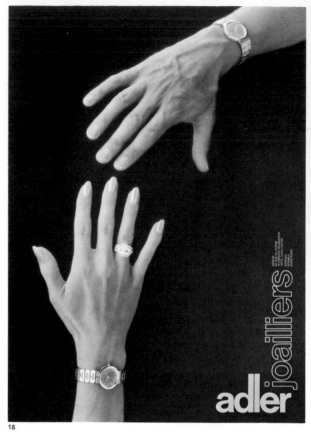

18

20

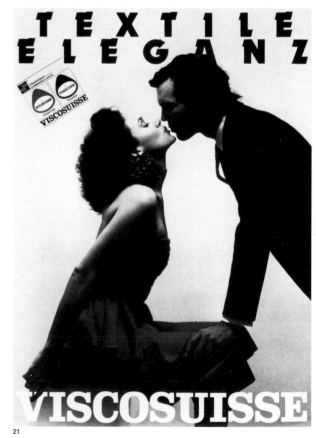

21

ARTIST / KÜNSTLER / ARTISTE:

17 Claude Jeanneret/Photo 2000
18 Jürgen Tapprich
19 Roger Bezombes
21 U. Fäsch
22 Roland Steiner
23 Dieter Schmitz
24 Hanspeter Rolly

DESIGNER / GESTALTER:

17 Mariano Moral/Didier Weiss
19 Roger Bezombes
20 Hans J. Holtmann
21 Peter Zumbühl
22 Piotr Müller
23 O. Bächler
24 Hanspeter Rolly

ART DIRECTOR:

17 Didier Weiss
18 René H. Bittel
19 Jean Pierre Rocher
20 Hans J. Holtmann
21 Peter Zumbühl
22 Piotr Müller
23 O. Bächler

AGENCY / AGENTUR / AGENCE:

17 Didier Weiss
18 Kenyon & Eckhardt SA
20 Hans J. Holtmann
21 Viscosuisse/Werbeabt.
22 GGK
23 Calida/Werbeabt.
24 Hanspeter Rolly

17 Poster for ladies' and gentlemen's gold watches of the brand *Concord*. Background stripes in beige, white and black. (SWI)
18 Poster for elegant watches and rings from the jewellers *Adler*. Brown background, dark beige lettering. (SWI)
19 Polychrome collage on white for an advertising poster for *Bally*. (FRA)
20 Poster to advertise the cosmetic institute Violette. Letter V in mid blue on violet ground, pink stripe. (SWI)
21 With this poster *Viscosuisse* advertises clothing made from synthetic-fibre textiles. Heading and model's dress in magenta. (SWI)
22 Full-colour poster for reasonably-priced nightwear from *Coop*. (SWI)
23 For *Calida* lingerie. Full-colour photograph on yellow background. (SWI)
24 Street poster for the Basle shoe store *Deiss*. (SWI)

17 Werbeplakat für eine Damen- und Herren-Gold-Quarzuhr der Marke *Concord*. Hintergrundstreifen in Beige, Weiss und Schwarz. (SWI)
18 Plakat im Weltformat für Schmuckuhren und einen Ring des Juweliers *Adler*. Brauner Hintergrund, dunkelbeige Schrift. (SWI)
19 Mehrfarbige Collage auf Weiss für ein Werbeplakat von *Bally*. (FRA)
20 Werbeplakat für das Kosmetikinstitut Violette. Buchstabe V in Mittelblau auf violettem Grund, pinkfarbener Strich. (SWI)
21 *Viscosuisse* wirbt mit diesem Plakat für Bekleidung aus Chemiefaser. Überschrift und Kleid des Modells in Magenta. (SWI)
22 Plakat für preisgünstige Schlafanzüge von *Coop*. In Farbe. (SWI)
23 Für *Calida*-Damenunterwäsche. Farbphoto auf gelbem Hintergrund. (SWI)
24 Strassenplakat für das Basler Schuhhaus *Deiss*. (SWI)

BALLY

roger bezombes

19

Der Slip, der nicht einschneidet

CALIDA

23

Echt Coop.

29.-

16.-
bis
22.-

22.-

22

Rally

DEISS

Schuhe·Marktplatz Basel

24

17 Affiche publicitaire pour une montre à quartz *Concord*, dames et messieurs, en or. Bandes de l'arrière-plan beige, blanc, noir. (SWI)
18 Affiche au format universel pour des montres-bijoux et une bague des joailliers *Adler*. Fond brun, texte beige foncé. (SWI)
19 Collage multicolore sur blanc pour une affiche publicitaire *Bally*. (FRA)
20 Affiche publicitaire pour l'institut de beauté *Violette*. Lettre V en bleu neutre sur fond violet, trait rose. (SWI)
21 La *Viscosuisse* fait sur cette affiche de la publicité pour les vêtements en fibres synthétiques. Titre et robe du modèle en magenta. (SWI)
22 Affiche pour les pyjamas à prix avantageux de la *Coop*. En couleur. (SWI)
23 Pour les slips *Calida* «qui ne marquent pas». Photo couleur. (SWI)
24 Affiche extérieure pour le chausseur bâlois *Deiss*. (SWI)

あかい心 しづかに 胸に染まる ✿資生堂香水[ZEN] 禅

25

小夜子・紅一点

26

BALLY

あかい心 しづかに 胸に染まる ✿資生堂香水[ZEN] 禅

27

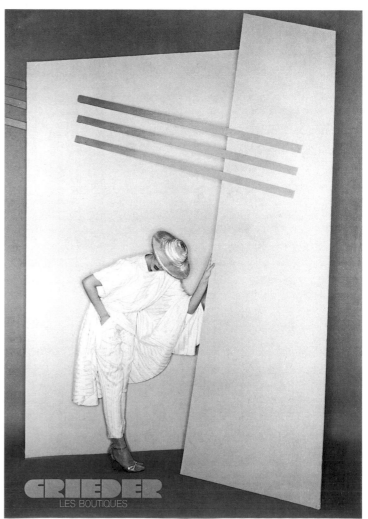

GRIEDER
LES BOUTIQUES

28

ARTIST / KÜNSTLER / ARTISTE:
25, 26, 29 Noriaki Yokosuka
27 Peter Kopp
28 Christian Coigny

DESIGNER / GESTALTER / MAQUETTISTE:
25, 26, 29 Makoto Nakamura
27 Rolf Hummel
28 Jean Paul Brunschwick

ART DIRECTOR / DIRECTEUR ARTISTIQUE:
25, 26, 29 Makoto Nakamura
27 Rodolphe Deville
28 Christian Coigny

AGENCY / AGENTUR / AGENCE – STUDIO:
25, 26, 29 Shiseido Co., Ltd.
27 Doyle Dane Bernbach
28 Bon Génie/Service Publicité

29

25, 26, 29 Posters for the Japanese cosmetic concern *Shiseido*. Fig. 25 is for the perfume "Zen"; Fig. 29 is for the perfume "Rêve d'Amour". (JPN)
27 The *Bally* shoes and matching handbag have a zigzag design in red, orange and blue, combined with black. From a long-running advertising campaign. (SWI)
28 Muted red and pink are the background colours of this poster for the *Grieder* boutiques. The model is wearing a white gold-threaded trouser-suit with a wide cape and golden accessories. The lettering underneath and the three stripes at the top of the poster are in a mauve shade. (SWI)

25, 26, 29 Plakate für den japanischen Kosmetikkonzern *Shiseido*. Abb. 25: Für das Parfum «Zen»; Abb. 29: für das Parfum «Rêve d'Amour». (JPN)
27 Die *Bally*-Schuhe mit Handtasche haben ein Zickzackmuster in Rot, Orange und Blau, kombiniert mit Schwarz. Aus einer langjährigen Werbekampagne. (SWI)
28 Gedämpftes Rot und Rosa sind die Hintergrundfarben dieses Plakats für die *Grieder*-Boutiquen. Das Modell trägt einen weissen, golddurchwirkten Hosendress mit weitem Umhang und goldene Accessoires. Die Schrift unten und die drei Streifen im oberen Teil sind mauvefarben. (SWI)

25, 26, 29 Affiches pour le groupe cosmétique japonais *Shiseido*. Fig. 25: pour le parfum «Zen»; fig. 29: pour le parfum «Rêve d'Amour». (JPN)
27 Ces chaussures *Bally* ont le même dessin rouge, orange et bleu en zigzag, combiné avec du noir. Il s'agit d'une affiche utilisée dans une campagne s'étendant sur plusieurs années. (SWI)
28 L'arrière-plan de cette affiche pour les boutiques *Grieder* est exécuté en rouge mat et en rose. Le modèle porte un ensemble pantalon blanc broché or avec une large cape et des accessoires dorés. Le texte du bas et les trois bandes du haut sont mauves. (SWI)

Fashion/Mode

30

31

30, 31 Poster and advertising board for *Araldit* adhesive. The car on the placard is real. (GBR)
32 The interior-furnishings company *Leiner* is here advertising its studio furniture in a sepia-toned photograph. "You never finish learning!" (AUT)
33 Poster from a campaign for the *Humana* collection of office chairs by *Knoll International*. (GER)
34 Poster to advertise driving mirrors produced by *Cipa*. (FRA)

30, 31 Plakat und Reklametafel für *Araldit*-Alleskleber. Abb. 30: «Klebt fast alles im Haus.» Abb. 31: «Klebt auch Teekannen-Henkel.» Auf die Tafel ist ein richtiges Auto montiert. (GBR)
32 Das Einrichtungshaus *Leiner* wirbt hier für seine Studiomöbel. Sepiafarbene Aufnahme. (AUT)
33 Plakat aus einer Kampagne für die *Humana*-Bürosessel-Kollektion von *Knoll International*. (GER)
34 Der Rückspiegelfabrikant *Cipa* wirbt mit diesem Plakat für seine Erzeugnisse. (FRA)

30, 31 Affiche et panneau publicitaire pour l'*Araldit,* qui «colle presque tout dans la maison» (30) et «même les anses des théières» (31). Une vraie auto est collée au panneau. (GBR)
32 Pour les meubles studio *Leiner*: «On n'en finit jamais d'apprendre!» Photo sépia. (AUT)
33 Affiche dans une campagne de *Knoll International* pour ses chaises de bureau *Humana*. (GER)
34 Affiche où le fabricant de rétroviseurs *Cipa* met en vedette ses produits. (FRA)

Industry/Industrie

ARTIST / KÜNSTLER / ARTISTE:

30, 31 Max Forsythe
32 Claude Buri
33 Jürgen Störk
34 Cheyco Leidmann

DESIGNER / GESTALTER / MAQUETTISTE:

32 Fritz Haubmann
33 Rudolf Beck
34 Marc Gobé/Gilles Plante

ART DIRECTOR / DIRECTEUR ARTISTIQUE:

30 Rob Kitchen
31 Ian Potter
32 Fritz Haubmann
33 Wolf Kaiser
34 Marc Gobé

AGENCY / AGENTUR / AGENCE – STUDIO:

30, 31 FCO Univas Ltd
32 Demner & Merlicek
34 Desgrippes Beauchant Gobé

32

33

unterwegs mit welti-furrer

35

ARTIST / KÜNSTLER / ARTISTE:

35 Celestino Piatti
36 Urs Schneider
37 Jürg Bernardt
38 Villemot
39 Poul Allan
40 Paul Christensen

DESIGNER / GESTALTER / MAQUETTISTE:

35 Celestino Piatti
36, 37 Urs Schneider
38 Villemot
39 Poul Allan
40 Bill Kumke

ART DIRECTOR / DIRECTEUR ARTISTIQUE:

36, 37 Urs Schneider
39 Poul Allan
40 David Bartels

AGENCY / AGENTUR / AGENCE – STUDIO:

36, 37 Atelier Jaquet
40 Bartels & Company

35 The coloured wheel signifies traffic on the move for the transport and storage firm *Welti-Furrer*. (SWI)
36, 37 Street advertising for *Schweppes*. Fig. 36 is a three-part poster from a campaign with woodcuts: "Now and again bitterly necessary"; Fig. 37 reads "Not just any bitter lemon". (SWI)
38 Poster by the artist Villemot for *Crosse & Blackwell's* tomato sauce. (FRA)
39 From a series of advertising posters for the coffeehouse *Café Gamst* in Denmark. (DEN)
40 Poster for the introduction of a new type of beer with less alcohol. The can is in white, red, dark blue and gold, with yellow beer showing inside and it is standing on a blue and white grid base. (USA)

35 Das farbige Rad symbolisiert das Unterwegssein der Transport- und Lagerfirma *Welti-Furrer*. (SWI)
36, 37 Strassenwerbung für *Schweppes*. Abb. 36: Dreiteiliges Plakat aus einer Kampagne mit Holzschnitten, hier für Quinine Water von *Schweppes*; Abb. 37: für *Schweppes* Bitter Lemon. (SWI)
38 Plakat des Künstlers Villemot für Tomatensauce von *Crosse & Blackwell*. (FRA)
39 Aus einer Serie von Werbeplakaten für das Kaffeehaus *Café Gamst* in Dänemark. (DEN)
40 Plakat für die Einführung einer neuen Biersorte mit wenig Alkohol. Bierdose in Weiss, Rot, Dunkelblau und Gold, die auf blauem Grund mit weissem Gitter steht. Im oberen Teil ist der Doseninhalt sichtbar. (USA)

35 Cette roue multicolore symbolise les activités de transport et d'entreposage de *Welti-Furrer*. (SWI)
36, 37 Publicité extérieure pour *Schweppes*. Fig. 36: affiche tripartite dans une campagne illustrée de gravures sur bois pour le Quinine Water de *Schweppes*; fig. 37: «pas n'importe quel Bitter Lemon». (SWI)
38 Affiche de l'artiste Villemot pour la sauce tomate *Crosse & Blackwell*. (FRA)
39 Affiche publicitaire dans une série réalisée en faveur du *Café Gamst* au Danemark. (DEN)
40 Affiche pour le lancement d'une bière à faible teneur en alcool. Boîte en blanc, rouge, bleu foncé et or reposant sur une grille blanche et un fond bleu. Le contenu de la boîte est visible en haut. (USA)

Varia

38

36

Nicht irgend ein Bitter Lemon

37

38

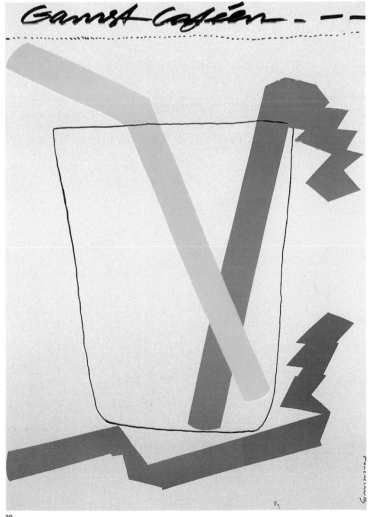

39

40

41

42

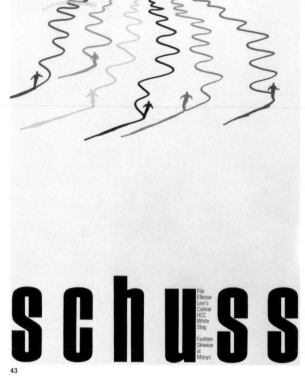

43

45

ARTIST / KÜNSTLER / ARTISTE:

41, 42 Stephen Green-Armytage
43 Brian Collentine
44 Jeff Jackson
45 Laurie Rosenwald
46 Hiro Nobuyama
47 Walter Adams

DESIGNER / GESTALTER / MAQUETTISTE:

43 Brian Collentine
44 Jeff Jackson
45 Laurie Rosenwald
47 Peter Vogt

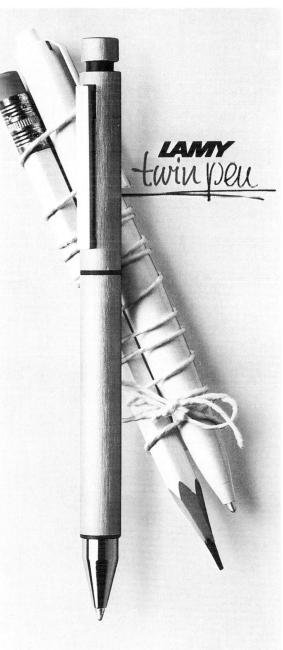

41, 42 Two posters from a series for *Levi's* "501" label. (USA)
43 Multi-coloured tracks on pale snow background and the word "schuss" in grey, to advertise fashion skiwear at the famous American store *Macys*. (USA)
44 Advertising for spring fashions by *Chetta B* in light blue and beige, with figures and graphics in black and white. (CAN)
45 A new-wave style poster for *Fiorucci* fashions. (USA)
46 Poster for a firm which newly changed over to film typesetting. The figures personify a famous loving couple. (JPN)
47 Shop-window poster to announce a two-way writing tool—a ballpoint and pencil in one. (GER)

41, 42 Zwei Plakate aus einer Serie für *Levi's* Jeans «501». (USA)
43 Verschiedenfarbene Spuren und Skifahrer sowie das Wort «schuss» in Grau auf hellem Grund werben für Skimode der entsprechenden Abteilung des Kaufhauses *Macys*. (USA)
44 Werbung für Frühlingsmode von *Chetta B*. In Hellblau und Beige, mit Figuren und Schrift in Schwarzweiss. (CAN)
45 Plakat im New-Wave-Stil für *Fiorucci*-Modegeschäfte. (USA)
46 Plakat einer Firma, die neu auf Photosatz umstellt. Die beiden Figuren verkörpern ein berühmtes Liebespaar. (JPN)
47 Schaufensterplakat für die Ankündigung eines Zwei-System-Schreibgeräts: Kugelschreiber und Bleistift in einem. (GER)

41, 42 Deux affiches dans une série réalisée pour les jeans *Levi's*, avec le numéro de modèle «501». (USA)
43 Chaque skieur laisse ici une trace de couleur différente. Publicité pour les modes de ski des grands magasins *Macys*. Le mot «schuss» apparaît en gris sur fond clair. (USA)
44 Publicité pour les modes de printemps de *Chetta B*. Bleu clair et beige, personnages et texte noir et blanc. (CAN)
45 Affiche nouvelle vague pour les boutiques mode *Fiorucci*. (USA)
46 Affiche d'une entreprise passant à la photocomposition. Les personnages représentent un couple d'amoureux célèbre. (JPN)
47 Affiche de vitrine annonçant la mise en vente d'un stylo-crayon combiné – deux systèmes en un. (GER)

ART DIRECTOR / DIRECTEUR ARTISTIQUE:

41, 42 Chris Blum
43 Richard Nodine
45 Franco Marabelli
46 Kenzo Nakagawa
47 Peter Vogt

AGENCY / AGENTUR / AGENCE – STUDIO:

41, 42 Foote Cone & Belding
43 Macys Graphic Design
44 Reactor Art & Design Ltd.
46 Bolt & Nuts Studio
47 Peter Vogt Grafik Design

48

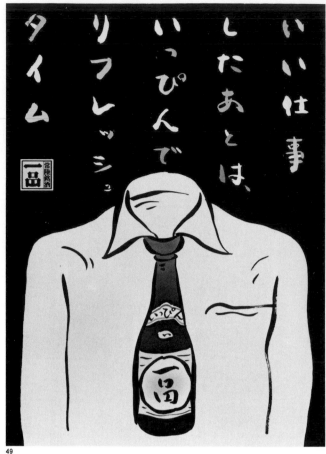

49

50

51

ARTIST / KÜNSTLER / ARTISTE:

48, 49 U. G. Sato
50 Yuzo Yamashita
51 Chuck Johnson
52 Teresa Fasolino
53 Alf Dietrich

DESIGNER / GESTALTER / MAQUETTISTE:

48, 49 U. G. Sato
50 Yuzo Yamashita
51 Chuck Johnson

ART DIRECTOR / DIRECTEUR ARTISTIQUE:

48, 49 U. G. Sato
50 Yuzo Yamashita
51 Bob Dennard
52 Milton Glaser
53 Göpf Horak

AGENCY / AGENTUR / AGENCE – STUDIO:

48, 49 Design Farm
50 Nakata Publicity
51 Dennard Creative
52 Milton Glaser, Inc.
53 BBWH

GRAND UNION'S FRESH FISH

52

Frisch geerntet
und sofort haltbar gemacht:
Unsere Gemüsekonserven

53

48, 49 Examples from an ad campaign for Sake. Fig. 48 shows a brownish-green bamboo sheath, bordeaux-red wine bottle on a white background. In Fig. 49 the shirt is white with a green Sake-bottle-necktie, on blackground. The colourful Japanese characters mean roughly "After successful work a well-earned, delicious Sake tastes good". (JPN)
50 Poster for salad sauces of Japanese and Chinese blend. Polychrome, strong blue background on white stock. (JPN)
51 For the Pizza Inn, a pastel-toned poster advertising quickly served take-away pizza slices. (USA)
52 Example from a series of posters hung in the *Grand Union* supermarkets. They are both decorative and informative. (USA)
53 Poster for the Swiss chain of supermarkets *Migros*, hung in the store to promote their tinned vegetables. "Freshly harvested and immediately rendered long-lasting, our vegetables." (SWI)

48, 49 Beispiele aus einer Werbekampagne für Sake. Abb. 48: Braungrüne Bambushülle, bordeauxrote Sakeflasche auf weissem Hintergrund; Abb. 49: weisses Hemd mit grüner Krawatten-Sakeflasche auf schwarzem Hintergrund. Die bunten japanischen Schriftzeichen bedeuten sinngemäss: «Nach gelungener Arbeit schmeckt ein guter, wohlverdienter Sake.» (JPN)
50 Für Salatsaucen nach japanischer und chinesischer Art. Mehrfarbig, blauer Hintergrund auf weissem Papier. (JPN)
51 Pizza Inn wirbt mit diesem pastellfarbenen Plakat für den Verkauf von Pizza-Schnitten über die Gasse. (USA)
52 Beispiel aus einer Serie von Plakaten, die in den Supermärkten von *Grand Union* hängen und sowohl dekorativ als auch informativ sind. Hier über Fische und Schalentiere. (USA)
53 Ladenplakat in den Supermärkten des Unternehmens *Migros* für den Gemüsekonservenverkauf im Winter. (SWI)

48, 49 Eléments d'une campagne publicitaire en faveur du saké. Fig. 48: gaine de bambou vert brun, bouteille de saké bordeaux sur fond blanc; fig. 49: chemise blanche, bouteille de saké en guise de cravate, fond noir. Le texte polychrome affirme qu'«après une bonne journée de travail, un bon saké bien mérité a un goût délicieux». (JPN)
50 Affiche pour des sauces à salades d'après des recettes chinoise et japonaise. En polychromie; fond bleu vif sur papier blanc. (JPN)
51 Affiche aux tons pastel où le Pizza Inn vante les mérites de ses tranches de pizza à l'emporter. (USA)
52 Exemple d'affiche dans une série décorative autant qu'instructive suspendue dans les supermarchés *Grand Union*, ici pour les poissons et fruits de mer. (USA)
53 Affiche de magasin pour la vente de conserves de légumes en hiver. Supermarchés de la coopérative suisse *Migros*. (SWI)

54

55

54, 55 The focal point is the number 25 in these posters from an anniversary campaign for *Chromolux* paper by *Zanders*. The posters are printed on *Chromolux* paper 700, 180 g/m². (GER)
56 Small-size poster for microphones in various colours from *Audio-Technica*. (JPN)
57 Example from an advertising campaign for *Kodak* films in duopacks. (SWI)
58 Poster as part of the graphic identity for *Harry's* ladies' fashions. (GER)
59 A sales-promotion poster for the firm National Semiconductor. (USA)

54, 55 Die Zahl 25 steht im Mittelpunkt dieser Jubiläums-Kampagne für *Chromolux*-Papier von *Zanders*. Gedruckt sind die Plakate auf *Chromolux* 700, 180 g/m². (GER)
56 Kleinformatiges Plakat für Mikrophone in verschiedenen Farben der Marke *Audio-Technica*. (JPN)
57 Beispiel aus einer Werbekampagne für *Kodak*-Filme im Duopack. (SWI)
58 Plakat als Teil der graphischen Ausstattung für *Harry's* Damenmoden. (GER)
59 Für die Verkaufsförderung lanciertes Plakat der Firma National Semiconductor. (USA)

Industry/Industrie

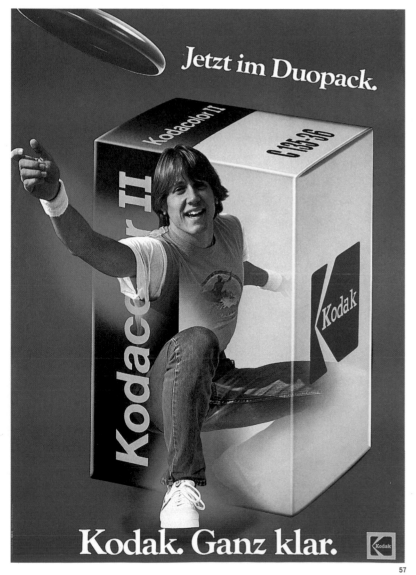

57

58

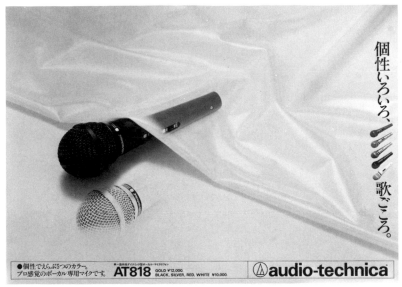

56

ARTIST / KÜNSTLER / ARTISTE:

54, 55 Siegbert Kercher
56 Susumu Endo
57 Jiri Vurma
59 David Campbell

DESIGNER / GESTALTER / MAQUETTISTE:

56 Susumu Endo
57 Ernst Herzog
58 Pierre Mendell
59 Gordon Mortensen

ART DIRECTOR / DIRECTEUR ARTISTIQUE:

56 Susumu Endo
57 Ernst Herzog
58 Pierre Mendell
59 Gordon Mortensen

AGENCY / AGENTUR / AGENCE – STUDIO:

57 Advico AG
58 Mendell & Oberer
59 Mortensen Design

54, 55 Le chiffre 25 est au centre de cette campagne anniversaire pour le papier *Chromolux* de *Zanders*.
Les affiches sont imprimées sur *Chromolux* 700 de 180 g/m². (GER)
56 Affichette pour les micros *Audio-Technica* en divers coloris. (JPN)
57 Exemple d'affiche dans une campagne publicitaire pour les films *Kodak* en duopack. (SWI)
58 Affiche réalisée pour bien ancrer l'image graphique des modes féminines *Harry's*. (GER)
59 Affiche de la National Semiconductor lancée pour la promotion des ventes. (USA)

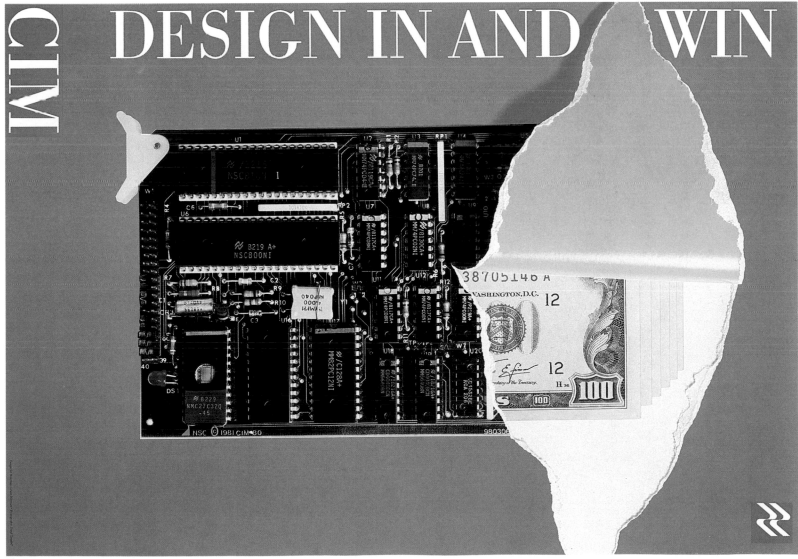

60

61

60, 61 From a series of posters for *Dunlop* sports shoes. Fig. 60: in soft pastel shades, Fig. 61: in various shades of blue and pale sand colour. (GBR)
62 For *Nike* sports shoes, alluding to John McEnroe's behaviour on the tennis court. (GBR)
63 A poster emphasizing the good performance of ski-trousers by *Killy*. (JPN)
64 For two *Eames* office seating programmes designed by Herman Miller, Inc. (USA)
65 Poster showing the versatile seating elements of the *Herman Miller* collection. (USA)

60, 61 Aus einer Reihe von Plakaten für *Dunlop*-Sportschuhe. Abb. 60 in zarten Pastelltönen, Abb. 61 in verschiedenen Blautönen und hellem Sandton. (GBR)
62 Für *Nike*-Sportschuhe, mit Anspielung auf John McEnroes Benehmen auf dem Tennisplatz. (GBR)
63 Die spezielle Ausstattung von *Killy*-Skihosen ist Gegenstand dieses Plakates. (JPN)
64 Für zwei *Eames*-Bürostuhlprogramme (Aluminium und Polster) der Herman Miller, Inc. (USA)
65 Plakat für verschiedene Modelle von Stühlen aus der *Hermann-Miller*-Kollektion. (USA)

透湿性、防風性、撥水性、ストレッチ性に優れた デュアルパンツ新登場!!

killy DUAL PANTS

63

McENROE SWEARS BY THEM.

NIKE

62

ARTIST / KÜNSTLER / ARTISTE:

60, 61 Neil Devonald
63 Shigeru Terada
64 Kathy Stanton
65 Earl Woods

DESIGNER / GESTALTER / MAQUETTISTE:

60, 61 Alf Menzies
63 Shigeru Terada
64 Barbara Loveland
65 Stephen Frykholm

ART DIRECTOR / DIRECTEUR ARTISTIQUE:

60, 61 Alf Menzies
62 Ian Potter
63 Shigeru Terada
64 Barbara Loveland
65 Stephen Frykholm

AGENCY / AGENTUR / AGENCE – STUDIO:

60, 61 Northern Design Unit
62 FCO Univas Ltd
63 Terada Illustration Office

Fashion/Mode
Industry/Industrie

60, 61 Exemples des affiches composant une série pour les chaussures sport *Dunlop*. Fig. 60: teintes pastel délicates; fig. 61: divers bleus, ainsi qu'un sable clair. (GBR)
62 Pour les chaussures sport *Nike*, préférées du tennisman John McEnroe (jeu de mots). (GBR)
63 Affiche mettant en évidence la configuration spéciale des pantalons de ski *Killy*. (JPN)
64 Pour deux programmes de sièges de bureau *Eames* (alu et rembourrés) de Herman Miller, Inc. (USA)
65 Affiche pour divers modèles de sièges figurant dans la collection *Herman Miller*. (USA)

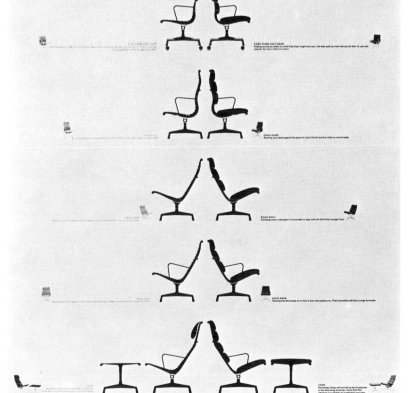

64

65

AES office automation makes the impossible possible. AES

66

67

ARTIST / KÜNSTLER / ARTISTE:

66, 67 James Marsh
68 Gary Meyer
69 Conny Winter

DESIGNER / GESTALTER / MAQUETTISTE:

66, 67 Paul Briginshaw
68 Budd Steinhilber
69 Conny Winter

ART DIRECTOR / DIRECTEUR ARTISTIQUE:

66, 67 Paul Briginshaw
68 Barry Deutsch
69 Conny Winter

AGENCY / AGENTUR / AGENCE – STUDIO:

66, 67 Greys Advertising
68 Steinhilber Deutsch & Gard

66, 67 Small-size posters with illustrations in full colour, for AES computers. (GBR)
68 This poster bears the title *"Visi* City", displayed by the computer producer *VisiCorp*. (USA)
69 Poster for the stairway and balustrade manufacturers *Müssig*. The model, a young student with ballet training, was attached to a lifeline fixed to a special corset underneath her dress, and suspended in the air from a crane. The photograph was later retouched and the line removed. A cardboard cone was placed under the girl's hair, and her hair and dress were then blown into position by wind machines. Conny Winter used no filter for this photograph. The shot was taken in brilliant sunshine, on a motorway bridge. Mirrors were used to enhance the light and shadow effects. (GER)

66, 67 Kleinformatige Plakate mit mehrfarbiger Illustration für AES-Computer, die «das Unmögliche möglich machen». (GBR)
68 *«Visi* City» ist der Titel dieses Plakates für den Computer-Hersteller *VisiCorp*. (USA)
69 Plakat für die Treppen- und Geländerbaufirma *Müssig*. Das Modell, eine Schülerin mit Ausbildung im klassischen Ballett, hängt am Seil eines Kranwagens, das an einem korsettartigen Spezialgürtel unter dem Kleid befestigt wurde. Das Seil wurde später wegretouchiert. Unter dem Haar des Mädchens befand sich ein Kern aus Pappe, zusätzlich wurden Haare und Kleid mit Windmaschinen in die richtige Position gebracht. Der Photograph, Conny Winter, benutzte für die Aufnahme keinen Filter. Sie entstand bei strahlendem Sonnenschein auf einer Autobahnbrücke. Für Aufhellungen wurden Spiegel verwendet. (GER)

66, 67 Affichettes aux illustrations polychromes pour les ordinateurs AES qui «rendent l'impossible possible». (GBR)
68 Cette affiche réalisée pour le fabricant d'ordinateurs VisiCorp s'intitule *«Visi* City». (USA)
69 Affiche pour le fabricant d'escaliers et de rampes *Müssig*. Le modèle, une jeune étudiante ayant suivi une formation de ballerine, est suspendue à une grue par une corde accrochée à une ceinture corsetée spéciale sous sa robe. Cette corde a été escamotée sur la photo définitive. La chevelure (qui repose sur un cône en carton) et la robe flottent au vent d'une soufflerie. Cette photo a été réalisée par un soleil éclatant sur un pont d'autoroute. Pour en éclaircir certains éléments, on a eu recours à divers miroirs. (GER)

68

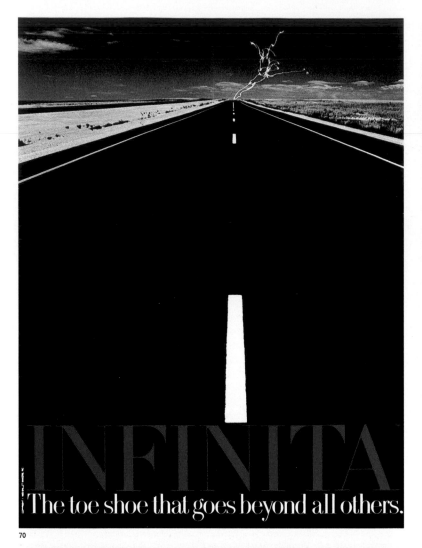

INFINITA
The toe shoe that goes beyond all others.

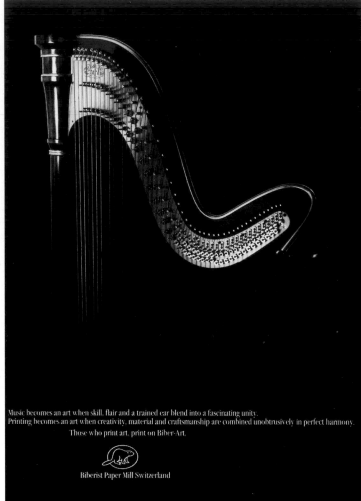

Music becomes an art when skill, flair and a trained ear blend into a fascinating unity.
Printing becomes an art when creativity, material and craftsmanship are combined unobtrusively in perfect harmony.

Those who print art, print on Biber-Art.

Biberist Paper Mill Switzerland

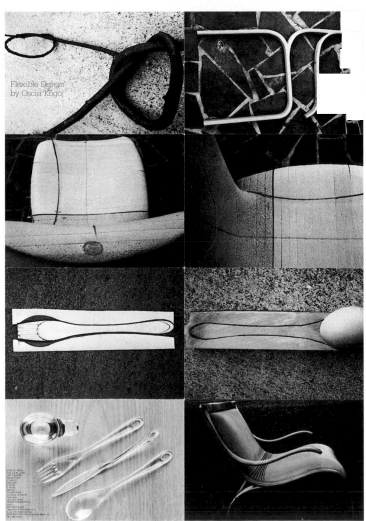

Flexible Design
by Oscar Kogoj

70 Poster sent by direct mail for *Infinita* ballet shoes by *Capezio*. (USA)
71 For *Biber* fine art paper, poster with colour photograph on dark ground. (SWI)
72 Advertising for *Quest* bicycles by *Spectrum* cycles. (USA)
73 The items designed by Oscar Kogoj, which this poster advertises, are adaptable to the many requirements of the user. (YUG)
74 Showroom-poster advertising *Steelcase* furniture. (USA)
75 Large-format poster for exclusive furniture under the *Tecno* brand. (SWI)

70 Als Direktwerbung versandtes Plakat für *Infinita*-Ballettschuhe von *Capezio*: «Der Ballettschuh, der über alle anderen hinausgeht.» (USA)
71 Plakat für *Biber*-Kunstdruckpapier. Farbaufnahme vor dunklem Grund. (SWI)
72 Werbung für *Quest*-Fahrräder von *Spectrum* Cycles. (USA)
73 Die von Oscar Kogoj entworfenen Gegenstände, für die dieses Plakat wirbt, sind flexibel in ihrer Anpassungsfähigkeit an die Bedürfnisse des Benutzers. (YUG)
74 Für Ausstellungsräume bestimmtes Plakat für *Steelcase*-Möbel. (USA)
75 Grossformatiges Plakat für anspruchsvolle Möbel der Marke *Tecno*. (SWI)

70 Affiche employée pour la publicité directe des chaussons de ballet *Infinita* de *Capezio*: «Le chausson de ballet qui dépasse tous les autres.» (USA)
71 Affiche pour le papier couché *Biber*. Photo couleur sur fond sombre. (SWI)
72 Publicité pour les vélos *Quest* fabriqués par *Spectrum* Cycles. (USA)
73 Les objets conçus par Oscar Kogoj et présentés sur cette affiche s'adaptent en souplesse aux besoins des utilisateurs. (YUG)
74 Affiche destinée aux locaux d'exposition des Ameublements *Steelcase*. (USA)
75 Affiche au grand format pour les meubles haut de gamme *Tecno*. (SWI)

74

75

ARTIST / KÜNSTLER / ARTISTE:

70 John Gruen
71 Jürg Erni
72 Michael Furman
73 Oscar Kogoj
74 John Boucher
75 Cyril Kobler

DESIGNER / GESTALTER / MAQUETTISTE:

70 Regina Ovesey
71 Armin Ehrismann
72 Michael Furman
73 Borislav Ljubičič/Oscar Kogoj
74 Roger Sliker
75 Jean-Pierre Blanchoud

ART DIRECTOR / DIRECTEUR ARTISTIQUE:

70 Frank Young
71 Armin Ehrismann
72 Michael Furman
74 Roger Sliker
75 Jean-Pierre Blanchoud

AGENCY / AGENTUR / AGENCE – STUDIO:

70 Ovesey & Co.
71 Max Kehl AG
72 Michael Furman
74 David Perkins & Associates

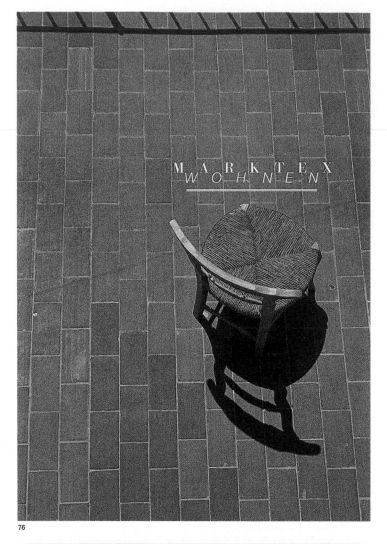

76

77

76 Poster for *Marktex* furniture to mark the occasion of the Cologne trade fair. (GER)
77 Summer is the subject of this poster for the Swiss department store ABM. Colour combination of blue, white and red on a sand-coloured ground. (SWI)
78 This Danish furniture-makers' poster marks twenty-five years of quality control. (DEN)
79 Screen-print poster for *Hickory* business furniture—an office chair with a difference. (USA)
80 A Christmassy look for *Bloomingdale's* in this poster designed for interior display. (USA)
81 Polychrome poster to commemorate the founding of the Mindset Corporation, manufacturers of computer hardware and software. (USA)

76 Anlässlich der Kölner Messe herausgegebenes Plakat für *Marktex*-Möbel. (GER)
77 Der Sommer ist Thema dieses Plakates für das Schweizer Kaufhaus ABM. Farbkombination von Blau-Weiss-Rot, sandfarbener Grund. (SWI)
78 Fünfundzwanzig Jahre Qualitätskontrolle ist der Titel dieses Plakates, das für Dänemarks Möbelhersteller wirbt. (DEN)
79 Siebdruckplakat für *Hickory*-Büromöbel: «Die neue Tradition». (USA)
80 Für den Innenaushang bestimmtes Plakat des Kaufhauses *Bloomingdale's*. (USA)
81 Mehrfarbiges Plakat zum Jahrestag der Gründung der Mindset Corporation, Hersteller von Computer-Hardware und -Software. (USA)

76 Affiche créée pour les meubles *Marktex* à l'occasion de la Foire de Cologne. (GER)
77 Cette affiche estivale des grands magasins suisses ABM se pare de coloris bleus, blancs et rouges sur fond sable. (SWI)
78 Ving-cinq ans de contrôle de la qualité, voilà ce qui est mis en exergue sur cette affiche de l'association danoise des fabricants de meubles. (DEN)
79 Affiche sérigraphique des meubles de bureau *Hickory* – «La nouvelle tradition». (USA)
80 Pour l'affichage intérieur dans les grands magasins newyorkais *Bloomingdale's*. (USA)
81 Affiche polychrome à l'occasion de l'anniversaire de la fondation de la Mindset Corporation, fabricant d'ordinateurs – hardware et software. (USA)

78

79

81

80

ARTIST / KÜNSTLER / ARTISTE:

77 Atelier U. Hiestand
78 Per Arnoldi
79, 81 Michael Vanderbyl
80 Jeanne Fisher

DESIGNER / GESTALTER / MAQUETTISTE:

76 Olaf Leu Design & Partner
77 Ursula Hiestand
78 Per Arnoldi
79, 81 Michael Vanderbyl

ART DIRECTOR / DIRECTEUR ARTISTIQUE:

77 Ursula Hiestand
79, 81 Michael Vanderbyl
80 John C. Jay

AGENCY / AGENTUR / AGENCE – STUDIO:

76 Olaf Leu Design & Partner
77 Atelier U. Hiestand
79, 81 Vanderbyl Design
80 Bloomingdale's

Industry/Industrie

Direct Mail/Direktwerbung
Publicité directe

ARTIST/KÜNSTLER/ARTISTE:

82 Kent Severson
83 Diane Padys
84 Philipp Messinger
85 Dennis Manarchy
86 Jürgen Spohn
87 David Deahl

DESIGNER/GESTALTER/MAQUETTISTE:

82 Charlie Clark
84 Rodger Browder
86 Jürgen Spohn
87 David Deahl

82 Invitation by an advertising agency to an open day. (USA)
83 Self-promotion for Diane Pady's photo studio, with the title "Allegro". (USA)
84 Invitation to participate in an annual competition, by which the best creative advertising can be determined and awarded. Black and white. (USA)
85 Poster as joint-venture advertisement by a photographer, a designer and a printer. Shoes and underwear in shocking pink, dress in ultramarine. (USA)
86 Black-and-white photograph with coloured rubber stamps, as self-promotion. (GER)
87 A pun on his name for photographer David Deahl's self-promotional poster. (USA)

82 Einladung einer Werbeagentur zu einem Tag der offenen Tür. (USA)
83 Eigenwerbung des Photostudios Diane Pady's mit dem Titel «Allegro». (USA)
84 Einladung zur Teilnahme an einem jährlichen Wettbewerb, bei dem die besten Leistungen auf dem Gebiet der Werbung ermittelt werden. In Schwarzweiss. (USA)
85 Als Gemeinschaftswerbung des Photographen, Designers und Druckers lanciertes Plakat. Schuhe und Slip in kräftigem Pink, Rock in Ultramarin. (USA)
86 Schwarzweissaufnahme mit verschiedenfarbigen Stempeln als Eigenwerbung. (GER)
87 Eigenwerbung des Photographen David Deahl mit einem Wortspiel. (USA)

82 Invitation d'une agence de publicité à une journée Portes Ouvertes. (USA)
83 Autopromotion du studio-photo Diane Pady's sous le titre d'«Allegro». (USA)
84 Invitation à participer à un concours annuel où sont primées les meilleures réalisations en matière de publicité. En noir et blanc. (USA)
85 Affiche lancée pour la promotion collective du photographe, du designer et de l'imprimeur. Chaussures et slip rose vif, jupe outremer. (USA)
86 Photo noir-blanc autopromotionnelle avec des tampons en diverses couleurs. (GER)
87 Autopromotion du photographe David Deahl assortie d'un jeu de mots. (USA)

U N D E R S T A T E M E N T

85

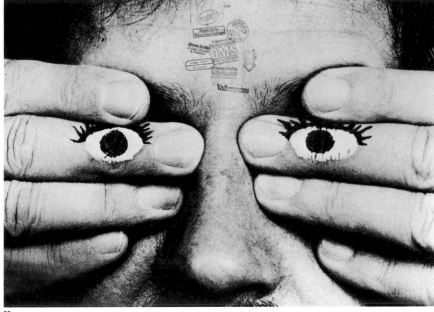

86

ART DIRECTOR / DIRECTEUR ARTISTIQUE:

82 Charlie Clark
83 André Sala
84 Rodger Browder
85 Jeff A. Barnes
87 David Deahl

AGENCY / AGENTUR / AGENCE – STUDIO:

82 Martin Williams Advertising
83 Portal Publications Ltd.
84 Dolph Miller & Assoc., Inc.
85 Barnes Design Office
86 Jurgen Spohn

87

88

89

90

91

ARTIST / KÜNSTLER / ARTISTE:

88, 89 Kozo Mio
90 Kiyoshi Awazu
91 Yoshihiko Shinoda
92 André Berg
93 Robert Mapplethorpe
94 Kazumi Kurigami

DESIGNER / GESTALTER / MAQUETTISTE:

88, 89 Hiroya Sugimoto
90 Kiyoshi Awazu
91 Yoshihiko Shinoda
92, 93 Shin Matsunaga
94 Takenobu Igarashi

ART DIRECTOR / DIRECTEUR ARTISTIQUE:

88, 89 Akira Iwano
90 Kiyoshi Awazu
91 Yoshihiko Shinoda
92, 93 Shin Matsunaga
94 Takenobu Igarashi

AGENCY / AGENTUR / AGENCE – STUDIO:

88, 89 TCD Corporation
91 Design Studio Art Work
94 Takenobu Igarashi Design

88, 89 For a chopping complex in the station of a regional railway company. Fig. 88 refers to the goods on offer by the 333 shops, Fig. 89 to plans made by women for the New Year. (JPN)
90 "A new spirit in Japan." Poster for a textile company in Kyoto. On the right are pictured traditional Japanese playing cards. (JPN)
91 "Don't say you're tired." Poster by a graphic designers' club for sport. (JPN)
92, 93 From a series of posters for a Japanese photographic magazine. Black-and-white photographs. (JPN)
94 Advertising poster for a book from the Takenobu Igarashi Design Studio entitled "Space Graphics". (JPN)

88, 89 Für ein Einkaufszentrum im Bahnhof einer regionalen Eisenbahngesellschaft. Abb. 88 bezieht sich auf das Angebot der 333 Geschäfte, Abb. 89 auf Pläne der Frau für das neue Jahr. (JPN)
90 «Ein neuer Geist in Japan.» Plakat für einen Textilhersteller in Kioto. Rechts traditionelle japanische Spielkarten. (JPN)
91 «Sag nicht, dass Du müde bist.» Plakat eines Graphik Designer Clubs für den Sport. (JPN)
92, 93 Aus einer Serie von Plakaten für eine japanische Photozeitschrift. Schwarzweissaufnahmen. (JPN)
94 Werbung für ein Buch des Takenobu Igarashi Design-Studios mit dem Titel «Raum-Graphik». (JPN)

88, 89 Pour un centre commercial installé dans les bâtiments d'une gare d'une compagnie ferroviaire régionale. La fig. 88 se rapporte à l'offre combinée des 333 commerces du centre, la fig. 89 aux projets des femmes pour l'année à venir. (JPN)
90 «Un nouvel esprit au Japon.» Affiche pour un fabricant de matières textiles de Kyōto. A droite, des cartes à jouer traditionnelles au Japon. (JPN)
91 «Ne dis pas que tu es fatigué.» Affiche d'un club de graphistes en faveur du sport. (JPN)
92, 93 Affiche dans une série créée pour un magazine-photo japonais. Photos noir et blanc. (JPN)
94 Publicité pour un ouvrage du studio de design Takenobu Igarashi, «Art graphique spatial». (JPN)

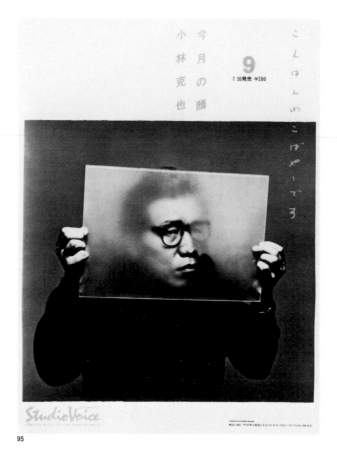

95

Chaque lundi

96

97

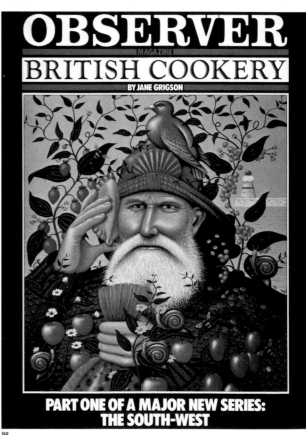

98

Publishers' Publicity
Verlagswerbung
Publicité d'éditeurs

58

99

95 Announcing a new issue of a magazine for men which chiefly contains interviews. Black-and-white photograph. (JPN)
96 Poster for *Le Point*, a political magazine which is published every Monday. In shades of orange and yellow, the ocean in light blue. (FRA)
97 Call-for-entries poster for a design competition with the motto "Visual Illusion". Bright green on red, black-and-white dogs. (JPN)
98 Poster to announce the first part of a new series on British cookery in the *Observer* weekly supplement. The Cornish fisherman is holding the traditional west-country "Cornish pasty". (GBR)
99, 100 Illustration and complete poster for a special series about New York in *The New York Times Magazine*. (USA)

95 Ankündigung einer neuen Ausgabe eines Journals für Männer, das vor allem Interviews enthält. Schwarzweiss-Aufnahme. (JPN)
96 Plakat für das politische Wochenmagazin *Le Point*, das jeweils montags erscheint. In Orange- und Gelbtönen, die Weltmeere in leuchtendem Blau. (FRA)
97 Aufruf zur Teilnahme an einem Design-Wettbewerb unter dem Motto «Visuelle Illusion». Grün auf Rot, Hunde schwarzweiss. (JPN)
98 Ankündigung einer Beitragsreihe über die britische Küche im Magazin der Zeitung *Observer*. Die Illustration bezieht sich auf den ersten Teil, der Rezepte aus dem Südwesten behandelt. (GBR)
99, 100 Illustration und vollständiges Plakat für eine spezielle Beitragsreihe über New York im Magazin der *New York Times*. (USA)

95 Lancement d'une nouvelle édition d'un magazine masculin qui comporte surtout des interviews. Photo noir et blanc. (JPN)
96 Affiche pour l'hebdo politique *Le Point*, paraissant le lundi. Tons orangés et jaunes; les océans apparaissent en tons bleus lumineux. (FRA)
97 Appel d'envois pour un concours de design intitulé «Illusion visuelle». Vert lumineux sur fond rouge, chiens noir et blanc. (JPN)
98 Annonce d'une série du magazine du quotidien *Observer* sur la cuisine britannique. L'illustration se rapporte au premier article consacré à la gastronomie du sud-est de l'Angleterre. (GBR)
99, 100 Illustration et affiche où elle figure, pour une série spéciale d'articles consacrés à la ville de New York dans le magazine publié par le *New York Times*. (USA)

100

ARTIST / KÜNSTLER / ARTISTE:

101 Hubert Kretzschmar
102 Chris Pfaff
103 Gilles Laraine
104 Richard Haughton
105 Andrzej Pagowski

DESIGNER / GESTALTER / MAQUETTISTE:

101 Hubert Kretzschmar
102 Franz Merlicek
103 Kenneth R. Cooke
104 John O'Brien
105 Andrzej Pagowski
106 Pierre Mendell

102

101

ART DIRECTOR / DIRECTEUR ARTISTIQUE:

101 Hubert Kretzschmar
102 Franz Merlicek
103 Kenneth R. Cooke
104 Roy Kohara
105 Ewa Popiolek
106 Pierre Mendell

AGENCY / AGENTUR / AGENCE – STUDIO:

101 Kretzschmar Studio
102 Demner & Merlicek
103 Landor Associates
104 Capitol Records, Inc.
106 Mendell & Oberer

101 Poster to advertise a new Rolling Stones record. (USA)
102 To promote the radio-drama editions by IBM Austria, an audioteque formed in cooperation with the Austrian radio and TV network (ORF) and an Austrian Society for Art and Culture. (AUT)
103 For a record by Miles Davis. Sombre figure and sepia-toned ground. (USA)
104 Polychrome poster for records and cassettes for a new-wave production with the title "The Flat Earth". (USA)
105 Poster to promote the sales of Beatles records. (POL)
106 Screen-print poster for a chain of video-lending shops and their blank video cassettes. (GER)

101 Plakatwerbung für eine neue Schallplatte der Rolling Stones. (USA)
102 Für die Hörspiel-Edition von IBM, eine Audiothek, die in Zusammenarbeit mit dem ORF und der N. Ö. Gesellschaft für Kunst und Kultur entsteht. Hintergrund in Brauntönen. (AUT)
103 Für eine Platte von Miles Davis. Dunkle Gestalt vor sepiafarbenem Hintergrund. (USA)
104 Mehrfarbiges Plakat für Schallplatten- und Tonbandaufnahmen einer New-Wave-Produktion unter dem Titel «Die flache Erde». (USA)
105 Für die Verkaufsförderung von Beatles-Schallplatten veröffentlichtes Plakat. (POL)
106 Siebdruckplakat für eine Kette von Video-Verleihgeschäften und ihre Produkte. (GER)

101 Publicité par voie d'affiche pour un nouveau disque des Rollings Stones. (USA)
102 Pour la Hörspiel-Edition d'IBM, une audiothèque réalisée avec le concours de l'ORF et de la Société d'art et de culture de Basse-Autriche. Fond en divers tons bruns. (AUT)
103 Pour un disque de Miles Davis. Personnage sombre sur fond sépia. (USA)
104 Affiche polychrome pour les enregistrements sur disque et bande magnétique d'une production nouvelle vague intitulée «La Terre plate». (USA)
105 Affiche servant à la promotion des ventes des disques des Beatles. (POL)
106 Affiche sérigraphique pour une chaîne de magasins vidéo et leurs produits. (GER)

103

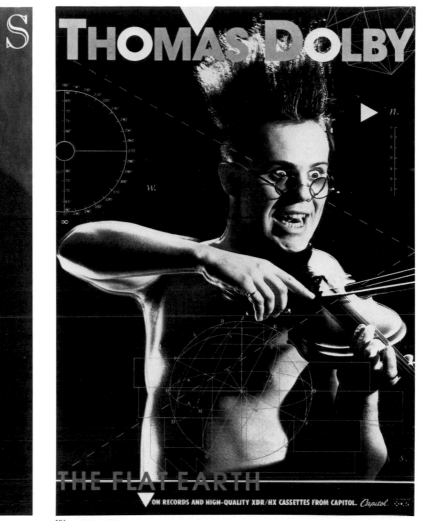

104

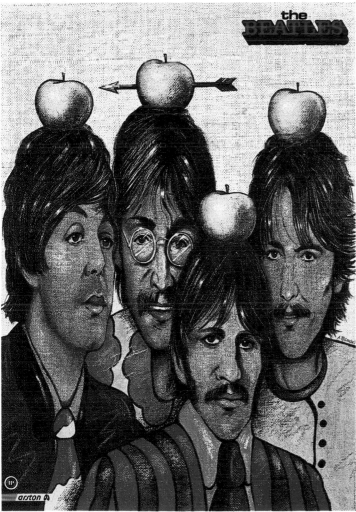

105

106

PATRICK COURATIN GRIMACE PRODUCTIONS PARIS

107

Direct Mail
Direktwerbung
Publicité directe

108

109

110

111

107 Promotional poster for the Parisian Patrick Couratin Grimace Productions, which is also available in shops. Title: "Cat on the Roof". (USA)
108, 109 In the year of the Olympics a poster gallery published polychrome posters under the motto "International Cat Games". (USA)
110, 111 Illustration and complete poster for a photo laboratory. It deals with the generous reductions in prices for poster formats. "An offer which one shouldn't sleep on." (USA)
112 Silkscreen poster for stuffed toy animals from *Forever Toys*. Red, black, green on white. (USA)

107 Promotions-Plakat für die Pariser Patrick Couratin Grimace Productions, das auch im Handel erhältlich ist. Titel «Die Katze auf dem Dach». (USA)
108, 109 Im Olympia-Jahr von einer Poster-Galerie herausgegebene mehrfarbige Plakate unter dem Motto «Internationale Katzen-Spiele». (USA)
110, 111 Illustration und vollständiges Plakat für ein Photolabor. Es geht um preisgünstige Abzüge im Posterformat, ein Angebot, das man nicht verschlafen sollte. (USA)
112 Siebdruckplakat für Stofftiere von *Forever Toys*. Rot, Schwarz, Grün auf Weiss. (USA)

107 Affiche promotionnelle pour les Patrick Couratin Grimace Productions de Paris, qui est aussi en vente comme poster. Son titre «Le Chat sur le toit». (USA)
108, 109 Affiches polychromes publiées par une galerie de posters l'année des Jeux Olympiques sous le titre de «Jeux de chats internationaux». (USA)
110, 111 Illustration et affiche complète pour un labo photo. Il s'agit d'épreuves à prix avantageux au format d'un poster, une offre qui devrait vous mettre en éveil. (USA)
112 Sérigraphie pour les animaux en peluche *Forever Toys*. Rouge, noir, vert sur blanc. (USA)

112

Publishers' Publicity
Verlagswerbung
Publicité d'éditeurs

ARTIST / KÜNSTLER / ARTISTE:

113 Björn Nyman
114 Charles Cramp
115 Stefano Massimo
116–118 Bruce Meek

DESIGNER / GESTALTER / MAQUETTISTE:

113 Pentti Pilve
114, 115 Peter Rose
116–118 Franz Merlicek

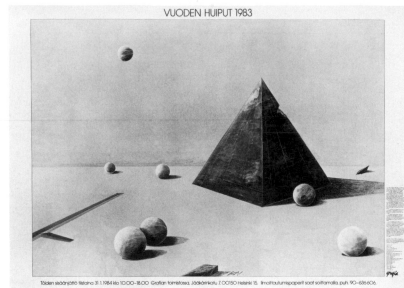

113

114

115

ART DIRECTOR / DIRECTEUR ARTISTIQUE:

113 Pentti Pilve
114, 115 Peter Rose
116–118 Franz Merlicek

AGENCY / AGENTUR / AGENCE – STUDIO:

113 Creator Oy
114, 115 GRC
116–118 Demner & Merlicek

113 Poster designed for interior display to announce a competition by which the best achievements in graphic design and advertising in Finland can be determined. Background in cool beige and light blue tones. (FIN)
114, 115 Examples from a series of posters with black-and-white photographs for *The Times* newspaper. The theme is the accuracy of the reporting in all the sectors. (GBR)
116–118 Posters for the newspaper *Kurier* which here present the results of a readership analysis. The main characteristics and types of reader are symbolized by the animal heads, for instance the crocodile represents the moneyed, brand- and fashion-conscious person, the beaver the industrious do-it-yourself home improver, etc. (AUT)

113 Für den Innenaushang bestimmtes Plakat mit Ankündigung eines Wettbewerbs, bei dem die besten Leistungen auf dem Gebiet des Graphik Designs und der Werbung in Finnland ermittelt werden. Hintergrund in kühlen Beige- und Hellblautönen. (FIN)
114, 115 Beispiele aus einer Serie von Plakaten mit Schwarzweissaufnahmen für die *Times*. Bei allen geht es um die Prägnanz und Genauigkeit in der Berichterstattung dieser Zeitung auf den verschiedenen Gebieten. (GBR)
116–118 Plakate für die Zeitung *Kurier*, die hier die Ergebnisse einer Leserschaftsanalyse darstellt. Die Haupteigenschaften der verschiedenen Gruppen werden treffend durch die Tierköpfe symbolisiert. (AUT)

113 Lancement d'un concours qui doit déterminer les meilleures réalisations finlandaises en matière d'art graphique et de publicité. Fond en couleurs fraîches, beige et bleu clair. Pour l'affichage intérieur. (FIN)
114, 115 Exemples d'affiches réalisées dans une série pour le *Times* à l'aide de photos noir et blanc. Il s'agit à chaque fois de démontrer la densité et la précision des reportages de ce journal dans divers domaines de l'information. (GBR)
116–118 Affiches pour le journal *Kurier* utilisant les résultats d'un sondage auprès des lecteurs. Les principales caractéristiques des divers groupes de lecteurs sont exprimées par des têtes d'animaux; ainsi le crocodile représente l'acheteur aisé épris de mode. (AUT)

116

117

118

119

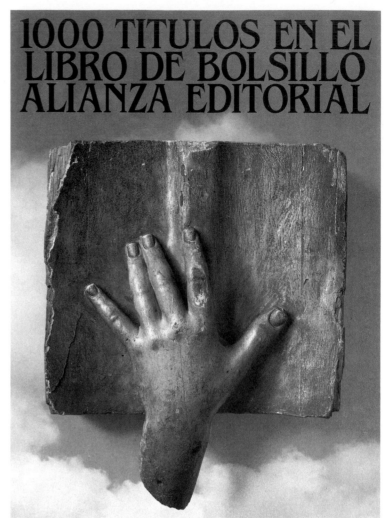

120

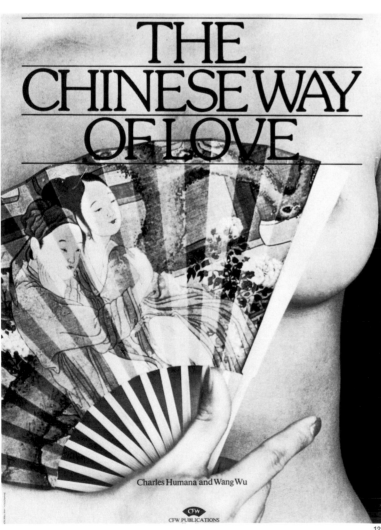

121

122

ARTIST / KÜNSTLER / ARTISTE:

119 Chris Moore
120 Daniel Gil
121 Raymond Hui
122 Pavel Jasanský
123 Leen Alting

DESIGNER / GESTALTER / MAQUETTISTE:

119 Andrew Kner
121 Hon Bing-Wah
122 Pavel Jasanský
123 Leen Alting

ART DIRECTOR / DIRECTEUR ARTISTIQUE:

119 Andrew Kner
121 Hon Bing-Wah

AGENCY / AGENTUR / AGENCE – STUDIO:

121 Kinggraphic

123

119 Polychrome poster for the announcement of a supplement in *The New York Times*, dealing with real-estate cooperatives. It is also available as a special issue. (USA)
120 For a publisher. Hand in a dark skin tone on a brown wooden book, blue sky, black lettering. (SPA)
121 Small-size poster with an oriental look for a book published in Hong Kong. (HKG)
122 Poster advertising a singer. (CSR)
123 Silkscreen poster for fashion from *Neels*. (NLD)

119 Mehrfarbiges Plakat für die Ankündigung eines auch als Separatdruck erhältlichen Sonderbeitrags der *New York Times* über Immobilien. (USA)
120 Plakat für einen Verlag. Hand in dunklem Hautton auf braunem Holzbuch, blauer Himmel mit weissen Wolken, schwarze Schrift. (SPA)
121 Kleinformatiges Plakat für ein Buch über chinesische Liebeskunst. (HKG)
122 Plakatwerbung für einen Sänger. (CSR)
123 Siebdruckplakat für Mode von *Neels*. (NLD)

119 Affiche polychrome annonçant un rapport spécial du *New York Times* sur le marché de l'immobilier, rapport aussi vendu séparément. (USA)
120 Affiche pour un éditeur. Main en ton de peau foncé sur livre en bois brun, ciel bleu, nuages blancs, texte noir. (SPA)
121 Affichette pour un ouvrage où sont relatées les pratiques amoureuses chinoises. (HKG)
122 Affiche publicitaire pour un chanteur. (CSR)
123 Sérigraphie pour les modes *Neels*. (NLD)

Publishers' Publicity
Verlagswerbung
Publicité d'éditeurs

Publishers' Publicity
Verlagswerbung
Publicité d'éditeurs

124 Poster to advertise the satirical science-fiction novel "Earth!". (ITA)
125 The author of the bestseller *The Name of the Rose* on a poster for the announcement of the publication of the paperback edition of this book. (ITA)
126 Poster for W. R. Grace in mid blue with black-and-white lettering. (USA)
127 "Kill the devil, save Supersaxo." Call for donations to finance a Swiss cartoon film. Black on white with red centre. (SWI)
128 Poster for the 75th anniversary of the publishing house *Rowohlt*. (GER)

124 Werbung für den satirischen Science-Fiction-Roman «Erde!». (ITA)
125 Der Autor des Bestsellers *Der Name der Rose* auf einem Plakat für die Ankündigung der Herausgabe dieses Buches im Taschenbuchformat. (ITA)
126 «Tüchtige Leute bilden eine bessere Firma.» Für W. R. Grace. (USA)
127 «Tötet den Teufel, rettet Supersaxo.» Spendenaufruf zugunsten eines Schweizer Zeichentrickfilms. Schwarz auf Weiss mit rotem Zentrum. (SWI)
128 Zum fünfundsiebzigjährigen Bestehen des *Rowohlt*-Verlags. (GER)

124 Publicité pour le roman de science-fiction satirique «Terre!». (ITA)
125 L'auteur du best-seller *Le Nom de la rose* figure sur cette affiche annonçant la parution du livre en poche. (ITA)
126 «A gens capables, sociétés prospères.» Pour W. R. Grace. (USA)
127 Appel public pour le financement du premier grand dessin animé suisse. Noir sur blanc, centre de la cible rouge. (SWI)
128 Affiche pour le 75e anniversaire des Editions *Rowohlt*. (GER)

124

125

126

127

Industry/Industrie

ARTIST / KÜNSTLER / ARTISTE:

129 Dietrich Ebert
131, 132 Katsu Yoshida
133 Brian Tattersfield
134, 135 Tino Erben

DESIGNER / GESTALTER / MAQUETTISTE:

130 Roger Pfund
131, 132 Mitsumasa Maeda
133 Minale, Tattersfield & Partners
134, 135 Tino Erben

ART DIRECTOR / DIRECTEUR ARTISTIQUE:

129 Dietrich Ebert
131, 132 Mitsumasa Maeda
134, 135 Tino Erben

AGENCY / AGENTUR / AGENCE – STUDIO:

129 Alain Fion
131, 132 J. Walter Thompson

24 Farben zum Ausmalen der Freizeit

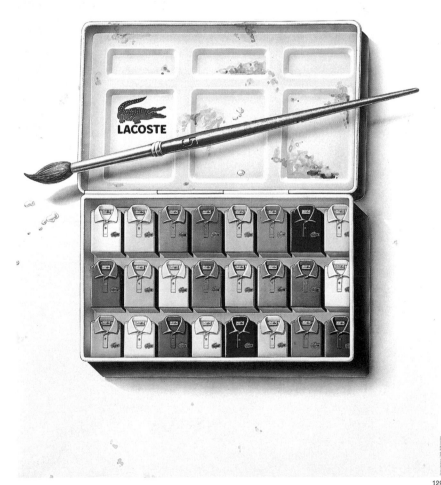

129

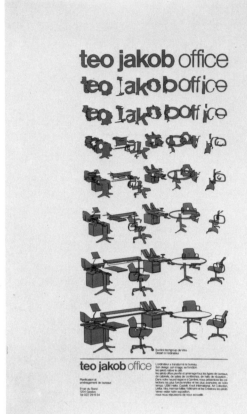

130

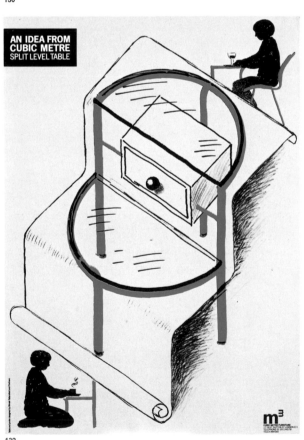

132

129 "24 colours for painting spare time" is the slogan on this poster to advertise leisure shirts by *Lacoste*. (GER)

130 Poster to mark the occasion of a trade fair, for office elements from *Teo Jakob*. A computer-aided design in mauve on white. (SWI)

131, 132 Examples from a poster campaign for *Bridgestone* bicycles to raise the image of this particular marque. The slogan chosen for the campaign was "The Body and the Bike". (USA)

133 A poster for a furniture-manufacturing firm. Colours are black and white with blue. (GBR)

134 Self-promotion for *Section N*, a firm concerned with form, environmental design and architecture. Black and white with yellow "cheese". (AUT)

135 Announcing a Christmas bazaar for *Section N* furnishing items. (AUT)

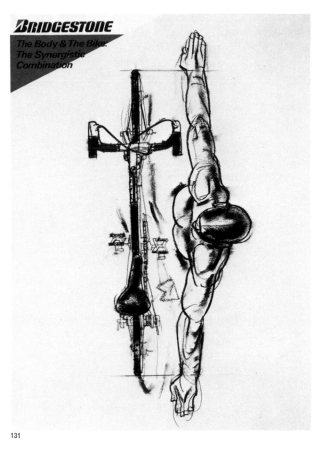

131

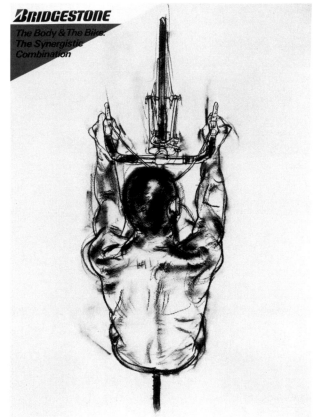

132

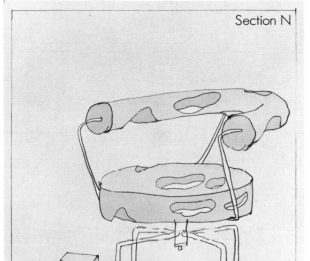

Section N

134

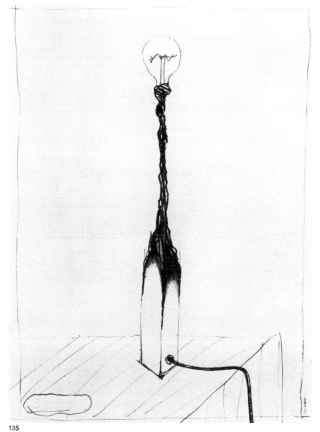

135

SHOULD YOU PLACE MORE FAITH IN A CAR THAN THE PEOPLE WHO MADE IT?

3 YEAR / 36,000-MILE LIMITED WARRANTY
(6 YEARS AGAINST RUST PERFORATION)

Every car enters the world accompanied by a testament of faith.

It's called a warranty, and it's one measure of the confidence, or apprehension, with which you can approach the purchase of an automobile.

It's also a compelling argument for buying a BMW. All BMW's are covered by a 3-year/36,000-mile limited warranty plus a 6-year limited warranty against rust perforation.

Which is a fitting testament to the quality and durability of a car that, as Car and Driver said of the 733i, "can take a limited amount of time and turn it into an experience to be savored for always."

For those unaccustomed to accepting such testaments on faith, we'll be pleased to arrange a test drive.

BMW **THE ULTIMATE DRIVING MACHINE.**

136

THE ONLY SERVICE PEOPLE IN THE WORLD BACKED BY THESE LETTERS OF RECOMMENDATION:

Essentially, there are two types of people who service BMW's: BMW-trained service technicians and all others. The former are the product of BMW's rigorous training courses, yearly update courses, plus instruction in the use of sophisticated electronic equipment and special BMW-authorized tools.

The extent of the training received by others is at best a guess.

Given the choice between credentials and conjecture, we suggest you do what we've done: make sure only BMW-trained service people service your BMW.

137

Industry/Industrie

136–141 Examples from a poster campaign with colour photographs to promote sales of the BMW car in the United States. Fig. 136 emphasizes the warranties offered; Fig. 137 refers to BMW's personnel service-training courses; Fig. 138 shows BMW model 633 CSi in white. Fig. 139: "The engine that powered an entire motorcycle company from 0 to 60 years." Fig. 140 is a poster to advertise the BMW company's marine engines and Fig. 141 portrays the new BMW 325 e which "affirms its dominance in the category it created". (USA)

136–141 Beispiele aus einer Plakatkampagne mit Farbaufnahmen für BMW in den Vereinigten Staaten. In Abb. 136 geht es um Garantie: «Sollen Sie mehr Vertrauen in ein Auto setzen als die Leute, die es gemacht haben?» Abb. 137 bezieht sich auf die Schulung des Service-Personals. Abb. 138: «Wie Puristen einen Klassiker der Zukunft von einem zeitgenössischen antiken Modell unterscheiden.» Abb. 139: «Die Maschine, die ein ganzes Motorrad-Unternehmen von 0 auf 60 Jahre antrieb.» Abb. 140 wirbt für BMW-Bootsmotoren. Abb. 141 betrifft die Einführung des 325er Modells. (USA)

136–141 Campagne d'affiches illustrées de photos couleur pour BMW aux Etats-Unis. Fig. 136: «Feriez-vous davantage confiance à une voiture que ceux qui l'ont fabriquée?» – la question de la garantie. Fig. 137 se rapporte à la formation des mécaniciens affectés au service après-vente. Fig. 138: «Comment les puristes distinguent un classique de l'avenir d'une antiquité contemporaine.» Fig. 139: «La machine qui a propulsé toute une entreprise de motos de 0 à 60 ans.» Fig. 140: moteurs BMW de canots automobiles; fig. 141: la nouvelle «325». (USA)

HOW PURISTS TELL A FUTURE CLASSIC FROM A CONTEMPORARY ANTIQUE.

THE BMW 633CSi

138

THE ENGINE THAT POWERED AN ENTIRE MOTORCYCLE COMPANY FROM 0 TO 60 YEARS.

139

140

141

Far East
Lufthansa

142

South America
Lufthansa

143

Near and Middle East
Lufthansa

144

Western Airlines SkiBirds

145

Tourism/Tourismus/Tourisme

ARTIST / KÜNSTLER / ARTISTE:

142–144 Jürg Andermatt
145 Don Weller
146 Ernst Strom

DESIGNER / GESTALTER:

145 Don Weller
146 Ernst Strom
147, 148 Wolf Magin

ART DIRECTOR / DIRECTEUR ARTISTIQUE:

145 Carl Leick

AGENCY / AGENTUR / AGENCE – STUDIO:

142–144 Lufthansa/Werbeabt.
145 The Weller Institute
for the Cure of Design
147, 148 Wolf Magin

142–144 Examples from a poster campaign for *Lufthansa*. Fig. 142 shows the Pokhara area of Nepal; Fig. 143: the Iguaçu waterfalls in Brazil; Fig. 144: the Rum wadi in Jordan. (GER)
145 *Western Airlines* advertises with this full-colour poster its flights to ski-resorts. (USA)
146 For Carnival 1984 (Fasching), a poster issued by the tourist authorities Munich. (GER)
147, 148 Posters in an unusual format from a campaign by the tourist office Mannheim. Fig. 147: white lettering on black and blue, Fig. 148: white on brown and black. (GER)

142–144 Beispiele aus einer Plakatkampagne für die *Lufthansa*. Abb. 142: Umgebung von Pokhara in Nepal; Abb. 143: Iguaçu-Wasserfälle in Brasilien; Abb. 144: Wadi Rum in Jordanien. (GER)
145 Die Fluggesellschaft *Western Airlines* wirbt hier für Flüge in Skigebiete. In Farbe. (USA)
146 Vom Fremdenverkehrsamt München herausgegebenes Plakat für den Fasching 1984. (GER)
147, 148 In ungewöhnlichem Format erschienene Plakate aus einer Kampagne des Verkehrsvereins Mannheim. Abb. 147: Weiss auf Schwarz und Blau, Abb. 148: Weiss auf Braun und Schwarz. (GER)

142–144 Exemples d'affiches de la compagnie aérienne *Lufthansa*. Fig. 142: les environs de Pokhara en Nepal; fig. 143: les cataractes d'Iguaçu en Brésil; fig. 144: Wadi Rum en Jordanie. (GER)
145 Publicité pour la desserte des stations de ski par les vols *Western Airlines*. Couleur. (USA)
146 Affiche de l'Office du tourisme de Munich à l'occasion du Carnaval 1984. (GER)
147, 148 Leur format insolite signale à l'attention ces affiches de l'Office du tourisme de Mannheim. Fig. 147: texte blanc sur noir et bleu, fig. 148: blanc sur brun et noir. (GER)

146

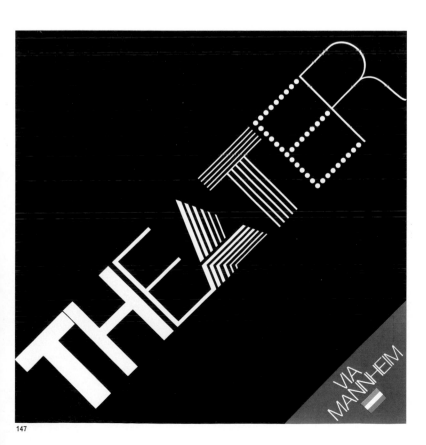

147

148

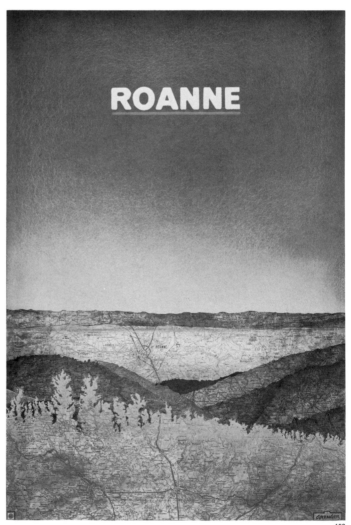

ARTIST / KÜNSTLER / ARTISTE:

149, 153 Barry Evans
150 Brian Shuel
151 Andrea Rauch
152 Granger

DESIGNER / GESTALTER / MAQUETTISTE:

149, 150, 153 Tony Fandino
151 Andrea Rauch
152 Granger

ART DIRECTOR / DIRECTEUR ARTISTIQUE:

151 Andrea Rauch
152 Jean Louis Biard

AGENCY / AGENTUR / AGENCE:

151 Graphiti

149, 150, 153 From a series of posters for the British Tourist Authority with the subject of Britain—Land of History and Land of Heritage. Fig. 149 portrays Brunel, construction engineer and shipbuilder, in front of some of his most famous engineering works, Fig. 150 shows the heroic figure-head on the "Cutty Sark", Fig. 153 Charles 1st and Oliver Cromwell with famous figures from art and science in 17th century Britain. (GBR)
151 "Art, Nature, Fantasy." Poster to promote Florence and its surroundings. (ITA)
152 Illustration for a poster displayed by the Tourist Office of Roanne on the Loire. (FRA)

149, 150, 153 Aus einer Serie von Plakaten für die britische Fremdenverkehrswerbung, deren Themen Grossbritanniens Geschichte und Verdienste sind. Abb. 149 zeigt Brunel, einen Ingenieur und Schiffsbauer, vor seinen Werken, Abb. 150 die heroische Galionsfigur der «Cutty Sark», Abb. 153 Charles I. und Oliver Cromwell, im Hintergrund Berühmtheiten der Künste und Wissenschaften im Grossbritannien des 17. Jahrhunderts. (GBR)
151 «Kunst, Natur, Phantasie.» Plakatwerbung für Florenz und Umgebung. (ITA)
152 Illustration für ein Plakat des Verkehrsbüros der Stadt Roanne an der Loire. (FRA)

149, 150, 153 Exemples d'affiches de l'Office national britannique du tourisme sur le thème de l'histoire glorieuse de la Grande-Bretagne. Fig. 149: l'ingénieur et constructeur naval Isambard Kingdom Brunel devant ses réalisations; fig. 150: l'héroïque figure de proue de la «Cutty Sark»; fig. 153: Charles 1er (son exécution à l'arrière-plan) et Oliver Cromwell avec, au fond, de grands noms des arts et des sciences de la Grande-Bretagne du XVIIe siècle. (GBR)
151 «L'art, la nature, l'imagination.» Affiche touristique pour Florence et sa région. (ITA)
152 Illustration pour une affiche du Syndicat d'initiative de la ville de Roanne. (FRA)

153

BRITAIN
Land of History
The King and the Protector

Tourism/Tourismus/Tourisme

154

155

154 A private railway company advertises excursions to the Lake of Geneva. (SWI)
155 "Smooth traffic, no parking problems" with Zurich's public transport. In full colour. (SWI)
156 Poster for the journal *House & Garden*. The photograph shows a view from a window in a sculptor's house. The foreground is black, the sky brilliant blue. (USA)
157 Street poster in black and white from a campaign for *Nordmende*. (GER)
158 Poster to celebrate the 100th anniversary of the Japanese prefecture of Toyama. (JPN)

154 Une compagnie de chemin de fer privée vante ses possibilités d'excursion au lac Léman. (SWI)
155 Publicité de la Régie des transports zurichois pour la fluidité du trafic. Couleur. (SWI)
156 Affiche pour le magazine *House & Garden*. La photo représente la vue qu'on a depuis la maison d'un sculpteur. Premier plan noir, ciel bleu lumineux. (USA)
157 Affiche extérieure en noir et blanc pour une campagne *Nordmende*. (GER)
158 Affiche diffusée pour le centenaire de la préfecture japonaise de Toyama. (JPN)

154 Eine private Eisenbahngesellschaft wirbt hier für Ausflüge an den Genfer See. (SWI)
155 Werbung der Verkehrsbetriebe Zürich für die öffentlichen Verkehrsmittel. In Farbe. (SWI)
156 Plakat für die Zeitschrift *House & Garden*. Die Aufnahme zeigt einen Ausblick aus dem Haus eines Bildhauers. Der Vordergrund ist schwarz, der Himmel leuchtendblau. (USA)
157 Strassenplakat in Schwarzweiss aus einer Kampagne für *Nordmende*. (GER)
158 Plakat zum hundertjährigen Bestehen der japanischen Präfektur Toyama. (JPN)

156

157

ARTIST / KÜNSTLER / ARTISTE:

154 Laurent Cocchi
155 P. Gmür
156 Sheila Metzner
157 Manfred Vogelsänger
158 Kazumasa Nagai

DESIGNER / GESTALTER / MAQUETTISTE:

154 Laurent Cocchi
155 H. M. Eggmann
156 Lloyd Ziff
157 Fritz Haase
158 Kazumasa Nagai

ART DIRECTOR / DIRECTEUR ARTISTIQUE:

155 G. Tscharner
156 Lloyd Ziff
157 Erwin Pfeffer/Harald Schweers
158 Kazumasa Nagai

AGENCY / AGENTUR / AGENCE – STUDIO:

154 Laurent Cocchi
155 G. Tscharner AG
156 House & Garden Magazine
157 Atelier Haase & Knels
158 Nippon Design Center

158

Zur Sache. NZZ

Schreibe mir, Du hörst von mir.

Schreibst Du ihr, so schreibt sie Dir.

162

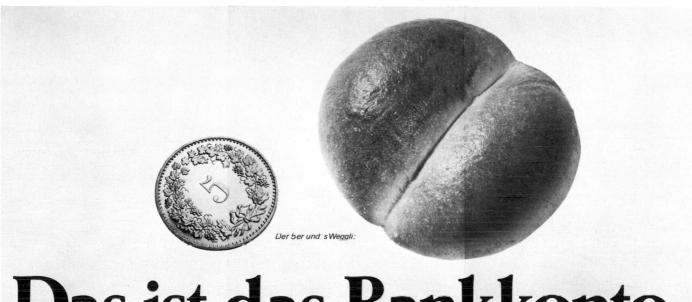

163

Varia

ARTIST / KÜNSTLER / ARTISTE:

160, 161 Jürgen Tapprich
162 Alf Dietrich
163 Jiri Vurma

DESIGNER / GESTALTER / MAQUETTISTE:

159 Charlie Hofer
160, 161 Bruno Albertin
163 Ruedi Külling

ART DIRECTOR / DIRECTEUR ARTISTIQUE:

159 Willi Bühler
160, 161 Bruno Albertin
162 Max Weber
163 Ruedi Külling

AGENCY / AGENTUR / AGENCE – STUDIO:

159 Adolf Wirz AG
160, 161 Young & Rubicam
162 Winzerhalde Grafik AG
163 Advico AG

159 Three-part poster from a long-running campaign for the *Neue Zürcher Zeitung*. (SWI)
160 "You hear from me" is taken literally in this three-part poster which is issued by the Swiss Post Office to introduce sound cassettes as a new method of communication. (SWI)
161 "You write to her, she'll write to you" (and perhaps seal it with a kiss), for the Swiss Post Office. (SWI)
162 Three-part poster in brown and beige from a campaign with the motto "Daily fresh" for products from the Migros Genossenschaft. (SWI)
163 You can have "the five cents and the bun" ("have your cake and eat it") if you make your financial transactions through the Swiss banks. (SWI)

159 Dreiteiliges Plakat aus einer langjährigen Kampagne für die *Neue Zürcher Zeitung*. (SWI)
160 «Du hörst von mir» ist hier wörtlich zu nehmen, denn die Schweizer Post wirbt mit diesem dreiteiligen Plakat für Tonbandkassetten als neues Mittel der Kommunikation. (SWI)
161 Nichtamtliches «Siegel» der Schweizer Post mit Aufmunterung zum Briefeschreiben. (SWI)
162 Dreiteiliges Plakat in Braun- und Beigetönen aus einer Kampagne unter dem Motto «Täglich frisch» für Lebensmittel von der Migros-Genossenschaft. (SWI)
163 Wenn man dieser Werbung der Schweizer Banken glauben will, so werden ihre Kunden den «Fünfer behalten und trotzdem das Brötchen bekommen». (SWI)

159 Affiche tripartite dans une campagne de longue durée du journal *Neue Zürcher Zeitung*. (SWI)
160 «Tu entendras parler de moi» est un slogan à prendre textuellement, car les PTT suisses font sur cette affiche tripartite de la publicité pour les envois de cassettes. (SWI)
161 Timbre non officiel (et pour cause) des PTT pour activer la poste aux lettres. (SWI)
162 Affiche tripartite, tons beiges et bruns, dans une campagne pour l'alimentation vendue par la Société coopérative Migros sous le slogan général de «Tous les jours frais». (SWI)
163 Si l'on en croit cette publicité des banques suisses, leurs clients peuvent avoir le beurre et l'argent du beurre, ou, comme on dit en Suisse, le sou et le petit pain. (SWI)

164

165

ARTIST / KÜNSTLER / ARTISTE:

165 Garth Bell
166 John Gladwin
167 Andy Post
168 Brian Collentine
170 Zenji Funabashi
171 Guy Billout

DESIGNER / GESTALTER:

164 Burkhard Neumann
165, 166 Garth Bell
167 Scott Eggers
169 Dan Reisinger
170 Sakae Kakigi

ART DIRECTOR:

165, 166 Garth Bell
167 Scott Eggers
168 Richard Nodine
169 Dan Reisinger
170 Sakae Kakigi

AGENCY / AGENTUR / AGENCE:

165, 166 Bell & Co.
167 Richards, Sullivan, Brock & Assoc.
168 Macys Graphic Design
169 Studio Reisinger
170 AZ Inc. Advertising

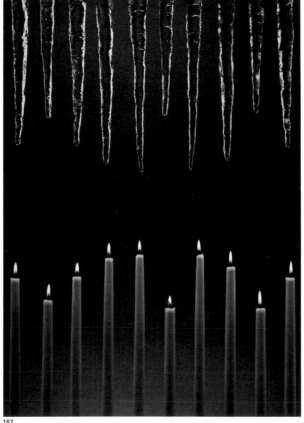

167

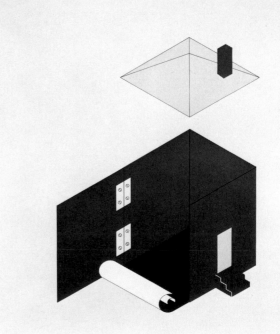

168

164 A winning poster from a competition under the title "450 Years Garamond", which was a joint advertising venture for the paper manufacturers *Zanders Feinpapiere* and the typographic workshop of Jöllenbeck & Schlieper. (GER)
165, 166 Two examples from a series of posters for the French typesetting firm *Compshop*. Fig. 165 was created after a graphic piece by Kurt Kranz and Fig. 166 is a colour photograph. (FRA)
167 A Christmas poster sent to their customers by the Rouse Company. (USA)
168 Announcement of a special carpet sale in *Macys* stores. (USA)
169 Poster for a furniture producer, also printed in red, blue and black. (ISR)
170 Call for entries by a Japanese annual of advertising graphics. The fish is white and violet. (JPN)
171 Poster for *China Seas*, makers of textiles and wall coverings. (USA)

164 Prämiertes Plakat aus einem Wettbewerb unter dem Titel «450 Jahre Garamond», das als Gemeinschaftswerbung für *Zanders Feinpapiere* und die Typographische Werkstatt Jöllenbeck & Schlieper verwendet wurde. (GER)
165, 166 Aus einer Serie von Plakaten für die Setzerei *Compshop*. Abb. 165 entstand nach einer Graphik von Kurt Kranz. (FRA)
167 Zu Weihnachten an Kunden versandtes Plakat der Rouse Company. (USA)
168 Ankündigung eines Teppich-Sonderverkaufs des Kaufhauses *Macys*. (USA)
169 Plakat für einen Möbelhersteller, das auch in Rot, Blau und Schwarz gedruckt wurde. (ISR)
170 Einladung zur Einsendung von Arbeiten für ein japanisches Jahrbuch der Werbegraphik. Kaltes Hellgrün und Rot, Fisch weiss und violett. (JPN)
171 Plakatwerbung für Textil-Design von *China Seas*. (USA)

Times Italic.

170

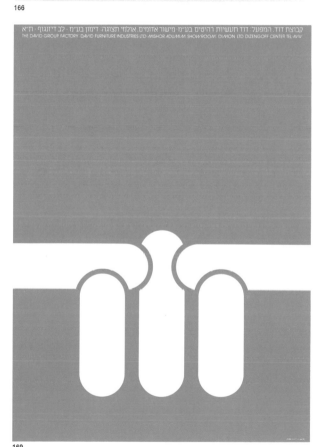

169

China Seas

CONTRACT DESIGNS · TEXTILES · WALLCOVERINGS

171

164 Affiche primée lors du concours «450 années de Garamond», utilisée pour la publicité collective de *Zanders Feinpapiere* et de l'Atelier Typographique Jöllenbeck & Schlieper. (GER)
165, 166 Eléments d'une série d'affiches réalisée pour l'atelier de composition *Compshop*. La fig. 165 s'inspire d'une composition de Kurt Kranz. (FRA)
167 Affiche destinée à Noël aux clients de la Rouse Company. (USA)
168 Annonce d'une vente spéciale de tapis aux grands magasins *Macys*. (USA)
169 Affiche pour un fabricant d'ameublements, dont il existe également une version en rouge, bleu et noir. (ISR)
170 Appel d'envois pour un annuel japonais de l'art publicitaire. Vert clair et rouge froids, poisson blanc et violet. (JPN)
171 Publicité par affiche pour le design *China Seas* en matière de textiles. (USA)

ARTIST / KÜNSTLER / ARTISTE:

172 Zenji Funabashi
173 David Kampa
174 Yusaku Tomoeda
175 Hickson-Bender

DESIGNER / GESTALTER / MAQUETTISTE:

172 Hidetaka Mochizuki
173 Woody Pirtle
174 Yusaku Tomoeda

ART DIRECTOR / DIRECTEUR ARTISTIQUE:

172 Hidetaka Mochizuki
173 Woody Pirtle
175 Doug Fisher/Bob Bender

172 With this poster the *Seiyu* store is offering the chance to customers to become the owner of an apple tree and its fruit for one year. Tree in bright blue, green and red, figure and lettering black on white stock. (JPN)
173 Poster to announce the opening of the nightclub "Tango" in Dallas. (USA)
174 Screen-print poster with a song text, as self-promotion for Yusaku Tomoeda. (JPN)
175 All colours (except bubble gum) match the floor and wall coverings of *Nevamar*. Correct placement and size of "bubbles" (rubber-, pingpong- and beach-balls) were important to depth and symmetry; overhead strobe lighting. (USA)

172 Das Kaufhaus *Seiyu* informiert hier über die Möglichkeit, für ein Jahr Besitzer eines Apfelbaumes und dessen Ertrag zu werden. Baum in Blau, Grün und Rot. (JPN)
173 Plakat aus Anlass der Eröffnung des Nachtclubs «Tango» in Dallas. (USA)
174 Siebdruckplakat mit einem Liedertext, als Eigenwerbung für Tomoeda. (JPN)
175 Alle Farben dieser Aufnahme (mit Ausnahme des Kaugummis) sind in der Kollektion der *Nevamar*-Boden- und Wandbeläge, für die das Plakat wirbt, vorhanden. (USA)

172 Les grands magasins *Seiyu* renseignent ici le public sur la possibilité d'être propriétaire d'un pommier et de sa récolte pendant une année. Arbre bleu lumineux, vert et rouge, personnage et texte noir sur papier blanc. (JPN)
173 Affiche pour l'inauguration du night-club «Tango» de Dallas. (USA)
174 Affiche sérigraphique avec une chanson; autopromotion de Tomoeda. (JPN)
175 Toutes les couleurs de cette photo (exception faite des couleurs du chewing-gum) se retrouvent dans les coloris des revêtements de sols et parois *Nevamar*. (USA)

172

173

174

175

AGENCY / AGENTUR / AGENCE – STUDIO:

172 Hot Art Co., Ltd.
173 Pirtle Design
174 T. I. Visual Planning
175 Lord, Sullivan & Yoder

Varia

176

177

178

179

Direct Mail
Direktwerbung
Publicité directe

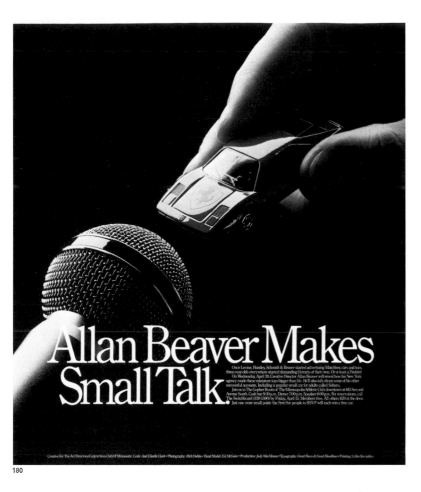

180

181

ARTIST / KÜNSTLER / ARTISTE:

176 Poul Allan
177 Adrianus Van der Elst
178 Renee Gettier-Street
179 Marie-Louise Cusack
180 Rick Dublin
181 Lou & Helen Fiorentino
182 John Collier

DESIGNER / GESTALTER / MAQUETTISTE:

176 Poul Allan
178 David R. Street/Renee Gettier-Street
179 Kalman Molnar
180 Charlie Clark
181 Lou Fiorentino

ART DIRECTOR / DIRECTEUR ARTISTIQUE:

176 Poul Allan
177 Lucchetta/Bacciocchi/Portinari
178 Dan Paiser
179 Marie Louise Cusack
180 Charlie Clark
181 Lou Fiorentino

AGENCY / AGENTUR / AGENCE – STUDIO:

176 Poul Allans Studio
177 Valter Bacciocchi
178 Streetworks Studio
179 Kalman Molnar Ltd
181 Visual Communications

176 Self-promotion poster for the Danish graphic designer Poul Allan. (DEN)
177 Poster printed on both sides at the start of a school term for the store *La Rinascente*. (ITA)
178 From a series of self-promotion posters for the Streetwork Studios entitled "Faces of American Literature". Screen print in moss green, pink and pinkish-beige on white. (USA)
179 Self-promotion poster for a studio specializing in illustration and graphics. Multi-coloured illustration on black background, yellow lettering on dull wine-red. (CAN)
180 Invitation to a lecture by the manager of an advertising agency about successful campaigns as, for example for the *Matchbox* make of toy cars. *Ferrari* on dark background. (USA)
181 Calendar poster with a colour photograph as advertising for a printer. (USA)
182 Poster for the Kansas City Art Directors Club, published in honour of a deceased member. The portrait is predominantly in brown tones. (USA)

176 Eigenwerbungsplakat für den dänischen Graphiker Poul Allan. (DEN)
177 Beidseitig bedrucktes Plakat des Mailänder Kaufhauses *La Rinascente* zum Schulanfang. (ITA)
178 Aus einer Serie von Eigenwerbungsplakaten des Streetwork Studios unter dem Titel «Gesichter der amerikanischen Literatur». Siebdruck in Moosgrün, Pink und Rosabeige auf Weiss. (USA)
179 Eigenwerbung eines Studios für Illustration und Graphik. Mehrfarbige Illustration vor schwarzem Hintergrund, Schrift gelb auf mattem Weinrot. (CAN)
180 Einladung zu einem Vortrag des Chefs einer Werbeagentur über erfolgreiche Kampagnen, wie z. B. für *Matchbox*-Spielautos. *Ferrari* vor dunklem Hintergrund. (USA)
181 Kalenderplakat mit Farbaufnahme als Werbung für eine Druckerei. (USA)
182 Plakat für den Kansas City Art Directors Club, das zu Ehren eines verstorbenen Mitglieds veröffentlicht wurde. Porträt überwiegend in Brauntönen. (USA)

176 Affiche autopromotionnelle du graphiste danois Poul Allan. (DEN)
177 Pour la rentrée scolaire. Grands magasins milanais *La Rinascente*. Impression biface. (ITA)
178 Affiche autopromotionnelle du Streetwork Studio. Série publiée sous le titre de «Visages de la littérature américaine». Sérigraphie en vert mousse, rose, beige rosé sur blanc. (USA)
179 Autopromotion d'un studio d'illustration et d'art graphique. Illustration polychrome sur fond noir, texte jaune sur bordeaux mat. (CAN)
180 Invitation à une conférence où le chef d'une agence de publicité oriente sur des campagnes couronnées de succès (les voitures *Matchbox* par exemple). *Ferrari* sur fond sombre. (USA)
181 Affiche-calendrier illustrée en couleurs. Publicité pour une imprimerie. (USA)
182 Affiche pour le Kansas City Art Directors Club publiée en l'honneur d'un membre décédé. Portrait exécuté surtout en tons bruns. (USA)

182

183

184

ARTIST / KÜNSTLER / ARTISTE:

183 Arthur Zelger
184 Heinz Looser
185 Makiko Hisamatsu
186 Ray Wood
187 Bob Conge
188 O & E Schwartz
189 Milton Glaser

DESIGNER / GESTALTER:

183 Arthur Zelger
184 Heinz Looser
185 Shigeyuki Hattori
186 Ray Wood
187 Bob Conge
188 O & E Schwartz
189 Milton Glaser

ART DIRECTOR:

184 Heinz Looser
185 Hidehiko Morii
186 Keith Bright
187 Robert MaHarry
188 O & E Schwartz
189 Milton Glaser

AGENCY / AGENTUR / AGENCE:

184 Heinz Looser
185 Nihon-Koutsu-Jigyo-Sya
186 Bright & Associates
187 Conge Design
188 O & E Schwartz
189 Milton Glaser, Inc.

186

187

183 Tourist-office advertising poster for the city of Innsbruck and area. (AUT)
184 Poster in bright colours on white background for a chair-lift to the Hoch Ybrig, a popular hiking and skiing resort. (SWI)
185 Poster with information about the sights to see in a national park, a joint-advertising venture of the railway and park management. In soft green, brown and grey tones. (JPN)
186 A poster issued by the Holland America shipping line for display in travel offices, here advertising a world cruise. In full colour. (USA)
187 "Technology blooms in the flower city"—a slogan to encourage more technology-minded firms to move to Rochester in New York State. (USA)
188 Tourist authority advertising for the beach of Haifa. Bright colours. (ISR)
189 From a long-running campaign by New York State, here for the sports opportunities and events held during the winter season. (USA)

183 Fremdenverkehrswerbung für die Stadt Innsbruck und Umgebung. (AUT)
184 Plakat in bunten Farben auf weissem Grund für eine Sesselbahn zum Hoch Ybrig, einem populären Wander- und Skigebiet. (SWI)
185 Plakat mit Informationen über die Sehenswürdigkeiten eines Nationalparks. Es ist eine Gemeinschaftswerbung der Eisenbahn und der Parkverwaltung. In sanften Grün-, Braun- und Grautönen. (JPN)
186 Für den Aushang in Reisebüros bestimmtes Plakat der Holland–Amerika–Schiffahrtslinie, die hier für eine Kreuzfahrt wirbt. In Farbe. (USA)
187 «Technologie blüht in der Blumenstadt.» Mit diesem Slogan wirbt die Stadt Rochester im Staat New York um Ansiedlung dieser Industrie. (USA)
188 Fremdenverkehrswerbung für den Strand von Haifa. Bunte Farben. (ISR)
189 Aus einer langjährigen Kampagne des Staates New York, hier für die Sportmöglichkeiten und Veranstaltungen in der Wintersaison. (USA)

185

188

183 Publicité touristique pour la ville d'Innsbruck et sa région. (AUT)
184 Affiche aux couleurs vives sur fond blanc pour un remonte-pente desservant le Hoch Ybrig, zone populaire de randonnées à pied et à ski. (SWI)
185 Affiche de renseignements sur les curiosités d'un parc national, réalisée en collaboration par les chemins de fer et l'administration du parc. Tons verts, bruns et gris atténués. (JPN)
186 Affiche de croisière de la compagnie de navigation Holland America, destinée aux agences de voyage. En couleur. (USA)
187 «La technologie fleurit dans la ville des fleurs.» Slogan de la ville de Rochester (Etat de New York) pour l'installation d'industries. (USA)
188 Publicité touristique pour la plage de Haïfa. Couleurs vives. (ISR)
189 Elément d'une campagne de longue durée de l'Etat de New York, ici en faveur de ses installations de sports et manifestations d'hiver. (USA)

189

artistry in sound
ONKYO

190

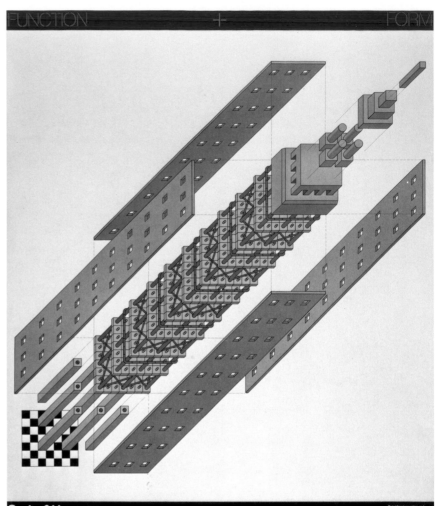

IBM

Syska & Hennessy

191

E A S T C O A S T

192

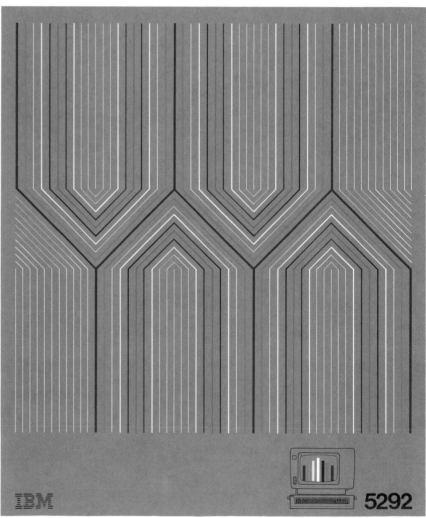

IBM 5292

193

ARTIST / KÜNSTLER / ARTISTE:

190 Yusaku Kamekura
192 Jeffrey Fisher
193 Ira Crane
194 Frans Zegger
195 Jung & Jung
196 Jim Jacobs
197 Bill Petersen

DESIGNER / GESTALTER / MAQUETTISTE:

190 Yusaku Kamekura
191 Michael Vanderbyl
193 Lou Fiorentino
194 André van Leeuwen/Hans Kroese
195 Hansjörg Oberholzer/Ruedi Ernst
196 Jim Jacobs
197 Gene Rosner/Jeff Callender

ART DIRECTOR / DIRECTEUR ARTISTIQUE:

190 Yusaku Kamekura
191 Michael Vanderbyl
192 Linda Warner
193 Lou Fiorentino
194 André van Leeuwen
195 Urs Fürer
196 Jim Jacobs
197 Cindy Halperin

AGENCY / AGENTUR / AGENCE – STUDIO:

191 Vanderbyl Design
193 Muir Cornelius Moore
194 KVH/GGK International
195 Adolf Wirz AG
196 Jim Jacobs' Studio, Inc.
197 Brown & Rosner

190 From a series for the audio products of Onkyo Corporation, incorporating 144 patterns. (JPN)
191 "Function and Form." Polychrome poster for Syska&Hennessy, an engineering bureau. (USA)
192 Image poster for the makers of *East Coast* jeans. In many colours. (AUS)
193 Advertising poster for a new colour-terminal from IBM. Various colours on grey. (USA)
194 "The bank near you." Poster for a savings-bank, in blue and white. (NLD)
195 Poster to advertise a personal computer by *Hewlett Packard*. (SWI)
196 For a typesetting/photo-copying firm called *Statcat*. In black, on yellow ground. (USA)
197 For a bank with the bear as symbol for security. Brown and blue. (USA)

190 Aus einer Serie für Audio-Produkte der Onkyo Corporation, hier mit 144 Mustern. (JPN)
191 «Funktion und Form.» Mehrfarbiges Plakat für Syska&Hennessy, ein Ingenieur-Büro. (USA)
192 Image-Plakat des Herstellers von *East-Coast*-Jeans. In vielen Farben. (AUS)
193 Werbung für einen neuen Farb-Terminal von IBM. Verschiedene Farben auf Grau. (USA)
194 «Die Bank in Ihrer Nähe.» Plakat für eine Sparkasse, in Blau und Weiss. (NLD)
195 Plakatwerbung für Personal-Computer von *Hewlett Packard*. (SWI)
196 Werbung einer Photokopieranstalt, welche die Katze im Namen hat. Schwarz auf Gelb. (USA)
197 Plakat einer Bank mit dem Bär als Symbol für Vorsorge und Sicherheit. Braun, Blau. (USA)

190 Affiche publiée dans une série pour les produits Audio (ici 144) de l'Onkyo Corp. (JPN)
191 «Forme et fonction.» Affiche couleur pour le bureau d'ingénieurs Syska&Hennessy. (USA)
192 Affiche de prestige du fabricant des jeans *East-Coast*. Nombreuses couleurs. (AUS)
193 Publicité pour un nouveau terminal couleurs d'IBM. Diverses couleurs sur fond gris. (USA)
194 «La banque près de chez vous.» Affiche pour une caisse d'épargne, bleu et blanc. (NLD)
195 Publicité par voie d'affiche pour les ordinateurs personnels *Hewlett Packard*. (SWI)
196 Publicité d'un atelier de photocopie au nom «félin». Noir sur jaune. (USA)
197 Affiche d'une banque. L'ours symbolise prévoyance et sécurité. Brun, bleu. (USA)

DIE KANT OP IS OOK'N DICHT BIJ HUISBANK.

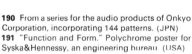
nutsspaarbank

194

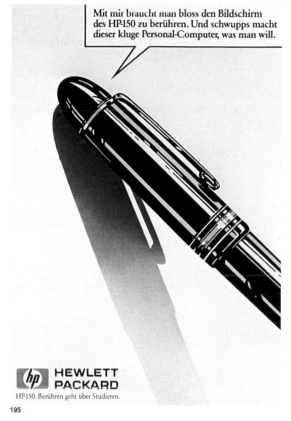

Mit mir braucht man bloss den Bildschirm des HP-150 zu berühren. Und schwupps macht dieser kluge Personal-Computer, was man will.

hp HEWLETT PACKARD

HP-150. Berühren geht über Studieren.

195

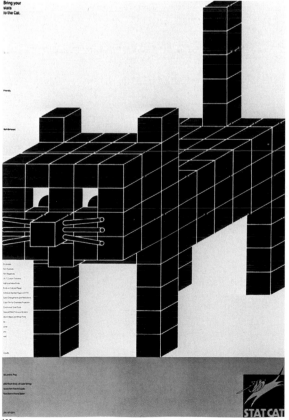

196

The Investment Plan. It Bears Consideration.

197

ARTIST / KÜNSTLER / ARTISTE:

198 Yves Lefèvre
199 Günter O. Lebisch/Erich Falkner
200 Geoff Senior
201 Fritz Henry Oerter
203 Raymond Pagès
204 János Flohr

DESIGNER / GESTALTER / MAQUETTISTE:

198 Yves Lefèvre
202 Ruth A. Leonard
203 Raymond Pagès
204 János Flohr

ART DIRECTOR / DIRECTEUR ARTISTIQUE:

199 Günter O. Lebisch
200 Alan Lofthouse
201 L. F. Kümper
202 Ruth A. Leonard
204 Katalin Benedek

AGENCY / AGENTUR / AGENCE – STUDIO:

199 Demner & Merlicek
200 Abbott Mead Vickers/SMS Ltd.
202 Salvato & Coe Associates
203 Air France/Service Publicité

198

199

Varia

198 The SNCB promotes its sleeping-car trains which also transport the passengers' cars. (BEL)
199 For the *Creditanstalt*, a house-finance company. (AUT)
200 The smaller *Volvo* "son" stands beside its "father". (GBR)
201 From a PR campaign for the firm *Haarmann & Reimer*, in Holzminden, makers of perfumes and aromas. (GER)
202 Poster in calendar form for a printer in Ohio. Colour-sample labels in rainbow colours on black ground. (USA)
203 Poster for *Air France Cargo*. In the background are shown transport goods in various languages. (FRA)
204 Poster with graphic representation of a reposing figure to be fed into a computer tomograph for medical records. (HUN)

198 Die SNCB wirbt mit diesem Plakat für ihre Schlafwagen-Züge, auf denen das eigene Auto mittransportiert wird. (BEL)
199 Plakat der *Creditanstalt* für die Hausfinanzierung. (AUT)
200 «Wie der Vater, so der Sohn.» Plakat für *Volvo*. (GBR)
201 Aus einer PR-Kampagne für die Firma *Haarmann & Reimer*, Duft- und Aromastoffe mit Sitz in Holzminden. (GER)
202 Plakat in Kalenderform für einen Drucker in Ohio. Farbmusteretiketten in Regenbogenfarben auf Schwarz. (USA)
203 Plakat für *Air France Cargo*. Im Hintergrund sind Transportgüter in diversen Sprachen aufgeführt. (FRA)
204 Poster mit graphischer Darstellung eines für Aufnahmen im Computer-Tomographen liegenden Menschen. (HUN)

198 Avec cette affiche, la SNCB vante ses possibilités de voyage en mettant l'auto sur le train. (BEL)
199 Affiche de la *Creditanstalt* (prêts hypothécaires). (AUT)
200 «Tel père, tel fils.» Affiche pour *Volvo*. (GBR)
201 Campagne de relations publiques des Parfums et Arômes *Haarmann & Reimer* installés à Holzminden. (GER)
202 Affiche en forme de calendrier pour un imprimeur de l'Ohio. Etiquettes d'échantillons arc-en-ciel sur noir. (USA)
203 Affiche pour *Air France Cargo*. Au fond, énumération des biens transportés, en diverses langues. (FRA)
204 Affiche-calendrier, avec la représentation assistée par ordinateur d'un humain examiné en tomographie. (HUN)

201

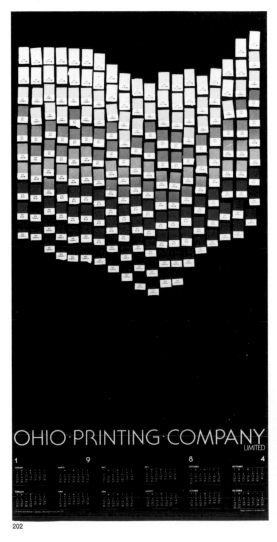

202

LIKE FATHER, LIKE SON.

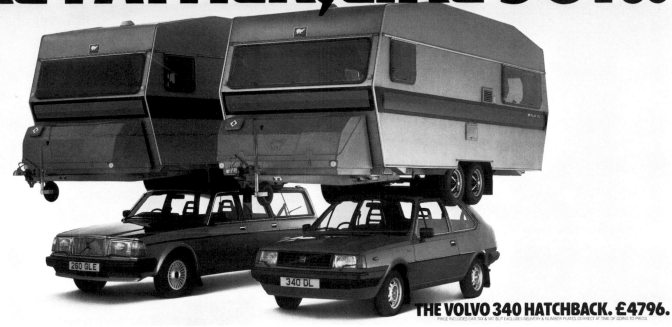

THE VOLVO 340 HATCHBACK. £4796.
PRICE INCLUDES CAR TAX & VAT BUT EXCLUDES DELIVERY & NUMBER PLATES. CORRECT AT TIME OF GOING TO PRESS.

200

203

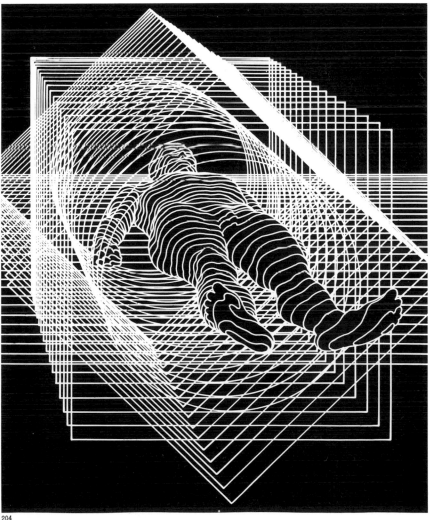

204

205

206

205 The yellow iris of the eye is the only spot of colour on this black-and-white illustration for the Befo Solarium's poster to advertise its services. (DEN)
206 Colour photograph as advertising poster for a *Yamaha* sailing boat. (JPN)
207 The focal point of this poster is a new bank-cheque design. Blue, white and grey table, black-and-white chequebook with green inner leaf, yellow pencil. (DEN)
208, 209 Two-part posters for the Japanese National Railways. The aim of the widely-dispersed advertising campaign with the slogan "Discover Japan" is to transport as many people as possible fast and safely to Japan's various recreation areas. (JPN)

205 Das Befo-Bräunungszentrum wirbt mit diesem Plakat für seine Dienste. Einziger Farbpunkt der Schwarzweiss-Illustration ist die gelbe Iris. (DEN)
206 Mehrfarbige Aufnahme als Werbeplakat für ein Segelboot der Marke *Yamaha*. (JPN)
207 Ein neues Bankscheck-Design diente als Auslöser für dieses Plakat. Blau-weiss-grauer Tisch, schwarzweisses Scheckheft mit grünem Innenblatt, gelber Griffel. (DEN)
208, 209 Zweiteilige Plakate des Nationalen Japanischen Eisenbahnunternehmens. Ziel der weitangelegten Werbekampagne mit dem Slogan «Entdecke Japan» ist es, möglichst viele Menschen sicher und schnell in verschiedene Erholungsgebiete Japans zu bringen. (JPN)

208

207

ARTIST / KÜNSTLER / ARTISTE:

205 Finn Nygaard
206 Toshikazu Furikado
207 Peter Bysted
208 Nobuyasu Toyokuni
209 Kazuyuki Otsubo

DESIGNER / GESTALTER / MAQUETTISTE:

206 Toru Nakagawa
208, 209 Hachiro Suzuki

ART DIRECTOR / DIRECTEUR ARTISTIQUE:

206 Toru Nakagawa
208, 209 Hachiro Suzuki

AGENCY / AGENTUR / AGENCE – STUDIO:

206, 208, 209 Dentsu Inc.
207 Peter Bysted Studio

205 Affiche du centre de bronzage Befo. Le seul point de couleur de cette illustration noir et blanc est l'iris jaune. (DEN)
206 Affiche-photo polychrome pour la publicité des voiliers *Yamaha*. (JPN)
207 Une nouvelle conception de chèque bancaire a servi de point de départ à cette affiche. Table bleu, blanc, gris, carnet de chèques noir-blanc, page intérieure verte, crayon jaune. (DEN)
208, 209 Affiches bipartites des Chemins de Fer Nationaux Japonais. La vaste campagne où elles sont intégrées sous le slogan de «Découvre le Japon» sert à amener le plus grand nombre dans diverses aires récréatives du Japon en alliant vitesse et sécurité. (JPN)

209

CONNECTIONS

John Massey — "One color next to another defines our universe. One color next to another establishes and connects the abstractions of form, perspective, volume, motion, space, light, dark, hope, fear, mystery and understanding, thus creating the human condition."

John Massey

Simpson
making paper...
perform!

210

ARTIST / KÜNSTLER / ARTISTE:

210 John Massey
211 Colin Forbes/Pentagram
212 John Casado/Casado Design
213 Stuart Ash/Gottschalk & Ash
214 Rudolph de Harak
215 Primo Angeli
216 Henry Wolf/
    Henry Wolf Productions

ART DIRECTOR:

210–216 James Cross

AGENCY / AGENTUR / AGENCE:

210–216 Cross Associates

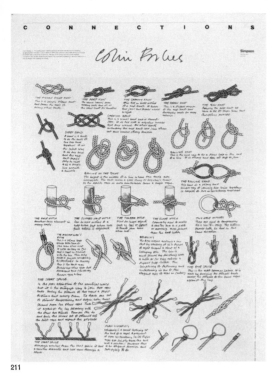

211

212

213

214

215

216

210–216 From a poster series for *Simpson* paper. The title is interpreted differently in each by a famous graphic designer. John Massey juxtaposes forms and colours to connect the abstractions of motion, space and hope etc. which create the universe; Colin Forbes believes that knots can best express ties which connect—with all their inherent variations; John Casado sees the dollar sign as the connecting symbol meaning "good design equals more profit for the client and the designer"; Stuart Ash thinks a connection is expressed when all the design components are in agreement—paper quality, typography, colour and form; Rudolph de Harak generates an optical illusion in his contrasting colour-connecting elements; Primo Angeli creates another kind of optical illusion in his colourful dessert for two; Henry Wolf sees man's relationship to his own self as the integral element of connections. Posters' format: 71×50,5 cm. (USA)

210–216 Aus einer Serie von Plakaten für *Simpson*-Papier, die «Zusammenhänge» illustrieren, wie sie von Graphikern erlebt werden: John Massey sieht im Universum ein Ineinanderfügen von Farbe, Form, Perspektive, Licht und Schatten; Colin Forbes empfindet die Idee des Knotens als eine simple Verbindung, die gleichzeitig unzählige Variationsmöglichkeiten bietet; John Casado meint, aus gutem Design entstünden verbindende finanzielle Vorteile für Auftraggeber und Gestalter; Stuart Ash arbeitet mit der Idee, dass eine Verbindung entsteht, wenn alle Komponenten wie Papierqualität, Typographie, Farbe und Form übereinstimmen; Rudolph de Harak erzeugt durch kontrastfarbene Verbindungselemente optische Illusionen; Primo Angeli kreierte eine farbenfrohe Dessertverbindung für zwei; Henry Wolf stellt die Beziehung des Menschen zu sich selbst als die essentielle dar. Plakatformat: 71×50,5 cm. (USA)

210–216 Divers exemples d'affiches figurant dans une série réalisée pour les papiers *Simpson* et illustrant des «connexions» comme les visualisent des artistes graphiques: John Massey voit dans l'univers l'interpénétration de la couleur, de la forme et de la perspective; Colin Forbes part du nœud, jonction simple susceptible de multiples configurations; John Casado perçoit les avantages financiers que le design de qualité vaut au client et à l'artiste; Stuart Ash estime que la vraie connexion naît de l'harmonisation de composantes telles que la qualité du papier, la typo, la couleur et la forme; Rudolph de Harak crée des illusions d'optique à partir d'éléments de jonction aux couleurs contrastantes; Primo Angeli réalise une «connexion dessert» savoureuse pour deux et haute en couleur de surcroît; Henry Wolf représente la relation de l'être humain à soi comme l'essentiel. Le format unitaire de toutes ces affiches est de 71×50,5 cm. (USA)

2

Cultural Posters
Kulturelle Plakate
Affiches culturelles

ARTIST / KÜNSTLER / ARTISTE:

217–224 Franciszek Starowieyski

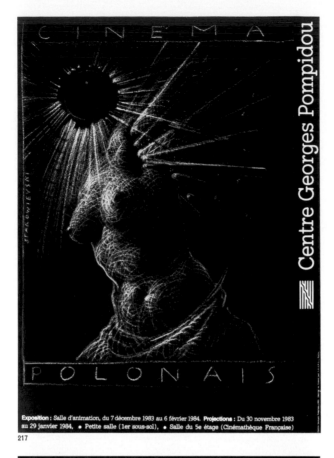

217

218

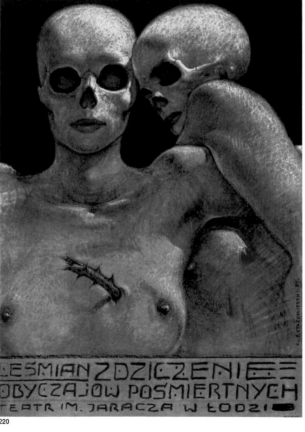

220

221

217–224 Examples from posters by the Polish artist Franciszek Starowieyski. Fig. 217: For an exhibition about Polish films in the Pompidou Centre, Paris; Fig. 218: "The Woman in Poster 1905–1980", for a poster exhibition in the Kochanowski Theatre in Opole; Fig. 219 is for a piece entitled "Outside Reality", performed in the Centre for Theatre Activities in Koszalin; Fig. 220: "The Degeneration of Morals after Death", poster for a play by Leśmian at the Jaracz Theatre in Lódź; Fig. 221 is for *Macbeth*, performed by the Municipal Theatre, Münster; Fig. 222: poster for a film by Lech J. Majewski: "The Cavalier"; Fig. 223 is a poster in brown-beige tones for the play "The Brother of our Lord" by Karol Wojtyła, the present Pope John Paul II; Fig. 224 is for a portrait exhibition by Krysztof Gierałtowski at a museum in Bonn. (POL)

217–224 Beispiele von Plakaten des polnischen Künstlers Franciszek Starowieyski. Abb. 217: Für eine Ausstellung über polnische Filme im Centre Pompidou Paris; Abb. 218: «Die Frau im Plakat 1905–1980» – für eine Plakatausstellung im Kochanowski-Theater in Opole; Abb. 219: für ein Stück mit dem Titel «Ausserhalb der Wirklichkeit», aufgeführt im Zentrum für Theateraktionen in Koszalin; Abb. 220: «Die Verwilderung der Sitten nach dem Tode» – Plakat für ein Stück von Leśmian am Jaracz-Theater in Lódź; Abb. 221: für *Macbeth*, aufgeführt von den Städtischen Bühnen Münster; Abb. 222: Plakat für einen Film von Lech J. Majewski: «Der Ritter»; Abb. 223: Plakat in braun-beigen Tönen für das Stück «Der Bruder unseres Herrn» von Karol Wojtyła, dem heutigen Papst Johannes Paul II.; Abb. 224: für eine Porträtausstellung von Krysztof Gierałtowski (POL)

219

223

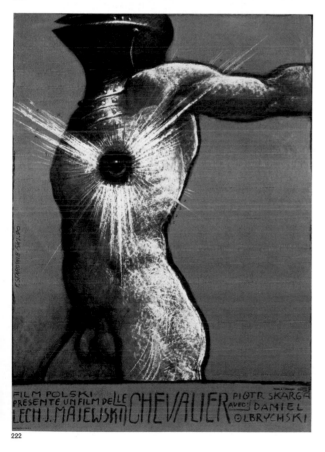

222

224

217–224 Exemples d'affiches créées par l'artiste polonais Franciszek Staro-wieyski. Fig. 217: pour une exposition de films polonais au Centre Pompidou de Paris; fig. 218: «La Femme dans l'affiche, 1905–1980», thème d'une exposition au Théâtre Kochanowski d'Opole; fig. 219: pour la pièce «En dehors du réel», jouée au Centre des actions théâtrales de Koszalin; fig. 220: «Le Dérèglement des mœurs après la mort»: affiche pour la pièce de Leśmian représentée au Théâtre Jaracz de Lódź; fig. 221: pour un *Macbeth* monté sur l'une des scènes du Théâtre municipal de Münster (RFA); fig. 222: affiche pour le film «Le Chevalier» de Lech J. Majewski; fig. 223: affiche aux tons beige brun pour la pièce «Le Frère de notre Seigneur» de Karol Wojtyła, aujourd'hui Jean-Paul II; fig. 224: pour une exposition des portraits de Krysztof Gierałtowski à Bonn. (POL)

225 Poster for the reopening of the Czech National Theatre in Prague. Black and red on gold-coloured background, white border. (CSR)
226 Full-colour theatre poster for the play *Tango* by Sławomir Mrożek. (POL)
227 A theatre poster by Roland Topor for the play *Marat Sade* by Peter Weiss. Hair "fashions" in red and grey, faces in dusky tones. (POL)
228 Polychrome poster for the pastorale *Aminta* by Torquato Tasso. (POL)
229 Poster for "History", a play by Witold Gombrowicz; green foot. (POL)
230 Theatre poster in shades of red, brown and beige. It was created as a project within a course of study for communications design at the University of Essen, in collaboration with the Municipal Theatre, Essen. (GER)

225 Plakat für die Neueröffnung des tschechischen Nationaltheaters Prag. Schwarz und Rot auf goldfarbenem Hintergrund, weisser Rand. (CSR)
226 Mehrfarbiges Theaterplakat für das Stück *Tango* von Sławomir Mrożek. (POL)
227 Von Roland Topor gestaltetes Theaterplakat für ein Stück von Peter Weiss: *Marat Sade*. «Haartrachten» in Rot und Grau, Gesichter in düsteren Farben. (POL)
228 Mehrfarbiges Plakat für die Pastorale *Aminta* von Torquato Tasso. (POL)
229 Plakat für «Geschichte», ein Theaterstück von Witold Gombrowicz. Grüner Fuss. (POL)
230 Theaterplakat in Rot-, Braun- und Beigetönen. Es entstand als Projektarbeit im Studiengang Kommunikationsdesign der Universität Essen, in Zusammenarbeit mit dem Theater der Stadt Essen. (GER)

225 Affiche pour la réouverture du Théâtre national tchèque de Prague. Noir et rouge sur fond or, bord blanc. (CSR)
226 Affiche de théâtre polychrome pour la pièce *Tango* de Sławomir Mrożek. (POL)
227 Affiche de théâtre créée par Roland Topor pour une pièce de Peter Weiss, *Marat Sade*. «Styles de coiffure» rouge et gris, visages aux couleurs lugubres. (POL)
228 Affiche polychrome pour la pastorale *Aminta* de Torquato Tasso. (POL)
229 Affiche pour la pièce «Histoire» de Witold Gombrowicz. Pied vert. (POL)
230 Affiche de théâtre aux tons rouges, bruns, beiges. C'est le résultat d'un travail sur un projet du programme d'études de design de communication de l'Université d'Essen, en collaboration avec le Théâtre municipal d'Essen. (GER)

225

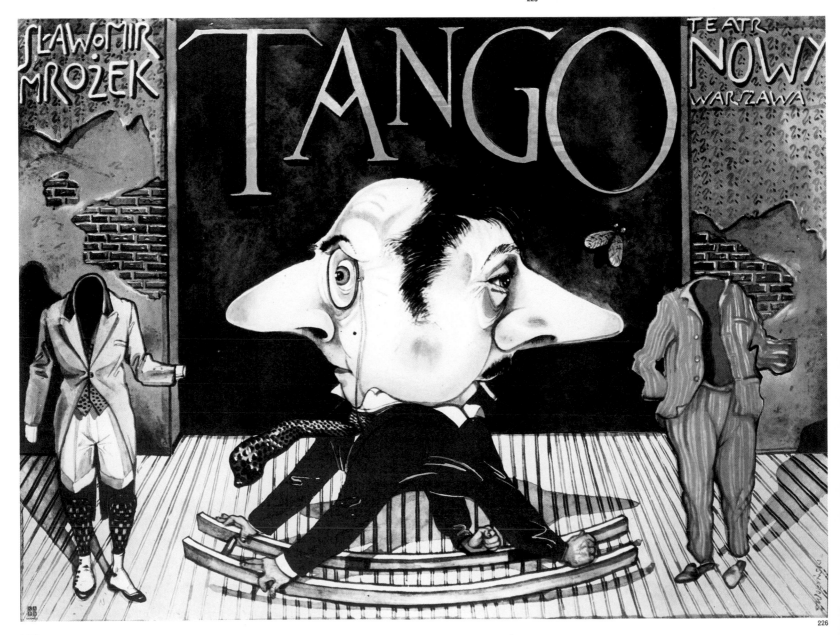

226

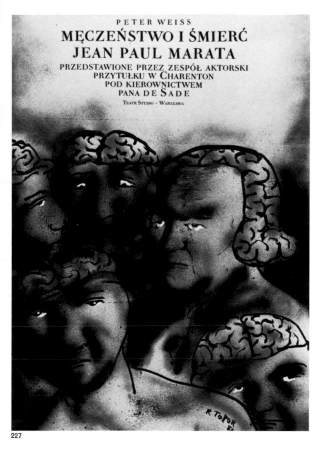

227

228

229

230

ARTIST / KÜNSTLER / ARTISTE:

225 Josef Flejšar
226 Wojciech Wolyński
227 Roland Topor
228 Jan Mlodozeniec
229 Henryk Tomaszewski
230 Andreas Rzadkowsky

DESIGNER / GESTALTER / MAQUETTISTE:

225 Josef Flejšar
227 Krzysztof Tyczkowski
230 Andreas Rzadkowsky

ART DIRECTOR / DIRECTEUR ARTISTIQUE:

226 Bohdan Cybulski
227 Jerzy Grzegorzewski
228 Adam Hanuszkiewicz
230 Sabine Tschierschky/
Heinz Ruhrmann

231

232

231 Theatre poster bearing a real postage stamp and the theatre rubber-stamp for the occasion of the world première of "The Radiation of Fatherhood", a play by Karol Wojtyła, Pope John Paul II. (POL)
232 Poster for Shakespeare's *Macbeth*. Various tones of red, on white. (POL)
233 Napoleon casts an eye on the hidden lady in this poster for Sardou's *Madame Sans-Gêne*. (POL)
234 Polish poster for a film about the suffering of the Jews. (POL)
235 An orange and red-toned poster for the first performance of a Polish play. (POL)
236 Theatre poster in yellow and brown shades for Friedrich Schiller's *Cabal and Love*. (POL)
237 Poster for the performance of Mario Vargas Llosa's "Pantaleon and his Lady Visitors". (POL)

231 Theaterplakat mit echter Briefmarke und Theaterstempel anlässlich der Welturaufführung des Stücks «Die Ausstrahlung der Vaterschaft» von Karol Wojtyła, Papst Johannes Paul II. (POL)
232 Plakat für *Macbeth* von William Shakespeare. Verschiedene Rottöne auf Weiss. (POL)
233 Napoleon im Hintergrund dieses Plakats für *Madame Sans-Gêne* von Victorien Sardou. (POL)
234 Polnisches Plakat für einen Film über die Leiden der Juden. (POL)
235 Premierenplakat in Orange- und Rottönen für ein polnisches Theaterstück. (POL)
236 Theaterplakat in Gelb- und Brauntönen für Friedrich Schillers *Kabale und Liebe*. (POL)
237 Plakat für die Aufführung von Mario Vargas Llosas «Pantaleon und seine Besucherinnen». (POL)

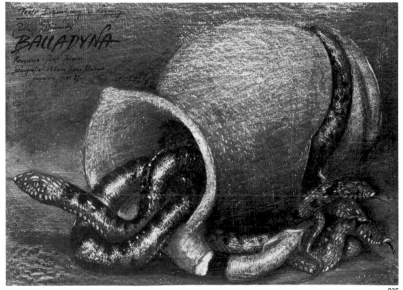

235

236

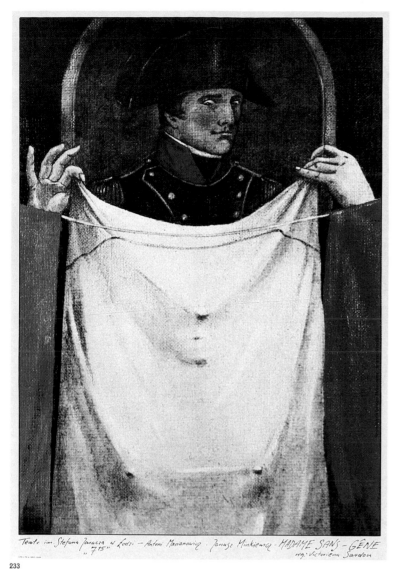

233

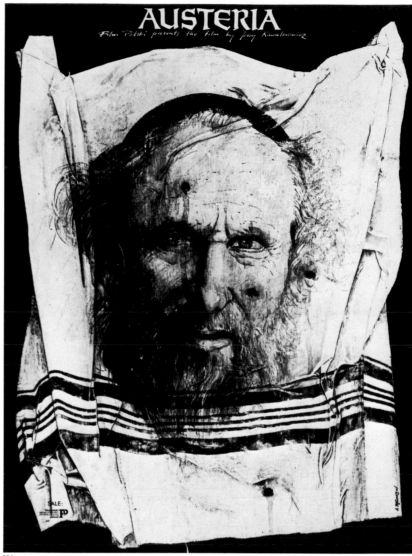

234

231 Affiche de théâtre pourvue d'un timbre véritable et d'un timbre du théâtre, pour la première mondiale du «Rayonnement de la paternité» de Karol Wojtyła alias Jean-Paul II. (POL)
232 Affiche pour le *Macbeth* de William Shakespeare. Divers rouges sur blanc. (POL)
233 Napoléon à l'arrière-plan de cette affiche de *Madame Sans-Gêne* de Victorien Sardou. (POL)
234 Affiche polonaise pour un film qui traite des souffrances des Juifs. (POL)
235 Affiche pour la première d'une pièce de théâtre polonaise. Divers orange et rouges. (POL)
236 Affiche de théâtre, divers jaunes et bruns, pour *Cabale et Amour* de Friedrich Schiller. (POL)
237 Affiche pour la pièce de Mario Vargas Llosa – «Pantaléon et ses visiteuses». (POL)

Theatre/Theater
Théâtre

ARTIST / KÜNSTLER / ARTISTE:

231–235 Andrzej Pagowski
236, 237 Mieczyslaw Gorowski

ART DIRECTOR / DIRECTEUR ARTISTIQUE:

231 Andrzej Marczewski
234 Miroslaw Galczynski

237

238

239

ARTIST / KÜNSTLER / ARTISTE:

238 Paul Valerry
239 Phil Risbeck
240 Hans Schleger & Associates
241 Yarom Vardimon
242, 244 Rolf-Felix Müller
243 John J. Sorbie
245 Manfred Hürrig
246, 247 Andreas Rzadkowsky

DESIGNER / GESTALTER / MAQUETTISTE:

239 Phil Risbeck
241 Yarom Vardimon
243 John J. Sorbie
246, 247 Andreas Rzadkowsky

ART DIRECTOR / DIRECTEUR ARTISTIQUE:

238 Heinz Gafert
239 Phil Risbeck
240 Pat Schleger
241 Yarom Vardimon
243 John J. Sorbie
245 Manfred Hürrig
246, 247 Sabine Tschierschky/
   Heinz Ruhrmann

AGENCY / AGENTUR / AGENCE – STUDIO:

238 Artist Vision Communication
239 CSU Art Dept.
243 Sorbie Roche

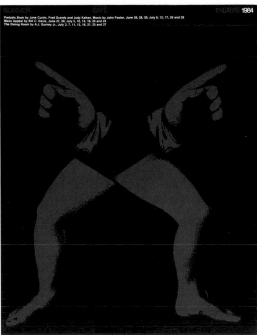

240

241

238 Poster to announce two one-act plays by Samuel Beckett. (GER)
239 For a performance of *Faust* by the OpenStage Opera at Lincoln Center. Colour runs from grey at bottom to red at top. (USA)
240 Fluid "living" S's (for symphony) which can be multiplied and re-arranged to form new designs thereby emphasizing the live perform-ances of the BBC's Symphony Orchestra. (GBR)
241 Poster for an exhibition of the artist group Radius with the symbol of this society. Green cogwheel, yellow paper on mauve ground. (ISR)
242 For the Municipal Theatre in Karl-Marx-Stadt. Black-and-white illustration on dull brown, rectangle with author and title of play in bright yellow. (GDR)
243 A poster announcing three different plays. (USA)
244 For Prokofiev's *Cinderella* on the stage in Gera. (GDR)
245 Poster for the Théâtre National de Belgique. (BEL)
246, 247 Poster created in collaboration with the Municipal Theatre Essen and the University of Essen. (GER)

238 Plakat für die Ankündigung von zwei Einaktern von Samuel Beckett. In Grautönen mit Weiss. (GER)
239 Für eine *Faust*-Aufführung der OpenStage Opera. Farbverlauf des Hintergrunds von unten grau zu oben rot. (USA)
240 S-Formen als Symbol für das Wort «Symphonie» in Schwarz und Weiss auf leuchtendgelbem Hintergrund. (GBR)
241 Plakat für eine Ausstellung der Künstlergruppe Radius mit dem Signet dieser Vereinigung. Hellvioletter Grund, grünes Zahnrad. (ISR)
242 Für das Städtische Theater in Karl-Marx-Stadt konzipiertes Plakat. Schwarzweiss-Illustration auf mattem Braun, leuchtendgelbes Recht-eck mit Autor und Titel des Stücks. (GDR)
243 Ankündigung von drei verschiedenen Theaterstücken. (USA)
244 Für die Bühnen der Stadt Gera konzipiertes Plakat. (GDR)
245 Plakat des Théâtre National de Belgique. (BEL)
246, 247 In Zusammenarbeit zwischen dem Theater der Stadt Essen und der Universität Essen realisierte Plakate. (GER)

238 Affiche annonçant deux pièces en un acte de Samuel Beckett. Divers gris, avec du blanc. (GER)
239 Pour une représentation du *Faust* de Goethe à l'OpenStage Opera. Le fond varie de gris (en bas) à rouge (en haut). (USA)
240 Divers S symbolisent le mot «symphonie» en noir et blanc sur fond jaune lumineux, sur cette affiche de l'orchestre de la BBC. (GBR)
241 Affiche pour une exposition du groupe artistique Radius, avec l'emblème du groupe. Fond violet clair, roue dentée verte. (ISR)
242 Affiche conçue pour le Théâtre municipal de Karl-Marx-Stadt. Illustration noir et blanc sur fond brun mat, rectangle jaune vif avec le nom de l'auteur et le titre de la pièce. (GDR)
243 Annonce de trois pièces de théâtre différentes. (USA)
244 Affiche réalisée pour les théâtres de la ville de Gera. (GDR)
245 Affiche du Théâtre national de Belgique. (BEL)
246, 247 Affiches créées conjointement par le Théâtre municipal d'Essen et l'Université de la même ville. (GER)

242

243

THEATRE NATIONAL
LA BALADE DU GRAND MACABRE
DE MICHEL DE GHELDRODE

Mise en scène : Bernard De Coster / décor et costumes : Thierry Bosquet / régie : Fernande Rousseau
Avec Georges Bossair / Michel Carcan / Gilbert Charles / Jean-Paul Connart /
Jean-Pierre Dauzun / Suzy Falk / Jean-Claude Frison / Isabelle Glorie / Alain Guilmard /
Tobias Kempf / Raymond Lescot / Jo Rensonnet /
Du 17 octobre au 10 novembre / Tous les soirs à 20 h 15. Attention: les 6, 7, 8 et 9 novembre, le rideau se lèvera à 19 h 30.
Matinées les 17, 20, 21, 24, 28 octobre et 4 novembre à 15 h. / Relâche les lundis et dimanches en soirée / Parking gratuit /
Location : Centre Rogier, de 11 à 18 H. Tél. 217.03.03 / auprès des délégués et agences du Théâtre National /
à l'Office du Tourisme de Bruxelles (TIB) (Teletib) Tél. 513.83.28 et 513.89.40

244

245

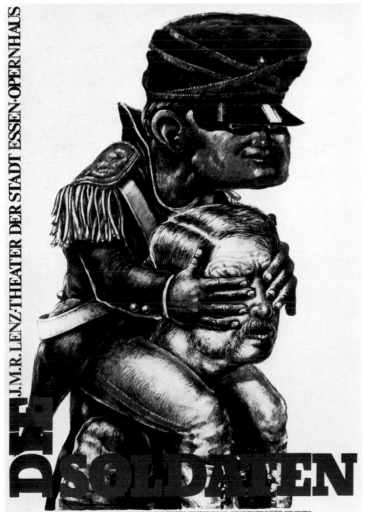

246

247

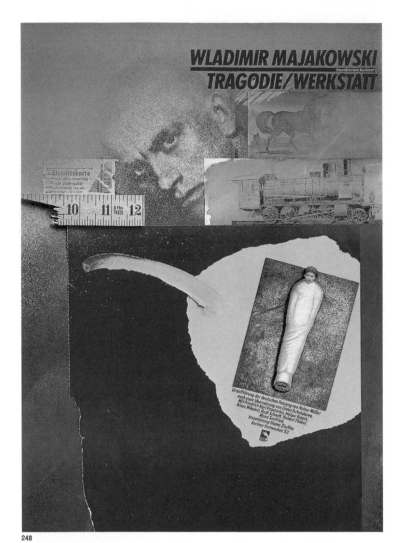

248

Theatre/Theater/Théâtre

ARTIST/KÜNSTLER/ARTISTE:
248–251 Holger Matthies

DESIGNER/GESTALTER/MAQUETTISTE:
248–251 Holger Matthies

ART DIRECTOR/DIRECTEUR ARTISTIQUE:
248–251 Holger Matthies

248–251 Holger Matthies, one of the world's leading poster artists, creates works mainly for the theatre, using a combination of media—three-dimensional items, photography and illustrations. His compositions are always strongly symbolic of their subject. Shown here are four examples. Fig. 248: Première poster for the play "A Tragedy" by Russian author Vladimir Mayakovsky; Fig. 249: Holger Matthies' contribution to the protection of the environment, "The desert quakes, the desert lives", an authentic shot; Fig. 250: theatre poster to announce the Hamburg theatre's summer programme; Fig. 251: Large-format poster for a theatre "collage" of Prussian scenes written by Heiner Müller. (GER)

248–251 Holger Matthies, ein international bekannter Plakatgestalter, hat diese vier Beispiele geschaffen und dabei verschiedene Medien miteinander kombiniert; aus Photographien, Illustrationen und Gegenständen sind Kompositionen mit Symbolcharakter entstanden. Abb. 248: Premierenplakat für das Stück «Tragödie» des russischen Autors Wladimir Maja-kowski; Abb. 249: Holger Matthies' Beitrag zum Thema Umwelt: Triumph der Natur über den Asphalt. Die Aufnahme ist authentisch; Abb. 250: Theaterplakat zur Ankündigung des Hamburger Sommerprogramms; Abb. 251: grossformatiges Plakat für eine Szenen-Collage über Preussen von Heiner Müller, im Schiller-Theater in Berlin. (GER)

248–251 Holger Matthies, affichiste de réputation internationale, est l'auteur de ces quatre exemples où il combine les approches de divers médias; des photos, des illustrations et des objets s'y agencent en des compositions au caractère symbolique. Fig. 248: affiche pour la première de la pièce «Tragédie» du Russe Vladimir Maïakovski; fig. 249: contribution de Holger Matthies au thème de l'environnement: le triomphe de la nature sur l'asphalte; la photo est authentique; fig. 250: affiche de théâtre annonçant le programme d'été de Hambourg; fig. 251: affiche au grand format pour une pièce de théâtre sous forme d'un collage des scènes prussiennes de Heiner Müller. (GER)

249

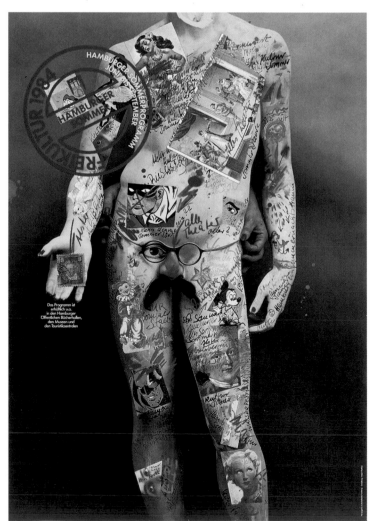

250

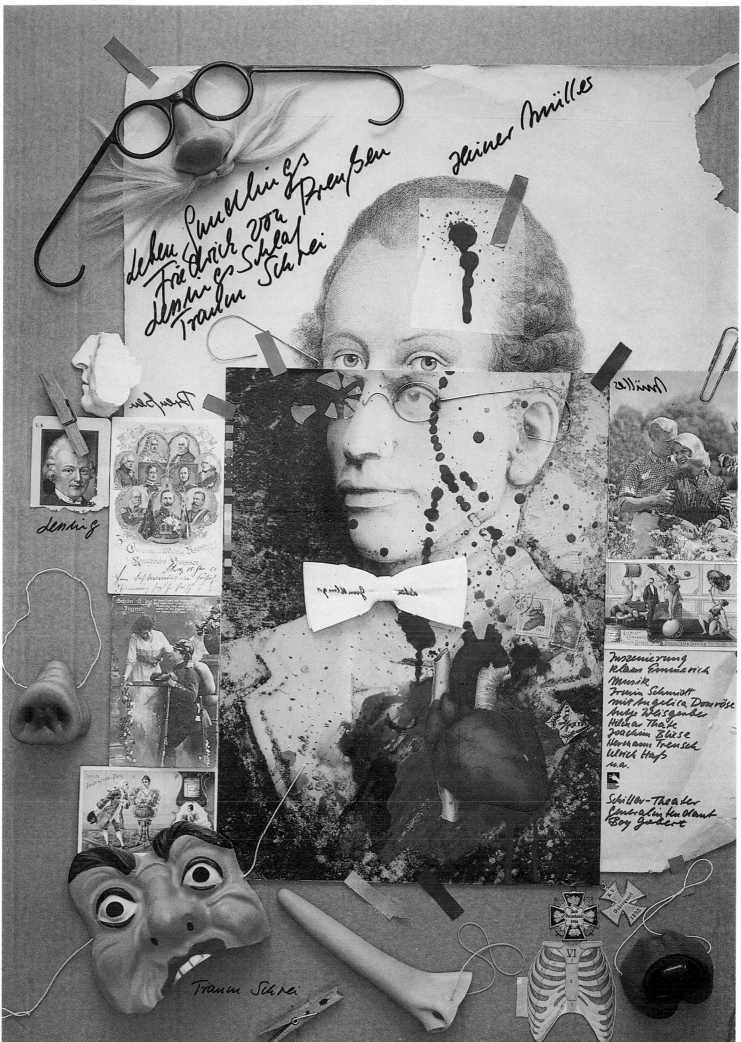

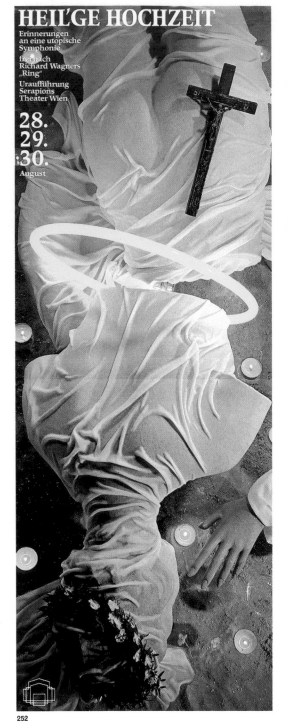

HEIL'GE HOCHZEIT

Erinnerungen
an eine utopische
Symphonie
frei nach
Richard Wagners
„Ring"
Uraufführung
Serapions
Theater Wien

**28.
29.
30.**
August

252

IM WANDEL DER ZEITEN

Ein musikalisches
Schauspiel für
die Alte Oper
von Harald Weiss

**26.
27.**
August

253

OPUS   ANTON WEBERN

Das Gesamtwerk
in zehn
Veranstaltungen
Die Junge Deutsche
Philharmonie
Künstlerische
Leitung:
Gary Bertini

254

252–254 Three examples from a series of four posters which Günther Kieser designed on commission of the Old Opera (Alte Oper) in Frankfurt/M. Uniform-size posters: 161×60 cm. (GER)
255 Large-format poster of the Hessian broadcasting company with programme tips for the Christmas festival. The Father Christmas figure on a beige-pink background can be cut out and assembled to make a jumping-Jack toy. (GER)
256 Poster to announce the 19th German Jazz Festival organized by the Hessian broadcasting company. In full colour. (GER)
257 Poster by Frieder Grindler for the performing season 1984/85 of the Baden Municipal Theatre in Karlsruhe. (GER)

252–254 Drei Beispiele aus einer Serie von vier Plakaten, die Günther Kieser im Auftrag der Alten Oper Frankfurt a. M. gestaltet hat. Einheitliches Plakatformat: 161×60 cm. (GER)
255 Grossformatiges Plakat des Hessischen Rundfunks mit Programmhinweisen für die Festtage. Die St.-Nikolaus-Figur auf dem rötlich beigen Hintergrund könnte theoretisch ausgeschnitten und zu einem Hampelmann montiert werden. (GER)
256 Plakat für die Ankündigung des vom Hessischen Rundfunk organisierten 19. Deutschen Jazz-Festivals. In Farbe. (GER)
257 Von Frieder Grindler konzipiertes Plakat für die Spielzeit 1984/85 des Badischen Staatstheaters Karlsruhe. (GER)

252–254 Trois des quatre affiches de Günther Kieser pour le vieil Opéra (Alte Oper) de Francfort-sur-le-Main. Format unitaire: 161×60 cm. (GER)
255 Affiche au grand format de la Radiodiffusion de Hesse avec des indications de programme pour les fêtes. Le Père Fouettard sur fond beige rosâtre peut se découper et être assemblé pour en faire un pantin. (GER)
256 Affiche pour le 19e Festival allemand du jazz organisé par la Radiodiffusion de Hesse. En couleur. (GER)
257 Affiche conçue par Frieder Grindler pour la saison 1984/85 du Badisches Staatstheater de Karlsruhe. (GER)

ARTIST / KÜNSTLER / ARTISTE:

252–256 Günther Kieser
257 Frieder Grindler

DESIGNER / GESTALTER / MAQUETTISTE:

252–256 Günther Kieser
257 Frieder Grindler

ART DIRECTOR / DIRECTEUR ARTISTIQUE:

252–256 Günther Kieser
257 Frieder Grindler

AGENCY / AGENTUR / AGENCE – STUDIO:

255, 256 Hessischer Rundfunk/
Abt. Publizistik

255

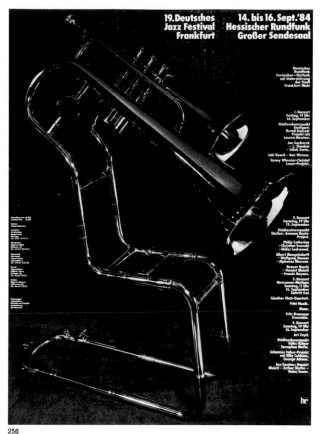

256

257

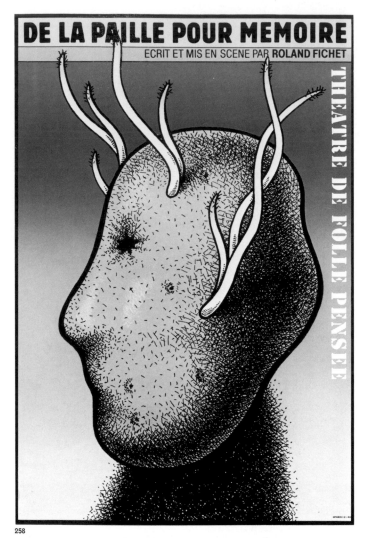

258

260

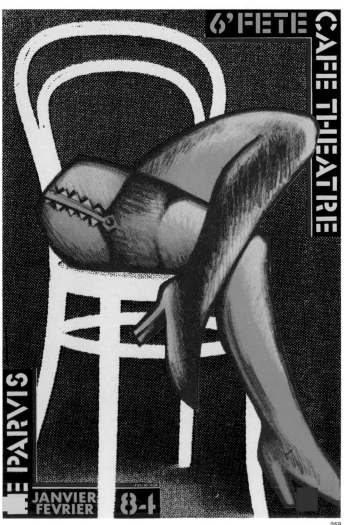

259

263

258 For a play by Roland Fichet at the Theatre of Mad Thoughts. (FRA)
259 Announcement of a festival at the Café-Theatre. (FRA)
260 "The Prison in the Town." Poster for an exhibition and assemblies at the Culture Centre of Amiens. (FRA)
261 Theatre poster for Rostand's *Cyrano de Bergerac* performed by the Royal Shakespeare Company. Gold-coloured and black profile. (GBR)
262 Polychrome poster for a world première by Michael Weller. (USA)
263 Poster for a play by Roland Fichet. Background anthracite-grey and black, "Théâtre" on a yellow stripe. (FRA)
264 Theatre poster with light brown photography in the background, depicting scenes of war and the aftermath. (DEN)
265 For a comic-opera by Kurt Weill and a musical revue. Black-and-white poster with the exception of the pink hand and the pink title stripes. (USA)

261

262

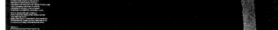

264

265

258 Für ein Theaterstück von Roland Fichet: «Stroh als Erinnerung.» (FRA)
259 Ankündigung eines Festivals des Café-Theaters. (FRA)
260 «Das Gefängnis in der Stadt.» Plakat für eine Ausstellung und Zusammenkünfte im Kulturzentrum von Amiens. (FRA)
261 Theaterplakat für ein Stück von Edmond Rostand, aufgeführt von der Royal Shakespeare Company. Goldfarbenes und schwarzes Profil. (GBR)
262 Mehrfarbiges Plakat für ein Stück von Michael Weller. (USA)
263 Plakat für ein Stück von Roland Fichet. Hintergrund anthrazit und schwarz, «Théâtre» auf gelbem Streifen. (FRA)
264 Theaterplakat mit hellbraunen Photographien im Hintergrund, die Kriegsszenen und Kriegsfolgen zeigen. (DEN)
265 Für eine komische Oper von Kurt Weill und eine Musikrevue. Hand und Titelstreifen in Pink, übriges Plakat in Schwarzweiss. (USA)

258 Affiche pour une pièce de théâtre de Roland Fichet. (FRA)
259 Annonce d'un festival du Café-Théâtre. (FRA)
260 «La Prison dans la ville.» Affiche pour une exposition et des réunions-débats à la Maison de la Culture d'Amiens. (FRA)
261 Affiche de théâtre pour le «Cyrano» d'Edmond Rostand, dans une mise en scène de la Royal Shakespeare Company. Profil or et noir. (GBR)
262 Affiche polychrome pour une pièce de Michael Weller. (USA)
263 Affiche pour une pièce de Roland Fichet. Arrière-plan anthracite et noir, mot «Théâtre» inscrit sur une bande jaune. (FRA)
264 Affiche de théâtre. Les photos brun clair du fond montrent des scènes et séquences de guerre. (DEN)
265 Pour un opéra bouffe de Kurt Weill et une revue musicale. Main et bandes de titre roses sur une affiche au demeurant noir et blanc. (USA)

266

267

Theatre/Theater/Théâtre

268

ARTIST / KÜNSTLER / ARTISTE:

266, 267, 269 Wiktor Sadowski
268 Jenko Radovan

DESIGNER / GESTALTER / MAQUETTISTE:

268 Jenko Radovan

ART DIRECTOR / DIRECTEUR ARTISTIQUE:

268 Jenko Radovan

266, 267, 269 Three theatre posters designed by Wiktor Sadowski for three different performances in the Wielki Theatre in Warsaw. Fig. 266 portrays a greyish-blue bird's head, dark blue tears, pink skin tone, white drape, dark blue background; Fig. 267: blue and white cathedral, blue snake, midnight-blue background, white lettering. (POL)
268 "Exercise in Style". Black-and-white theatre poster with dark grey "speech-bubbles". (YUG)

266, 267, 269 Von Wiktor Sadowski gestaltete Theaterplakate für drei verschiedene Aufführungen im Wielki-Theater in Warschau. Abb. 266: graublauer Vogelkopf, dunkelblaue Träne, beige-rosa Hautton, weisses Tuch, dunkelblauer Hintergrund; Abb. 267: blau-weisser Dom, blaue Schlange, nachtblauer Hintergrund, weisse Schrift. (POL)
268 «Stilübung.» Schwarzweisses Theaterplakat mit schwarzgrauen Sprechblasen. (YUG)

266, 267, 269 Affiches de théâtre créées par Wiktor Sadowski pour trois pièces jouées au Théâtre Wielki de Varsovie. Fig. 266: tête d'oiseau bleu gris, larme bleu foncé, peau rose beige, étoffe blanche, fond bleu foncé; fig. 267: dôme blanc bleu, serpent bleu, fond bleu nuit, texte blanc. (POL)
268 «Exercice de style.» Affiche de théâtre noir et blanc, bulles gris noir. (YUG)

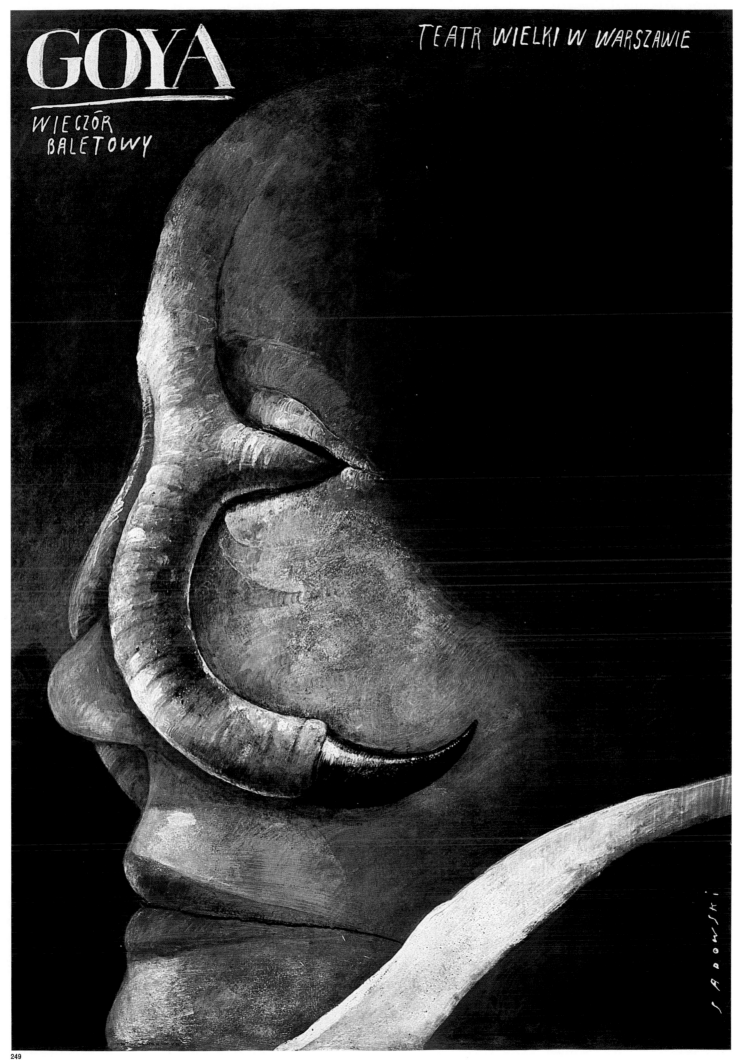

GOYA

WIECZÓR
BALETOWY

TEATR WIELKI W WARSZAWIE

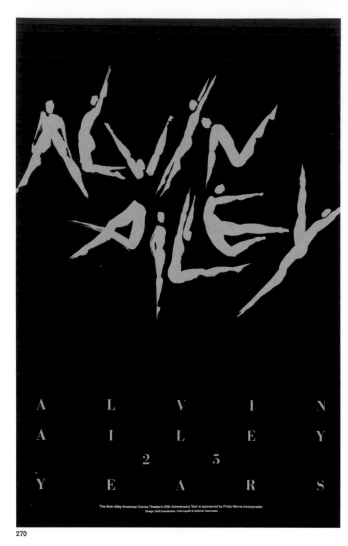

270

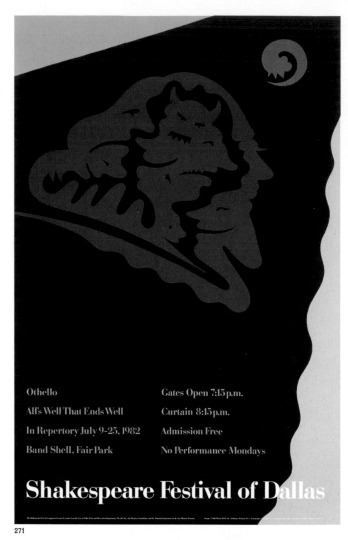

Othello

All's Well That Ends Well

In Repertory July 9-25, 1982

Band Shell, Fair Park

Gates Open 7:15 p.m.

Curtain 8:15 p.m.

Admission Free

No Performance Mondays

Shakespeare Festival of Dallas

271

272

273

ARTIST / KÜNSTLER / ARTISTE:

270 Steff Geissbuhler
271, 275 Woody Pirtle
272–274 Jan Sawka
276 Paul Davis

DESIGNER / GESTALTER / MAQUETTISTE:

270 Steff Geissbuhler
271, 275 Woody Pirtle
272–274 Jan Sawka
276 Paul Davis

ART DIRECTOR / DIRECTEUR ARTISTIQUE:

270 Steff Geissbuhler
271, 275 Woody Pirtle
272–274 Jan Sawka

AGENCY / AGENTUR / AGENCE – STUDIO:

270 Chermayeff & Geismar
271, 275 Pirtle Design

270 Poster for the 25th anniversary of the Alvin Ailey American Dance Theater. Dancing figures in lilac, lettering in green and white on black. (USA)
271, 275 Posters for the annual Shakespeare Festival in Dallas. The bard's features are shown in profile in Fig. 271 and outlined in stars in Fig. 275. (USA)
272–274 Three posters for performances of plays by Samuel Beckett. All the posters are in black and white with one additional colour. Fig. 273: Skin-toned hands and faces; Fig. 274: deep yellow rocking-chair. Poster format: 35.5×56 cm. (USA)
276 Poster in muted colours for the announcement of two performances held during the Shakespeare Festival in New York. (USA)

270 Zum 25jährigen Bestehen des Alvin Ailey American Dance Theater konzipiertes Plakat. Tanzende Figuren in Lila, Schrift in Grün und Weiss auf Schwarz. (USA)
271, 275 Plakate für das jährliche Shakespeare-Festival in Dallas. Die Gesichtszüge des Dichters sind im Profil (271) und als Sternbild (275) angedeutet. (USA)
272–274 Drei Plakate für Aufführungen von Samuel-Beckett-Theaterstücken. Alle Plakate sind in Schwarzweiss mit einer zusätzlichen Farbe. Abb. 273: hautfarbene Hände und Gesichter; Abb. 274: dunkelgelber Schaukelstuhl. Plakatformat: 35,5× 56 cm. (USA)
276 Plakat in matten Farben für die Ankündigung von zwei Aufführungen anlässlich des Shakespeare-Festivals in New York. (USA)

270 Affiche réalisée pour le 25e anniversaire de l'Alvin Ailey American Dance Theater. Danseurs lilas, texte vert et blanc sur fond noir. (USA)
271, 275 Affiches pour le Festival Shakespeare annuel de Dallas. Le visage de l'auteur apparaît en profil (fig. 271) et sous forme d'une constellation (fig. 275). (USA)
272–274 Trois affiches pour des pièces de Samuel Beckett. Elles sont toutes en noir et blanc, avec une couleur supplémentaire. Fig. 273: mains couleur chair, visages de même; fig. 274: rocking-chair jaune foncé. Format des affiches: 35,5×56 cm. (USA)
276 Affiche aux teintes mates annonçant deux représentations dans le cadre du Festival Shakespeare de New York. (USA)

275

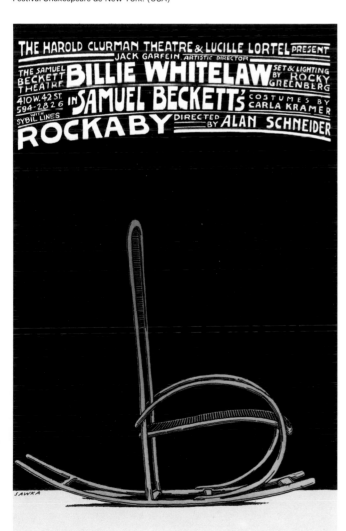

274

276

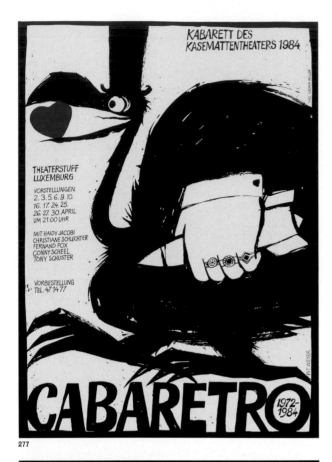

277

278

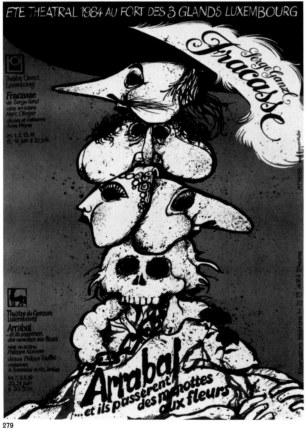

279

280

Theatre/Theater/Théâtre

ARTIST / KÜNSTLER / ARTISTE:

277, 279, 280 Pit Weyer
278 Manfred Hürrig/M. Parascan
281 Volker Pfüller

ART DIRECTOR / DIRECTEUR ARTISTIQUE:

278 Manfred Hürrig

277 For a cabaret programme in the Kasematten Theatre, Luxemburg. (LUX)
278 "Story of a Horse", a performance at the National Theatre of Belgium, based on a work by Leo Tolstoy. Yellow background. (BEL)
279 Theatre poster for two plays, *Fracasse* and *Arrabal*, performed in the Théâtre Ouvert and in the Théâtre du Centaure. Black, white and red on pale violet. (LUX)
280 Black-and-white poster for the performance of two one-act plays: Absurd Theatre by Eugene Ionesco and Samuel Beckett. (LUX)
281 Film poster by the GDR artist Volker Pfüller for *The Patrioteer*, after the novel by Heinrich Mann. The poster is in black and white with the exception of the brown underlined title. (GDR)

277 Für ein Kabarett-Programm im Kasematten-Theater Luxemburg. (LUX)
278 «Geschichte eines Pferdes.» Plakat mit gelbem Hintergrund für ein im Théâtre National de Belgique aufgeführtes Stück. (BEL)
279 Theaterplakat für zwei Stücke, *Fracasse* und *Arrabal*, aufgeführt im Théâtre Ouvert und im Théâtre du Centaure. Schwarz, weiss und rot auf hellviolettem Hintergrund. (LUX)
280 Schwarzweisses Plakat für die Aufführung zweier Einakter: Absurdes Theater von Eugene Ionesco und Samuel Beckett. (LUX)
281 Filmplakat des DDR-Künstlers Volker Pfüller. Ausser dem braun unterstrichenen Titel ist das Plakat schwarzweiss. (GDR)

277 Pour un programme de cabaret au Théâtre des Casemates de Luxembourg. (LUX)
278 Affiche sur fond jaune pour une pièce jouée au Théâtre National de Belgique. (BEL)
279 Affiche de théâtre pour deux pièces, *Fracasse* et *Arrabal*, montée au Théâtre Ouvert et au Théâtre du Centaure. Noir, blanc, rouge sur violet clair. (LUX)
280 Affiche noir et blanc pour la représentation de deux pièces en un acte d'Eugène Ionesco et de Samuel Beckett. (LUX)
281 Affiche de cinéma de l'artiste est-allemand Volker Pfüller. Il s'agit du *Sujet de l'Empereur*, d'après le roman de Heinrich Mann. A part le titre souligné en brun, l'affiche est en noir et blanc. (GDR)

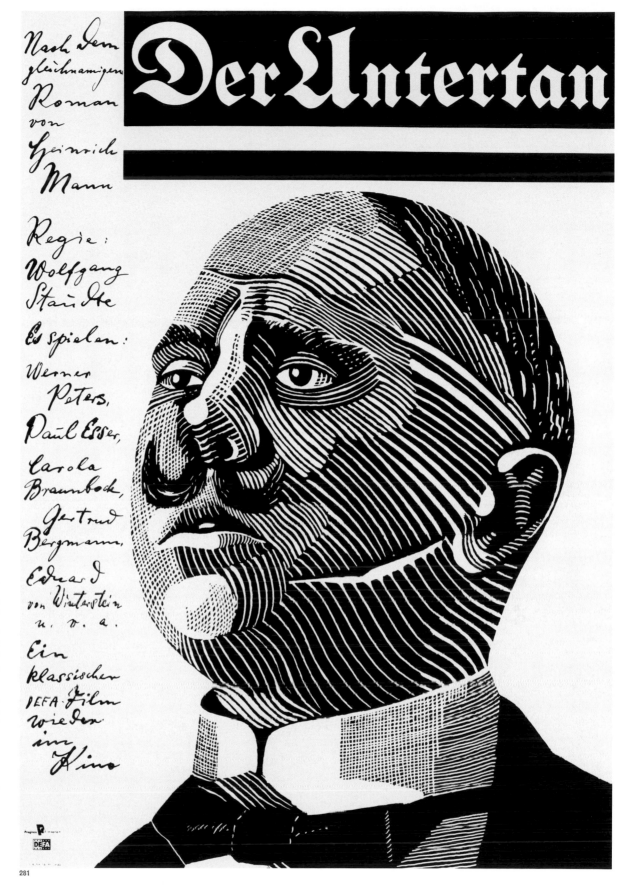

281

119

282

ARTIST / KÜNSTLER / ARTISTE:

282–284 Stephan Bundi
285, 286 Heinz Jost

DESIGNER / GESTALTER / MAQUETTISTE:

282–284 Stephan Bundi
285, 286 Heinz Jost

ART DIRECTOR / DIRECTEUR ARTISTIQUE:

285, 286 Heinz Jost

AGENCY / AGENTUR / AGENCE – STUDIO:

282–284 Atelier Bundi

282 Poster for an open-air performance of *Till Eulenspiegel.* Screen print in brown and yellow. (SWI)
283 "Project without Title", written and performed by two actresses, describing their lives as women—the day-dreams and the reality. Screen-print poster. (SWI)
284 "Do something impossible" is the heading on this poster by Stephan Bundi. The anamorphoses require the viewer to find the correct angle from which to view in order for the face to appear normal. One observation point where both faces appear undistorted does not exist. The designer calls this kind of posters "Poster Theatre". (SWI)
285 Ballet comes to three theatres in Berne—literally "on the winged feet" of this dancer. (SWI)
286 Screen-print poster for the first performance of a fairy-tale containing circus slots, and which should encourage children to attempt the unusual—thereby the inversion of the title Kolumbus to "Submulok". (SWI)

282 Plakat für eine Freilichtaufführung der *Ballade vom Eulenspiegel.* Siebdruck in Braun und Gelb. (SWI)
283 In der hier angekündigten Veranstaltung schildern zwei Schauspielerinnen ihr Leben als Frau, die Vorstellung und die Realität. Siebdruck. (SWI)
284 «Plakattheater» nennt Stephan Bundi sein Plakat mit zwei nach einem geometrischen System verzerrten Gesichtern. Der Betrachter muss den Standort finden, der ihm einen unverzerrten Kopf zeigt; einen für beide Köpfe richtigen Blickwinkel gibt es nicht. (SWI)
285 Das Ballett kommt nach Bern – buchstäblich mit beflügelten Schritten. (SWI)
286 Siebdruckplakat für die Uraufführung eines Kindermärchens, das Zirkuseinlagen enthält und Mut zum Ungewöhnlichen machen soll. Daher auch die Umkehrung des Namens Kolumbus, der zu «Submulok» wird. (SWI)

282 Pour une représentation en plein air de la *Ballade de Till l'Espiègle.* Sérigraphie en tons brun et jaune. (SWI)
283 Dans la représentation annoncée ici, «Projet sans titre», deux actrices relatent leur vie de femme sur les plans fantasmatique et réel. Sérigraphie. (SWI)
284 «Théâtre affichiste», voilà le titre que Stephan Bundi donne à cette affiche où deux visages se trouvent distordus géométriquement. C'est à l'observateur de trouver l'angle sous lequel la distorsion est annulée pour l'un des visages (pas pour les deux). (SWI)
285 Le ballet vient à Berne – sur des jambes ailées. (SWI)
286 Affiche sérigraphique pour la première d'un conte pour enfants avec des jeux de cirque scéniques. Le nom de Kolumbus (Christophe Colomb) inversé en Submulok documente un désir d'insolite, d'aventure. (SWI)

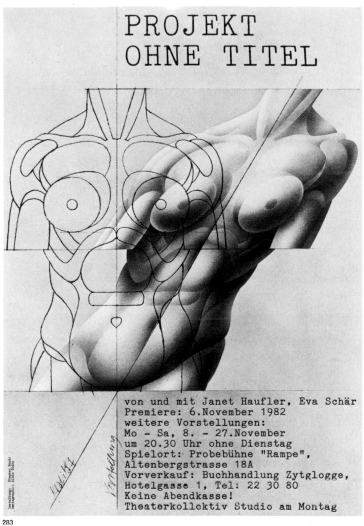

PROJEKT
OHNE TITEL

von und mit Janet Haufler, Eva Schär
Premiere: 6.November 1982
weitere Vorstellungen:
Mo - Sa, 8. - 27.November
um 20.30 Uhr ohne Dienstag
Spielort: Probebühne "Rampe",
Altenbergstrasse 18A
Vorverkauf: Buchhandlung Zytglogge,
Hotelgasse 1, Tel: 22 30 80
Keine Abendkasse!
Theaterkollektiv Studio am Montag

283

Tue etwas Unmögliches

284

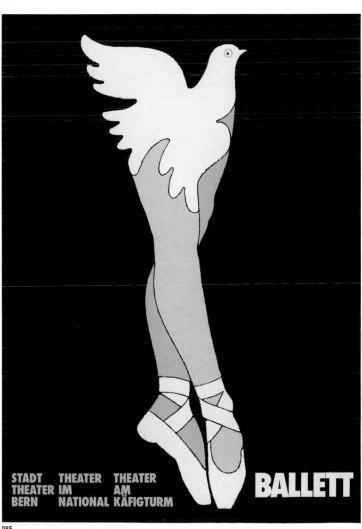

STADT   THEATER   THEATER
THEATER IM   AM
BERN   NATIONAL KÄFIGTURM   **BALLETT**

285

286

287

ARTIST / KÜNSTLER / ARTISTE:

287, 288 Jacques Richez
289 Michael Mathias Prechtl
290 Rolf-Felix Müller
291 Andrzej Pagowski
292 Holger Matthies

DESIGNER / GESTALTER / MAQUETTISTE:

287, 288 Jacques Richez
289 Michael Mathias Prechtl
292 Holger Matthies

ART DIRECTOR / DIRECTEUR ARTISTIQUE:

287, 288 Jacques Richez
292 Holger Matthies

288

Theatre/Theater/Théâtre

287, 288 Illustration and complete poster for a performance by the Théâtre de Villeneuve-d'Ascq in France. (FRA)
289 Polychrome poster for the Munich People's Theatre. From back left: Molière, Anzengruber, M. L. Fleisser, Goldoni, Aristophanes (as a bust), Shakespeare, L. Thoma, Nestroy. Front: Lisl Karlstadt and Karl Valentin; as children Ö. v. Horvath and Therese Giehse. (GER)
290 Poster for a puppet-show. Colourful figures and yellow rectangle on white ground. (GDR)
291 For the performance of a play entitled "Dog Heart". In brown tones. (POL)
292 For Ibsen's *Lady from the Sea*. Woodcut in black and white. (GER)

287, 288 Illustration und vollständiges Plakat für eine Aufführung des Théâtre de Villeneuve-d'Ascq, Frankreich. (FRA)
289 Mehrfarbiges Plakat für das Münchner Volkstheater, mit Gruppenbild seiner «Hausdichter». Von oben links: Molière, Anzengruber, M. L. Fleisser, Goldoni, Aristophanes (als Büste), Shakespeare, Ludwig Thoma, Nestroy, unten Lisl Karlstadt und Karl Valentin; als Kinder Ödön v. Horvath und Therese Giehse. (GER)
290 Plakat für eine Puppenbühne. Mehrfarbige Figuren und gelbes Feld auf Weiss. (GDR)
291 Für die Aufführung eines Stückes mit dem Titel «Hundeherz». In Brauntönen. (POL)
292 Für eine Aufführung von Ibsens *Die Frau vom Meer*. Xylographie in Schwarzweiss. (GER)

287, 288 Illustration et affiche complète pour le Théâtre de Villeneuve-d'Ascq. (FRA)
289 Affiche polychrome pour le Théâtre populaire de Munich. De gauche à droite: Molière, Anzengruber, M. L. Fleisser, Goldoni, Aristophane (sous forme d'un buste), Shakespeare, L. Thoma, Nestroy; en bas: Lisl Karlstadt, Karl Valentin; Ö. v. Horvath et Therese Giehse apparaissent sous les traits de deux enfants. (GER)
290 Affiche pour un théâtre de marionnettes. Polychromie, champ jaune sur blanc. (GDR)
291 Pour la représentation de la pièce «Cœur de chien». Divers bruns. (POL)
292 Pour une représentation de *La Femme de la mer* d'Ibsen. Xylographie, noir-blanc. (GER)

290

289

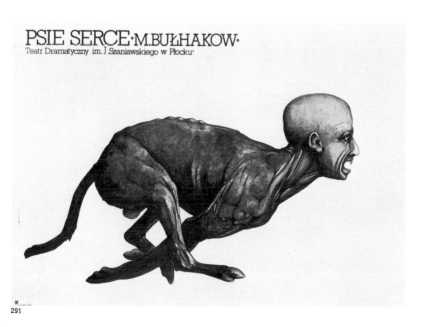

PSIE SERCE · M.BUŁHAKOW ·
Teatr Dramatyczny im. J.Szaniawskiego w Płocku

DIE FRAU VOM MEER

293

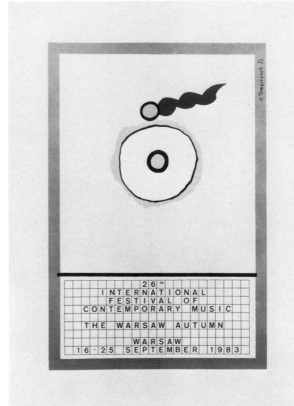

294

295

296

ARTIST / KÜNSTLER / ARTISTE:

293 Andrzej Pagowski
294 Henryk Tomaszewski
295 Pet Halmen
296 Axel Weigand
297 Boris Bućan

DESIGNER / GESTALTER:

295 Pet Halmen
296 Axel Weigand
297 Boris Bućan

ART DIRECTOR / DIRECTEUR ARTISTIQUE:

295 Pet Halmen
296 Sabine Tschierschky / Erich vom Endt
297 Boris Bućan

297

293 Announcement of a festival for jazz pianists in Poland. Dinner jacket and keyboard in black and white, face and background in various colours. (POL)
294 "The Warsaw Autumn." Polychrome illustration with lettering in red and green, gold-coloured frame, on white stock. (POL)
295 Poster in blue and green tones for Verdi's *Aida* which opened the opera season of the Lyric Opera of Chicago. (USA)
296 Announcing the opera *Cardillac* by Paul Hindemith. In green shades with gold, lettering in magenta and violet. (GER)
297 Poster for Stravinsky's ballets *Petrouchka* and *The Firebird*. Black-and-white bird with red beak and red shoes, background pale green. (YUG)

293 Ankündigung eines Festivals für Jazz-Pianisten in Polen. «Kleidung» schwarzweiss, Gesicht und Hintergrund mehrfarbig. (POL)
294 «Der Warschauer Herbst.» Plakat für ein internationales Festival zeitgenössischer Musik. Mehrfarbige Illustration, Schrift rot und grün, Umrandung goldfarben auf Weiss. (POL)
295 Plakat in Blau- und Grüntönen für eine Aufführung von Verdis *Aida* zur Eröffnung der Opern-Saison 1983 in Chicago. (USA)
296 Für eine Aufführung von P. Hindemiths Oper *Cardillac*. Vorwiegend Grüntöne mit Gold, Schrift Magenta und Violett. (GER)
297 Plakat für Ballettaufführungen von Strawinskys *Petruschka* und *Der Feuervogel*. Vogel schwarzweiss mit rotem Schnabel und roten Schuhen, Hintergrund grünweiss. (YUG)

293 Annonce d'un festival du piano de jazz en Pologne. «Habit» noir et blanc, visage et arrière-plan polychromes. (POL)
294 «L'automne de Varsovie.» Affiche pour un festival international de musique contemporaine. Illustration polychrome, texte rouge, vert, encadrement or sur blanc. (POL)
295 Affiche en divers bleus et verts pour une représentation d'*Aida* de Verdi ouvrant la saison d'opéra 1983 à Chicago. (USA)
296 Annonce d'une représentation de l'opéra *Cardillac* de Paul Hindemith. Verts prédominants, or, texte magenta et violet. (GER)
297 Affiche pour des représentations des ballets *Petrouchka* et *l'Oiseau de feu* de Stravinski. Oiseau noir-blanc, bec rouge, chaussures rouges, fond blanc vert. (YUG)

298

299

ARTIST / KÜNSTLER / ARTISTE:

298–300 Holger Matthies
301 Frieder Grindler
302 Dave Brüllmann
303 Evelyn Schwark
304 Roger Pfund
305 Daniel de Quervain

DESIGNER / GESTALTER / MAQUETTISTE:

298–300 Holger Matthies
301 Frieder Grindler
302 K. Domenic Geissbühler
303 Evelyn Schwark
304 Roger Pfund
305 Heinz Jost

ART DIRECTOR / DIRECTEUR ARTISTIQUE:

298–300 Holger Matthies
301 Frieder Grindler
302 K. Domenic Geissbühler
303 Evelyn Schwark
304 Roger Pfund
305 Heinz Jost

AGENCY / AGENTUR / AGENCE – STUDIO:

302 K. Domenic Geissbühler
304 Roger Pfund

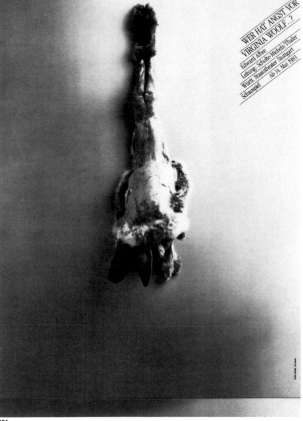

301

302

298, 299 For the 1983/84 and 84/85 seasons of a Lüneburg theatre. (GER)
300 Poster to announce Delibes' *Coppelia* during the Bergedorf Ballet Days held in Hamburg. (GER)
301 For a performance of Edward Albee's play *Who's Afraid of Virginia Woolf?* at the Municipal Theatre Stuttgart. Photograph in black and white. (GER)
302 Poster for Arthur Honegger's opera based on Paul Claudel's text , *Joan of Arc at the Stake*, performed at the Kongresshaus, Zurich. (SWI)
303 *Gimme Shelter* by Barrie Keefe. Poster for a performance of this play at the Schauspielhaus Kassel. (GER)
304 For Jules Romains' medical satire *Dr. Knock or the Triumph of Medicine* produced at the Migros Cultural Centre in Geneva. (SWI)
305 Poster with black-and-white photograph for a theatre in Berne. (SWI)

298, 299 Allegorien zu den Programmen des Treffpunkts Neues Theater im Stadttheater Lüneburg für die Spielzeiten 1983/84 und 84/85. (GER)
300 Plakat für die Ankündigung einer Ballett-Aufführung anlässlich der Bergedorfer Ballett-Tage. (GER)
301 Aphorismus zu Edward Albees *Wer hat Angst vor Virginia Woolf?*, aufgeführt vom Württ. Staatstheater Stuttgart. Schwarzweissaufnahme. (GER)
302 Plakat für eine Inszenierung des Zürcher Opernhauses. (SWI)
303 «Gib mir Obdach.» Plakat für die Aufführung eines Stückes von Barrie Keefe am Schauspielhaus Kassel. (GER)
304 Für eine Inszenierung von Jules Romains' Ärztesatire *Dr. Knock oder der Triumph der Medizin*. (SWI)
305 Plakat mit Schwarzweissaufnahme für das Stadttheater Bern. (SWI)

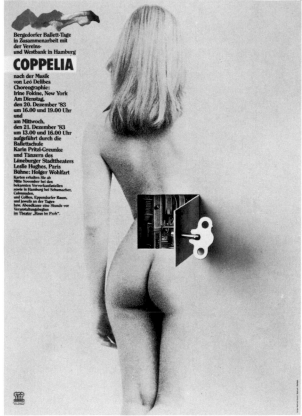

298, 299 Composition allégorique pour les programmes du Treffpunkt Neues Theater au Théâtre municipal de Lüneburg, saisons 1983/84 et 84/85. (GER)
300 Affiche annonçant une représentation de ballet dans le cadre des Journées de ballet de Bergedorf. (GER)
301 Composition en forme d'aphorisme pour le *Qui a peur de Virginia Woolf?* d'Edward Albee au Staatstheater de Stuttgart. Photo noir et blanc. (GER)
302 Affiche pour une représentation à l'Opéra de Zurich. (SWI)
303 «Prends-moi chez toi». Affiche pour la représentation de cette pièce de Barrie Keefe au Schauspielhaus de Kassel. (GER)
304 Pour une représentation de la satire bien connue de Jules Romains sur les médecins, *Dr Knock ou le triomphe de la médecine.* (SWI)
305 Affiche-photo noir et blanc pour le Théâtre municipal de Berne. (SWI)

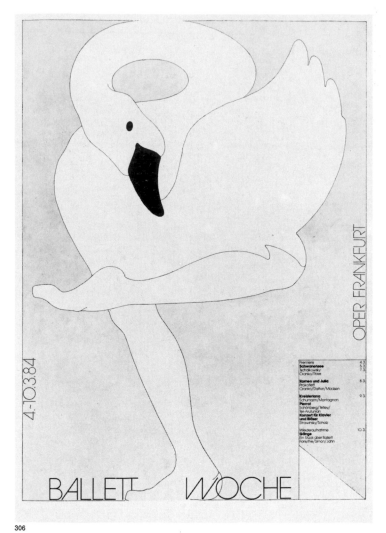

306

307

308

309

ARTIST/KÜNSTLER/ARTISTE:

306 Günther Kieser
307 Yarom Vardimon
308 Reinhold Luger
309 Alan E. Cober
310 PW, Inc.
311 Gary Overacre

DESIGNER/GESTALTER:

306 Günther Kieser
307 Yarom Vardimon
308 Reinhold Luger
310 Julius Friedman
311 David Bartels

ART DIRECTOR:

306 Günther Kieser
307 Yarom Vardimon
309 Dave Foote
310 Julius Friedman
311 David Bartels

AGENCY/AGENTUR/AGENCE:

310 Images
311 Bartels & Company

310

311

306 Announcing a ballet week held by the Frankfurt Opera Company, with Tchaikovsky's *Swan Lake* as opening performance. In soft shades, with the exception of the beak. (GER)
307 Poster for the 10th anniversary of the Israel Sinfonietta. The large sun as focal point relates to the orchestra's domicile in the desert town of Beer-Sheva. (ISR)
308 For a performance of Puccini's *Tosca* during the Bregenz music festival. (AUT)
309 Poster with polychrome illustration to mark the centenary of the New York Metropolitan Opera, for which occasion also a special-issue postage stamp was produced. (USA)
310 Promotion for the Louisville Orchestra, Kentucky, designed by Julius Friedman. (USA)
311 Small-size poster to announce a competition for high-school pupils to recognize the various bird-calls. Predominantly in green tones. (USA)

306 Für die Ankündigung einer Ballett-Woche der Oper Frankfurt, die mit Tschaikowskis *Schwanensee* eröffnet wird. In zarten Farben, mit Ausnahme des Schnabels. (GER)
307 Plakat zum zehnjährigen Bestehen der Israel Sinfonietta. Die Sonne im Mittelpunkt der Illustration ist ein Hinweis auf den Sitz des Orchesters in der Wüstenstadt Beer Sheva. (ISR)
308 Für eine Aufführung von Puccinis Oper *Tosca* während der Bregenzer Festspiele. (AUT)
309 Plakat mit mehrfarbiger Illustration zum hundertjährigen Bestehen der New Yorker Metropolitan Opera, anlässlich dessen auch eine Sonderbriefmarke herausgegeben wurde. (USA)
310 Als Werbung für das Orchester der Stadt Louisville veröffentlichtes Plakat. (USA)
311 Hier wird ein Studentenwettbewerb angekündigt, bei dem es um das Bestimmen von Vogelarten geht. Vorwiegend in Grüntönen gehaltenes, kleinformatiges Plakat. (USA)

306 Annonce d'une semaine du ballet à l'Opéra de Francfort, avec le *Lac des Cygnes* de Tchaïkovski en guise d'ouverture. Teintes délicates, à l'exception du bec. (GER)
307 Affiche pour le 10e anniversaire de l'Israël Sinfonietta. Le soleil surdimensionné rappelle que cet orchestre a son siège dans la ville de Beersheba en bordure du désert. (ISR)
308 Pour une représentation de l'opéra *Tosca* de Puccini au Festival de Bregenz. (AUT)
309 Affiche illustrée en polychromie pour le centenaire du Metropolitan Opera de New York, commémoré entre autres par l'émission d'un timbre spécial. (USA)
310 Affiche publiée pour asseoir l'image de l'orchestre de Louisville (Kentucky). (USA)
311 Annonce d'un concours estudiantin d'ornithologie – savoir reconnaître les diverses espèces. Affichette où prédominent les verts. (USA)

312

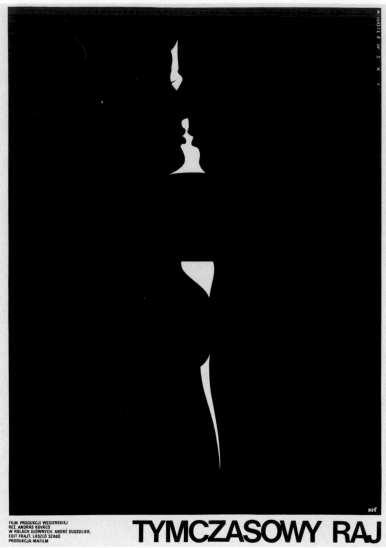

FILM PRODUKCJI WĘGIERSKIEJ
REŻ. ANDRÁS KOVÁCS
W ROLACH GŁÓWNYCH: ANDRÉ DUSSOLIER,
EDIT FRAJT, LÁSZLÓ SZABÓ
PRODUKCJA: MAFILM

TYMCZASOWY RAJ

313

315

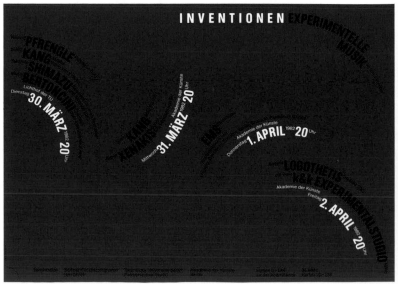

316

314

ARTIST / KÜNSTLER / ARTISTE:

312, 315 Boris Sokolow
313 Mieczyslaw Wasilewski
314 Erhard Grüttner
317 Fernando Medina
318 Čedomir Kostović

DESIGNER / GESTALTER / MAQUETTISTE:

312, 315 Boris Sokolow
313 Mieczyslaw Wasilewski
316 Nicolaus Ott/Bernard Stein

ART DIRECTOR / DIRECTEUR ARTISTIQUE:

317 Fernando Medina
318 Čedomir Kostović

AGENCY / AGENTUR / AGENCE – STUDIO:

316 Internationales Design Zentrum, Berlin
317 Fernando Medina Design

312, 315 Posters to announce variety shows in Leningrad—"Troika" and "Sailors' Variety". (USR)
313 Black-and-white poster for a film entitled "The Temporary Paradise". (POL)
314 Polychrome screen-print poster for "The Last Days" at a theatre in East Berlin. (GDR)
316 Announcement of a programme with experimental music performed at universities in Berlin. (GER)
317 Tintin and Milou with a computer code, as homage to their creator Hergé. (SPA)
318 Poster in soft red and yellow shades for a production of Aristophanes' *The Birds*. (YUG)

312, 315 Plakate für die Ankündigung von Varieté-Theatern – «Troika» und «Matrosen-Varieté». (USR)
313 Schwarzweiss-Plakat für einen Film mit dem Titel «Das provisorische Paradies». (POL)
314 Mehrfarbiges Siebdruckplakat für eine Aufführung des Theaters im Palast, Ostberlin. (GDR)
316 Bekanntgabe eines Programms mit experimenteller Musik an Berliner Hochschulen. (GER)
317 Tintin und Milou mit Computer-Code, als Hommage an ihren Schöpfer Hergé. (SPA)
318 Plakat in zarten Rot- und Gelbtönen für eine Aufführung von Aristophanes' *Die Vögel*. (YUG)

312, 315 Affiche pour les spectacles de variétés «Troïka» et «Variétés pour matelots». (USR)
313 Annonce noir et blanc pour un film intitulé «Paradis provisoire». (POL)
314 Affiche sérigraphique polychrome pour une représentation du Théâtre du Palais, Berlin-Est. (GDR)
316 Annonce d'un programme de musique expérimentale dans les universités de Berlin. (GER)
317 Tintin et Milou et un code d'ordinateur, en hommage à leur créateur Hergé. (SPA)
318 Affiche aux teintes rouges et jaunes délicates, pour *Les Oiseaux* d'Aristophane. (YUG)

317

318

319

321

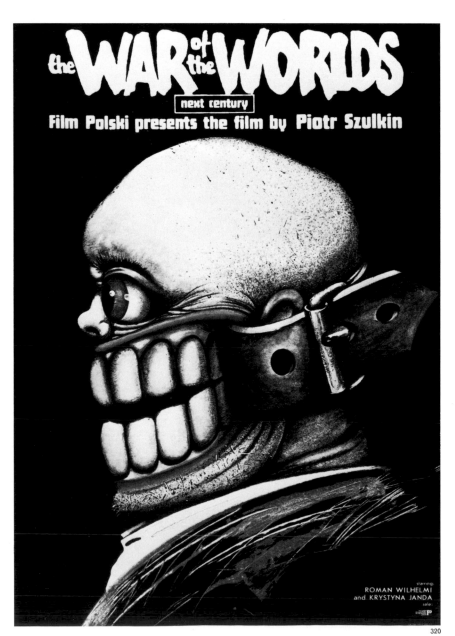

320

324

319 Poster in black and white to promote a Yugoslavian film. (POL)
320 Poster with multi-coloured illustration on a black ground for the film *The War of the Worlds*. (POL)
321 Announcement of an American film entitled *The Black Stallion*. Pale blue on black background, lettering white and black. (HUN)
322 Poster in sepia for the film *The German Sisters* by M. von Trotta. (HUN)
323 Announcement of the film *The War of the Worlds* (s. also Fig. 320). Red skirt on dark brown background, red border. (POL)
324 For an exhibition of posters by the Polish designer M. Gorowski. (POL)
325 Black-and-white poster for a film from the GDR. (POL)
326 For a film entitled "Autumn Holiday". In black and white. (POL)

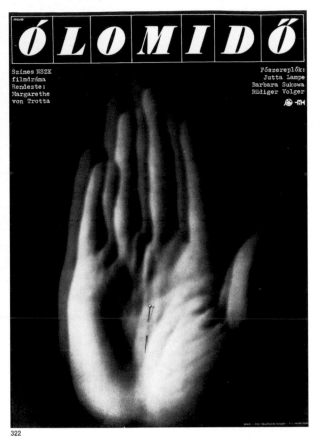

322

323

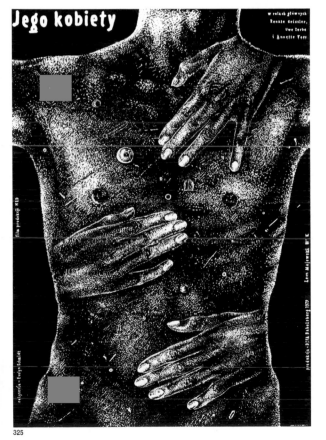

325

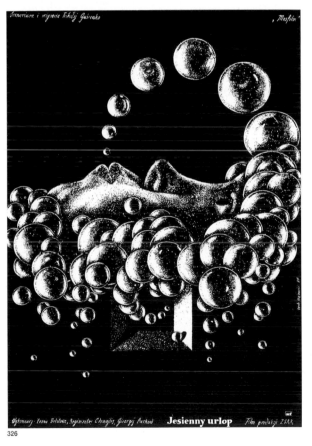

326

ARTIST / KÜNSTLER / ARTISTE:

319 Andrzej Piwoński
320 Andrzej Pagowski
321 Katalin Rónyi
322 Istvań Farago
323 Andrzej Pagowski/
Krystyna Hoffmann
324 Mieczyslaw Gorowski
325, 326 Lech Majewski

ART DIRECTOR / DIRECTEUR ARTISTIQUE:

323 Magda Glogowska

AGENCY / AGENTUR / AGENCE – STUDIO:

321 Magyar Hirdető

319 Plakat in Schwarzweiss für einen jugoslawischen Film. (POL)
320 Plakat mit mehrfarbiger Illustration auf schwarzem Grund für den Film *Kampf der Welten*. (POL)
321 Ankündigung eines amerikanischen Films mit dem Titel *Der schwarze Hengst*. Hellblau auf schwarzem Grund, Schrift weiss und schwarz. (HUN)
322 Plakat in Sepia für den Film *Die bleierne Zeit* von M. von Trotta. (HUN)
323 Ankündigung eines Films mit dem Titel *Kampf der Welten* (s. auch Abb. 320). Rotes Kleid auf schwarzbraunem Grund, roter Rand. (POL)
324 Für eine Ausstellung von Plakaten des Polen M. Gorowski. (POL)
325 Schwarzweiss-Plakat für die Ankündigung eines Films aus der DDR. (POL)
326 Für einen Film mit dem Titel «Herbsturlaub». In Schwarzweiss. (POL)

319 Affiche noir et blanc pour un film yougoslave. (POL)
320 Affiche illustrée en polychromie sur fond noir pour le film *La Guerre des mondes*. (POL)
321 Annonce d'un film américain intitulé *Le Talon noir*. Bleu clair sur fond noir, texte blanc et noir. (HUN)
322 Affiche sépia pour le film *Les Années de plomb* de M. von Trotta. (HUN)
323 Annonce de la projection de *La Guerre des mondes* (voir aussi la fig. 320). Robe rouge sur fond brun noirâtre, bord rouge. (POL)
324 Pour une exposition de l'œuvre affichiste du Polonais M. Gorowski. (POL)
325 Affiche noir et blanc pour la projection d'un film de RDA. (POL)
326 Pour un film intitulé «Vacances d'automne». Noir et blanc. (POL)

327

328

ARTIST / KÜNSTLER / ARTISTE:

327 Wieslaw Walkuski
328 Mieczyslaw Wasilewski
329 Stane Jagodič
330, 331 Klára Tamás Blaier
332 Valentino Bintchev

ART DIRECTOR / DIRECTEUR ARTISTIQUE:

332 Ivan Andonov

330

331

327 Poster for the announcement of a film by Ingmar Bergman entitled "From the Life of the Marionettes". Illustration in brown tones on pale bordeaux-red, white lettering. (POL)
328 For the performance of a Hungarian film in Poland. In black and white. (POL)
329 Poster with colour photograph for the announcement of a film festival. (YUG)
330 Poster in brown and white for a Rumanian film production. (RUM)
331 Announcement of a film entitled "Impossible Love". In shades of brown. (RUM)
332 A small-size poster which is printed on both sides for the announcement of a Bulgarian film entitled "White Magic". (BUL)

327 Plakat für die Ankündigung eines Films von Ingmar Bergman mit dem Titel *Aus dem Leben der Marionetten*. Illustration in Brauntönen auf hellem Bordeauxrot, Schrift weiss. (POL)
328 Für die Aufführung eines ungarischen Films in Polen. In Schwarzweiss. (POL)
329 Plakat mit Farbaufnahme für die Ankündigung eines Film-Festivals. (YUG)
330 Plakat in Braunweiss für eine rumänische Filmproduktion. (RUM)
331 Ankündigung eines Films mit dem Titel «Die unmögliche Liebe». In Brauntönen. (RUM)
332 Beidseitig bedrucktes, kleinformatiges Plakat für die Ankündigung eines bulgarischen Films mit dem Titel «Weisse Magie». (BUL)

327 Affiche annonçant la projection du film d'Ingmar Bergman: *De la vie des marionnettes*. Illustration en divers bruns sur bordeaux clair, texte blanc. (POL)
328 Pour la projection d'un film hongrois en Pologne. Noir et blanc. (POL)
329 Affiche avec photo couleur pour un festival du cinéma. (YUG)
330 Affiche blanc brunâtre pour le film roumain «Mourir blessé d'amour de vivre». (RUM)
331 Annonce d'un film intitulé «Amour impossible». Divers bruns. (RUM)
332 Affichette de cinéma imprimée des deux côtés servant à la promotion d'une production bulgare intitulée «Magie blanche». (BUL)

329

Films/Filme

332

135

ARTIST / KÜNSTLER / ARTISTE:

333 Masaaki Hiromura
334 Takenobu Igarashi
335 Jim Jacobs
336 Niklaus Troxler
338 Mieczyslaw Wasilewski
339 Paul Davis

DESIGNER / GESTALTER / MAQUETTISTE:

335 Orlando Castro
336 Niklaus Troxler
337 Klaus Mohr
338 Mieczyslaw Wasilewski
339 Paul Davis

ART DIRECTOR / DIRECTEUR ARTISTIQUE:

333 Ikko Tanaka
334 Takenobu Igarashi
335 Orlando Castro
336 Niklaus Troxler

AGENCY / AGENTUR / AGENCE – STUDIO:

334 Takenobu Igarashi Design
335 Jim Jacobs' Studio Inc.
336 Niklaus Troxler Grafik Studio

333

334

336

337

333 For a series of concerts held in the Seibu Theatre of *Parco* stores. (JPN)
334 Announcement of the 16th Summer Jazz Festival in Japan. White letters bordered in blue, red and green, on turquoise. (JPN)
335 Polychrome poster for free performances given by the Dallas orchestra, opera-, theatre- and ballet companies, held in Dallas parks. (USA)
336 Announcement of a concert held during the Willisau Jazz Festival in summer. Blue, green and black on white background. (SWI)
337 For a concert organized by the German broadcasting station WDR in cooperation with a Russian agency. Yellow and white on red ground. (GER)
338 Poster for the tenth anniversary of a culture centre. In black and white, with a wine-red title ground. (POL)
339 Poster for the announcement of a circus performance. (USA)

333 Für eine Konzertreihe im Seibu-Theater der Kaufhauskette *Parco*. (JPN)
334 Ankündigung eines regelmässig stattfindenden Sommer-Jazz-Festivals. Blau-rot-grün umrandete weisse Buchstaben auf türkisfarbenem Grund. (JPN)
335 Mehrfarbiges Plakat für kostenlose Veranstaltungen von Konzerten, Theater-, Ballett- und Opernaufführungen in den Parks von Dallas. (USA)
336 Bekanntgabe eines Konzerts innerhalb des Willisauer Jazz-Festivals. Blau, Grün und Schwarz auf weissem Grund. (SWI)
337 Für ein Konzert, das vom WDR in Zusammenarbeit mit einer russischen Agentur organisiert wurde. Gelb und Weiss auf rotem Grund. (GER)
338 Zum zehnjährigen Bestehen eines Kulturzentrums veröffentlichtes Plakat in Schwarzweiss, mit weinrotem Feld. (POL)
339 Plakat für die Ankündigung von Zirkusvorstellungen. (USA)

335

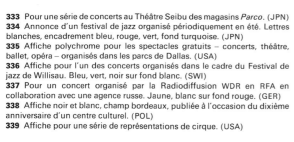

338

333 Pour une série de concerts au Théâtre Seibu des magasins *Parco*. (JPN)
334 Annonce d'un festival de jazz organisé périodiquement en été. Lettres blanches, encadrement bleu, rouge, vert, fond turquoise. (JPN)
335 Affiche polychrome pour les spectacles gratuits – concerts, théâtre, ballet, opéra – organisés dans les parcs de Dallas. (USA)
336 Affiche pour l'un des concerts organisés dans le cadre du Festival de jazz de Willisau. Bleu, vert, noir sur fond blanc. (SWI)
337 Pour un concert organisé par la Radiodiffusion WDR en RFA en collaboration avec une agence russe. Jaune, blanc sur fond rouge. (GER)
338 Affiche noir et blanc, champ bordeaux, publiée à l'occasion du dixième anniversaire d'un centre culturel. (POL)
339 Affiche pour une série de représentations de cirque. (USA)

339

Films/Filme

ARTIST / KÜNSTLER / ARTISTE:
340–346 Paul Brühwiler

DESIGNER / GESTALTER / MAQUETTISTE:
340–346 Paul Brühwiler

ART DIRECTOR / DIRECTEUR ARTISTIQUE:
340–346 Paul Brühwiler

340 Poster announcing a series of free film performances in Zurich. (SWI)
341–346 Posters for the Swiss Cultural Foundation "Pro Helvetia" which were devoted to Swiss films. Fig. 341 relates to the first film by Jean Choux, a poetic work about the Lake of Geneva region and its inhabitants. Fig. 342 informs about "The Little Escapades" by Yves Yersin. Fig. 343 is for *Montauk*, "a film reading" of Max Frisch's story, directed by Richard Dindo. Fig. 344 is a black-and-white poster for a documentary film about a deaf, dumb and blind child. Fig. 345: "Handicapped Love"—a documentary film by Marlis Graf. Fig. 346 concerns a film by Daniel Schmid "Tonight or Never". (SWI)

340 Plakat für eine Reihe von kostenlosen Filmvorführungen in Zürich. (SWI)
341–346 Von der Schweizer Kulturstiftung Pro Helvetia veröffentlichte Plakate, die dem Schweizer Film gewidmet sind. Abb. 341 betrifft den ersten Film von Jean Choux, ein poetisches Werk über den Genfer See und seine Anwohner. Abb. 342 informiert über *Die kleinen Freiheiten* von Yves Yersin. Abb. 343 stellt Richard Dindos «filmische Lesung» von Max Frischs *Montauk* vor. Abb. 344 zeigt ein Schwarzweiss-Plakat für einen Film über das Leben eines taubstummen und blinden Kindes. Abb. 345 informiert über einen Dokumentarfilm von Marlis Graf. Abb. 346 betrifft einen Film von Daniel Schmid über Dekadenz, Tod, Verführung, Gefühle. (SWI)

340 Affiche pour une série de films projetés gratuitement à Zurich. (SWI)
341–346 Affiches consacrées au cinéma suisse et publiées par la Fondation culturelle Pro Helvetia. La fig. 341 concerne le premier film de Jean Choux, une œuvre poétique sur le lac Léman et sa population. La fig. 342 renseigne sur *Les Petites Fugues* d'Yves Yersin. La fig. 343 présente l'interprétation cinématographique du *Montauk* de Max Frisch par Richard Dindo. La fig. 344, en noir et blanc, se rapporte à la vie d'Ursula, enfant sourd-muet et aveugle. Fig. 345: un documentaire de Marlis Graf, *Amour contrarié*. Fig. 346: *Cette nuit ou jamais*, film de Daniel Schmid sur la séduction et la mort. (SWI)

341

340

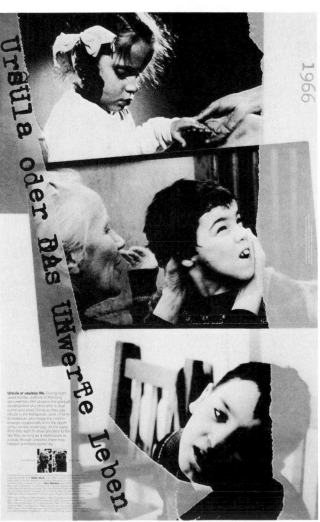

344

The little escapes. An old farm-hand, wasted by hard work and self-sacrificing devotedness, finally gets his old-age pension and simultaneously discovers for the first time the feeling of freedom, i.e. the pleasures of leisure and of personal creativeness. As a consequence, his outlook changes, he discovers other persons, the landscape, the sky. His bicycle frees him from the bonds of his all too tiny patch of land, which he had to cultivate for his masters, and provides him with quasi-mystical transports, during which he learns – for the first time – to fathom his own strength and vulnerability.

342

343

"Max Frisch, JOURNAL I–III"

1981

Max Frisch, Journal I–III. Dindo, one of the most sensitive documentary filmmakers, calls this film «a filmic reading» of Max Frisch's story «Montauk» (1974). Investigating into the writer's past and present wherein about he depicts in an intricate form Frisch's inner biography as well as his own search for a father image. In interpreting memories of past events this important director comes near to feature filming.

behinderte Liebe

Handicapped Love by Marlies Graf, who used to work herself as an independent filmmaker.

1979

345

Heute Nacht oder nie

Tonight or never. During the celebration of Saint Johannes in Bohemia the servants in aristocratic household take their master's place and play their role for one night. Daniel Schmid, who is exceptional in his ability to evoke decadence and ornamental effects of persons, opens with «Tonight or never» his series of works which suggest in images of fascinating beauty the thrill of death and enticement, showing how intense feelings in a time of decline can be.

Daniel Schmid, born 1941 in Flims, 1962 Matura at the Free University of Berlin.

1972

346

Български игрален филм   режисьор ИВАНКА ГРЪБЧЕВА

сценарист Георги Богданов   **ЗЛАТНАТА РЕКА**   композитор Митко Щерев   оператор Емил Вагенщайн   художник Валентина Младенова

В гл. роли: Петър Слабаков, Михаил Михайлов, Никола Чиприянов, Стойне Павлин и др.

347

ZLO POD SLUNCEM

ANGLICKÝ FILM
DETEKTIVNÍ PŘÍBĚH
PODLE ROMÁNU
AGATHY CHRISTIE
S PETEREM USTINOVEM
V HLAVNÍ ROLI
REŽIE: GUY HAMILTON
DÁLE HRAJÍ:
JANE BIRKINOVÁ
COLIN BLAKELY
NICHOLAS CLAY
JAMES MASON
RODDY MCDOWALL
SYLVIA MILESOVÁ
DENIS QUILLEY
AJ.

348

Grand Prix „Kryształowy Globus"
na MFF w Karlowych Warach '80

Film produkcji NRD
Występują: Jutta Wachowiak,
Regimantas Adomajtis, Slivka Budinová,
Ewa Ziętek

Narze-czona

Reżyseria: Günther Rücker,
Günter Reisch

Produkcja
DEFA - TV NRD

349

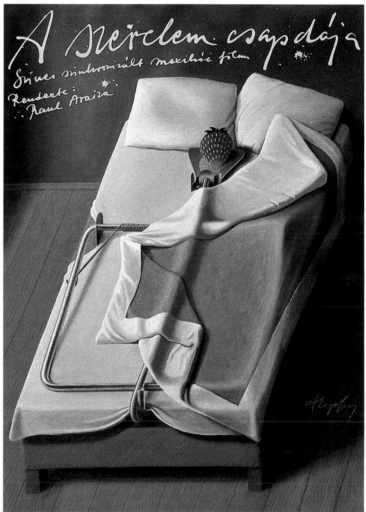

350

ARTIST / KÜNSTLER / ARTISTE:

347 Christo Aleksiev
348 Jan Tomaňek
349 Lech Majewski
350 Andras Alapfy
351 Leszek & Grazyna Drzewiński

DESIGNER / GESTALTER / MAQUETTISTE:

348 Jan Tomaňek
350 Andras Alapfy

ART DIRECTOR / DIRECTEUR ARTISTIQUE:

348 Jan Tomaňek
350 Andras Alapfy

347 Poster for the announcement of a film entitled "The Golden River". (BUL)
348 Poster for the performance of the English film based on Agathe Christie's novel *Evil Under the Sun*, in which Peter Ustinov plays the role of Hercule Poirot. Polychrome illustration on a white background, black lettering. (CSR)
349 Poster in black-and-white with greyish-blue, for an East-German film production shown in Poland, concerning the Nazi regime. (POL)
350 For an announcement of a Mexican film shown in Hungarian cinemas. The film is a love story. (HUN)
351 Poster for the filming of the uncompleted historical novel *Peter I* by Aleksei Nikolayevich Tolstoy. The illustration is predominantly in violet and greyish-green tones. (POL)

347 Plakat für die Ankündigung eines Films mit dem Titel «Der goldene Fluss». (BUL)
348 Plakat für die Aufführung eines englischen Films nach dem Kriminalroman *Das Böse unter der Sonne* von Agatha Christie, mit Peter Ustinov in der Rolle des Hercule Poirot. Mehrfarbige Illustration auf weissem Grund mit schwarzer Schrift. (CSR)
349 Plakat in Schwarzweiss mit Graublau für eine DDR-Filmproduktion über das Nazi-Regime. (POL)
350 Für die Ankündigung eines mexikanischen Films in ungarischen Kinos. Es handelt sich um eine Liebesgeschichte. (HUN)
351 Plakat für eine Verfilmung des unvollendet gebliebenen historischen Romans *Peter I* von Aleksej Nikolajewitsch Tolstoj. Illustration überwiegend in Violett- und Graugrüntönen. (POL)

347 Affiche pour la projection d'un film intitulé «Le Fleuve d'or». (BUL)
348 Affiche pour la projection d'un film anglais tiré du roman policier *Le Mal sous le Soleil* d'Agatha Christie, avec Peter Ustinov dans le rôle d'Hercule Poirot. Illustration en polychromie sur fond blanc. Le texte apparaît en noir. (CSR)
349 Affiche noir et blanc, avec du bleu gris, pour un film est-allemand consacré au nazisme. (POL)
350 Affiche pour la projection d'un film mexicain dans les cinémas de Hongrie. Il s'agit d'une histoire d'amour. (HUN)
351 Affiche pour la version cinématographique du roman historique inachevé d'Alekseï Nikolaïevitch Tolstoï, *Pierre I*er. Illustration où prédominent les violets et les verts gris. (POL)

351

352

352 Poster for the announcement of the film *The Draughtsman's Contract*. Multi-coloured collage, background in brown tones. (GBR)
353 *The Moon in the Gutter*. The foreground of this film poster is in blood-red, the background is mainly in shades of blue. (GBR)
354 Poster in water-colours for a play "Without Desires" based on a work by Peter Handke. (ITA)
355 Poster for a *Defa* film production, in green tones with various colour accents. (GDR)
356 Announcement of an annual cinematographic reproduction of the worst television advertising shown throughout the past year. In full colour. (USA)
357 Poster with black-and-white photographs for an exhibition of pictures out of Pierpaolo Pasolini's films. Red and black lettering on white. (ITA)

352 Für die Ankündigung eines Films mit dem Titel *Mord im englischen Garten*. Mehrfarbige Collage, Hintergrund in Brauntönen. (GBR)
353 Ankündigung des Films *Der Mond in der Gosse*. Vordergrund blutrot, Hintergrund vorwiegend in Blautönen. (GBR)
354 Plakat in Aquarellfarben für ein Stück nach Peter Handkes *Wunschloses Unglück*. (ITA)
355 Für eine *Defa*-Filmproduktion, in Grüntönen mit verschiedenen Farbakzenten. (GDR)
356 Ankündigung einer jährlich stattfindenden Filmvorführung der schlechtesten Fernsehwerbung des vergangenen Jahres. In Farbe. (USA)
357 Plakat mit Schwarzweiss-Aufnahmen für eine Ausstellung von Bildern aus den Filmen Pierpaolo Pasolinis. Schrift rot und schwarz auf Weiss. (ITA)

352 Affiche de cinéma pour le film intitulé *Meurtre dans un jardin anglais*. Collage polychrome sur fond brunâtre. (GBR)
353 Pour la projection du film *La Lune dans le caniveau*. Premier plan rouge sang, fond principalement interprété en tons bleus. (GBR)
354 Affiche aux teintes d'aquarelle pour une pièce d'après le récit *Malheur sans désirs* de Peter Handke. (ITA)
355 Affiche pour un film *Defa*. Divers verts avec une distribution marquée des couleurs. (GDR)
356 Annonce de la projection annuelle de la plus mauvaise publicité télévisée de l'année écoulée. En couleur. (USA)
357 Affiche illustrée de photos noir et blanc, pour une exposition de photos des films de Pierpaolo Pasolini. Texte rouge et noir. (ITA)

353

354

355

356

357

ARTIST / KÜNSTLER / ARTISTE:

352, 353 Nichola Bruce / Mike Coulson
354 Andrea Rauch
355 Dieter Heidenreich
356 Alex Murawski
357 Marisa Rizzato

DESIGNER / GESTALTER / MAQUETTISTE:

354 Andrea Rauch
356 David Bartels
357 Marisa Rizzato

ART DIRECTOR / DIRECTEUR ARTISTIQUE:

352 Mary Jane Walsh
353 Paul Webster
354 Andrea Rauch
356 David Bartels
357 Marisa Rizzato

AGENCY / AGENTUR / AGENCE – STUDIO:

352, 353 Muscle Films / Kruddart
354 Graphiti
356 Bartels & Company
357 Coopstudio

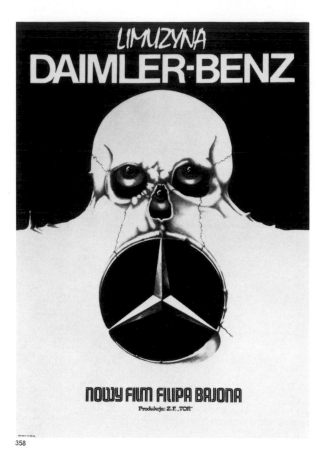

358

359

361

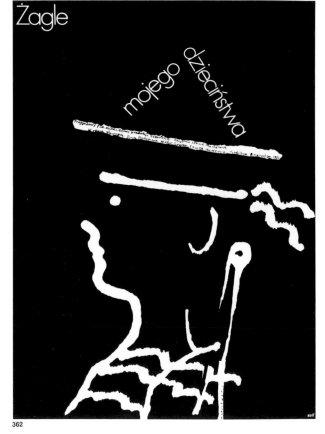

362

358 Poster in black and white for the announcement of a film. (POL)
359 Black-and-white poster for the performance of an East-German film in Hungarian cinemas: "Your Escape Nears its End". (HUN)
360 Poster for a Polish film, in green and red on white. (POL)
361 Screen-print poster for Peter Bogdanovich's film Saint Jack. (POL)
362 "The Sailing Boats of my Childhood". Poster in dark blue with white for a Russian film production. (POL)
363 Screen-print poster in grey, green, yellow, orange and pink for the announcement of a winter film programme. (GDR)
364 Poster for the performance of a criminal film. (CSR)
365 For the announcement of a Czech film comedy. (CSR)

358 Plakat in Schwarzweiss für die Ankündigung eines Films. (POL)
359 Schwarzweisses Plakat für die Aufführung eines ostdeutschen Films in ungarischen Kinos: «Deine Flucht nimmt ein Ende». (HUN)
360 Plakat für einen polnischen Film, in Grün und Rot auf Weiss. (POL)
361 Siebdruckplakat für die Ankündigung eines amerikanischen Films. (POL)
362 «Die Segelboote meiner Kindheit.» Plakat in Dunkelblau mit Weiss für eine russische Filmproduktion. (POL)
363 Siebdruckplakat in Grau, Grün, Gelb, Orange und Rosa für die Ankündigung eines Winter-Filmprogramms. (GDR)
364 Plakat für die Vorführung eines Kriminalfilms. (CSR)
365 Ankündigung einer tschechischen Filmkomödie. (CSR)

360

364

363

365

358 Affiche noir et blanc annonçant un nouveau film. (POL)
359 Affiche noir et blanc pour la projection d'un film est-allemand sur les écrans hongrois: «Ta Fuite prendra fin». (HUN)
360 Affiche pour un film polonais, vert et rouge sur blanc. (POL)
361 Affiche sérigraphique pour un film américain. (POL)
362 «Les Voiliers de mon enfance.» Affiche bleu foncé, avec du blanc, pour un film soviétique. (POL)
363 Affiche sérigraphique en gris, vert, jaune, orange et rose pour un programme de projection cinématographique en hiver. (GDR)
364 Affiche pour la projection d'un film policier. (CSR)
365 Affiche de cinéma pour une comédie tchèque. (CSR)

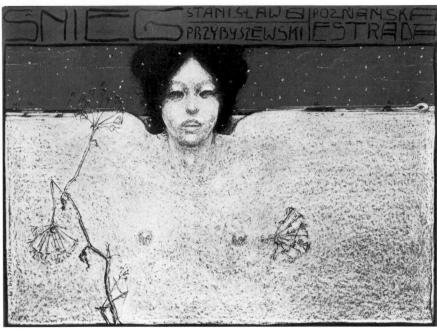

366

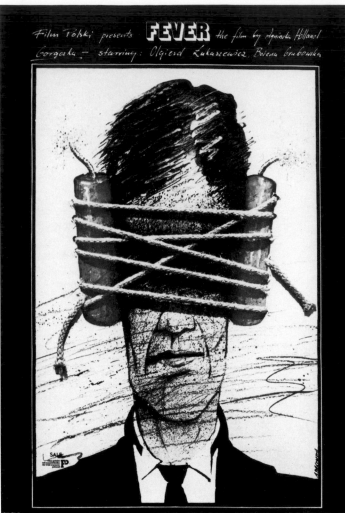

367

368

ARTIST / KÜNSTLER / ARTISTE:

366 Franciszek Starowieyski
367 Andrzej Pagowski
368 Klára Tamás Blaier
369, 370 Waldemar Swierzy
371 Jan Mlodozeniec
372 Roman Cieslewicz

ART DIRECTOR / DIRECTEUR ARTISTIQUE:

369 Anna Mieczynska
370 Grazyna Maria Szpyra
372 Andrzej Zielinski

366 Poster for a play entitled "Snow" performed by a theatre and music group in Poznan. (POL)
367 Poster with polychrome illustration for a Polish film entitled "Fever". (POL)
368 "Fruits of the Forest" is the title of the Rumanian film which this poster is announcing. (RUM)
369 For an exhibition of drawings, posters and poster-designs by Waldemar Swierzy. (POL)
370 Poster for an exhibition devoted to poster-design in France, from Toulouse-Lautrec to Alain Le Quernec. Brush strokes in various colours, Toulouse-Lautrec's portrait in sepia. (POL)
371 Multi-coloured poster for a performance of Molière's *The School for Wives*. (POL)
372 For an exhibition of works by Polish artist Roman Cieślewicz in a Warsaw gallery. (POL)

366 Plakat für ein vom Posener Podium aufgeführtes Stück mit dem Titel «Schnee». (POL)
367 Plakat mit mehrfarbiger Illustration für einen polnischen Film mit dem Titel «Fieber». (POL)
368 «Früchte des Waldes» ist der Titel des mit diesem Plakat angekündigten rumänischen Films. (RUM)
369 Für eine Ausstellung mit Zeichnungen, Plakaten und Plakatentwürfen von Waldemar Swierzy. (POL)
370 Plakat für eine Ausstellung, die dem Plakatschaffen in Frankreich – von Toulouse-Lautrec bis Alain Le Quernec – gewidmet ist. Pinselstriche in vielen Farben, Porträt Toulouse-Lautrecs in Sepia. (POL)
371 Mehrfarbiges Plakat für eine Aufführung von Molières *Die Schule der Frauen*. (POL)
372 Für eine Ausstellung des polnischen Künstlers Roman Cieślewicz in einer Warschauer Galerie. (POL)

366 Affiche pour une pièce jouée au théâtre Podium de Poznań et intitulée «Neige». (POL)
367 Affiche illustrée en polychromie, pour un film polonais intitulé «Fièvre». (POL)
368 Le film roumain annoncé par cette affiche porte le titre de «Fruits de la forêt». (RUM)
369 Pour une exposition des dessins, affiches et projets d'affiches de Waldemar Swierzy. (POL)
370 Affiche pour une exposition consacrée à l'affiche française, de Toulouse-Lautrec à Alain Le Quernec. Coups de pinceau en diverses couleurs, portrait de Toulouse-Lautrec en sépia. (POL)
371 Affiche polychrome pour une représentation de la pièce *l'Ecole des femmes* de Molière. (POL)
372 Pour une exposition de l'œuvre de Roman Cieślewicz dans une galerie d'art de Varsovie. (POL)

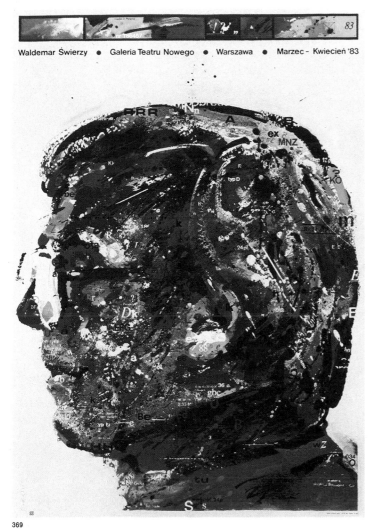

369

Plakat Francuski
Biuro Wystaw Artystycznych
Zamość – Rynek Wielki 14/2
Styczeń **1983** Janvier
Luty Février

Affiche Française

pod Toulouse Lautrec wg **Alain le Quernec**

przedstawia
Władysław
Serwatowski
présente

370

Molière

TEATR POLSKI w Szczecinie

SZKOŁA ŻON

371

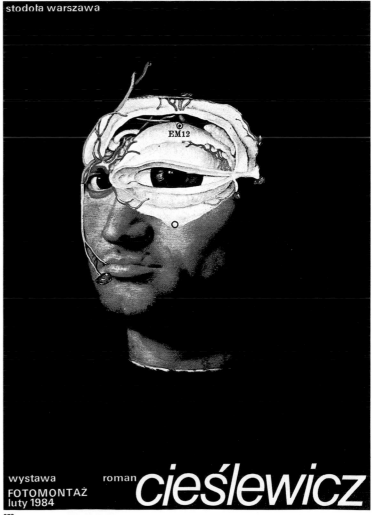

stodoła warszawa

EM12

wystawa
FOTOMONTAŻ
luty 1984

roman cieślewicz

372

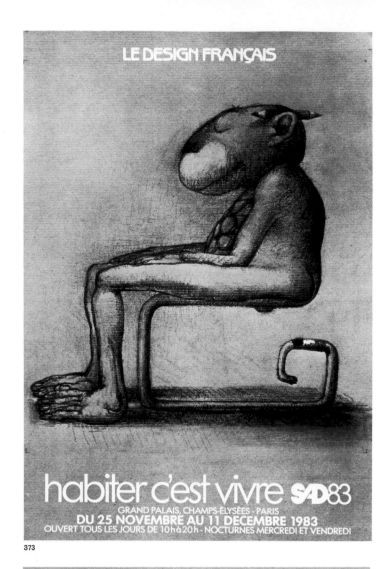

373

374

375

378

373 "Living means Life". Poster with a brown packing-paper similarity and few coloured strokes, for an exhibition of French furnishing design. (FRA)
374 Poster for the announcement of a Walt Disney festival. (ITA)
375 Poster in soft pastel shades for the announcement of a three-day symposium dedicated to literature for young people. (FRA)
376 Poster for an exhibition of humorous graphics centering on the theme of money. Red head with blue, hand outlined in green. (ITA)
377 Poster in predominantly violet tones for an exhibition devoted to Gahan Wilson's macabre humour. (GER)
378 For an exhibition of posters by Rolf-F. Müller. (GDR)
379 Poster for an exhibition of early German posters. (GDR)
380 Polychrome poster for a comics festival. (GER)

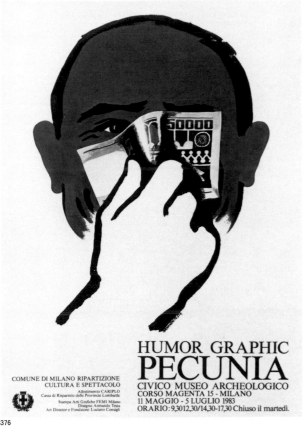

376

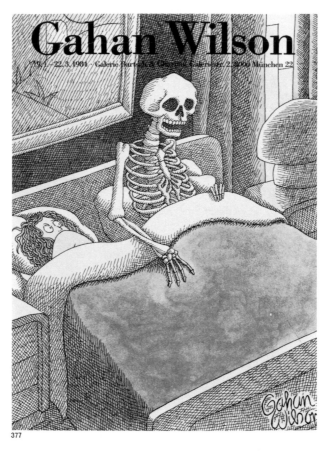

377

379

380

ARTIST / KÜNSTLER / ARTISTE:

373 André François
374 Andrea Rauch
375 Jean Claverie
376 Armando Testa
377 Gahan Wilson
378 Rolf Felix Müller
379 Helmut Brade
380 Alain Le Quernec

DESIGNER / GESTALTER / MAQUETTISTE:

374 Tapiro
375 Jean Claverie
376 Antonio Pepe
377 Bartsch & Chariau
380 Alain Le Quernec

ART DIRECTOR / DIRECTEUR ARTISTIQUE:

374 Tapiro/Andrea Rauch
375 Jean Claverie
376 Armando Testa
380 Alain Le Quernec

AGENCY / AGENTUR / AGENCE – STUDIO:

374 Graphiti
376 Armando Testa S. p. A.

373 «Wohnen heisst leben.» Plakat mit Packpapiercharakter und wenigen Farbstrichen für eine Ausstellung französischen Designs. (FRA)
374 Plakat für die Ankündigung eines Walt-Disney-Festivals. (ITA)
375 Bekanntgabe eines dreitägigen Symposiums, das der Jugendliteratur gewidmet ist. Plakat in sanften Pastelltönen. (FRA)
376 Geld ist das Thema der hier angekündigten Ausstellung humoristischer Graphik. Roter Kopf mit Blau, Hand grün umrandet. (ITA)
377 Vorwiegend in Violettönen gehaltenes Plakat für eine Ausstellung, die dem makabren Humor Gahan Wilsons gewidmet ist. (GER)
378 Für eine Ausstellung der Plakate von Rolf-F. Müller. (GDR)
379 Dem Ausstellungsthema angepasstes Plakat in dunklen Farben. (GDR)
380 Bekanntgabe einer Comic-Messe in Erlangen. Mehrfarbig. (GER)

373 Affiche style papier d'emballage, usant de quelques traits couleur pour présenter une exposition du design français appliqué à l'habitat. (FRA)
374 Affiche annonçant un festival Walt Disney. (ITA)
375 Affiche annonçant l'organisation d'un symposium de trois jours consacré aux livres pour la jeunesse. Teintes pastel délicates. (FRA)
376 L'argent, voilà le thème de l'exposition d'humour graphique annoncée sur cette affiche. Tête rouge, avec du bleu, main silhouettée en vert. (ITA)
377 Affiche aux tons violets prédominants pour une exposition de l'œuvre humoristique macabre de Gahan Wilson. (GER)
378 Pour une exposition de l'œuvre affichiste de Rolf-F. Müller. (GDR)
379 Pour une exposition d'affiches anciennes. Couleurs sombres. (GDR)
380 Pour un Salon de la bande dessinée à Erlangen. En polychromie. (GER)

149

381 Poster for the announcement of a film festival in Houston, Texas. Black and white with red and greenish-beige. (USA)
382 For an exhibition of works by London art-students over the last three decades. In black and white with two shades of brown. (GBR)
383 For an exhibition of business calendar award-winners. (GBR)
384 Large-format poster for an exhibition of drawings by citizens of Geneva—from Liotard to Hodler—held in the museum Rath in Geneva. Polychrome portraits on grey ground. (SWI)
385 For the 31st Bernese exhibition representing Swiss trade, agriculture, commerce and industry. Yellow hat, red collar. (SWI)
386 For an exhibition of etchings by various artists. Black and white on beige, red title. (SWI)
387, 388 Illustration and complete poster for an exhibition of children's book illustrations in New York. (USA)

381 Plakat für die Ankündigung eines Filmfestivals in Houston. Schwarzweiss mit Rot und grünlichem Beige. (USA)
382 Für eine Ausstellung von Arbeiten Londoner Kunststudenten aus drei Jahrzehnten. Schwarzweiss mit zwei Brauntönen. (GBR)
383 Für eine Ausstellung prämierter Geschäftskalender. (GBR)
384 Grossformatiges Plakat für eine Ausstellung mit Genfer Zeichnungen – von Liotard bis Hodler – im Genfer Rath-Museum. Mehrfarbige Abbildungen auf grauem Grund. (SWI)
385 Ankündigung der 31. Berner Ausstellung für Handwerk, Landwirtschaft, Handel und Industrie. Gelber Hut, roter Kragen. (SWI)
386 Für eine Ausstellung von Radierungen verschiedener Künstler. Schwarzweiss auf Beige, Titel rot. (SWI)
387, 388 Illustration und vollständiges Plakat für eine Ausstellung von Kinderbuchillustrationen in New York. (USA)

381 Affiche annonçant un festival du film à Houston. Noir et blanc avec deux couleurs vives: rouge et beige vert. (USA)
382 Pour une exposition des travaux d'artistes issus des écoles d'art du centre de Londres; noir et blanc, deux bruns. (GBR)
383 Pour une exposition de calendriers d'entreprises primés. (GBR)
384 Affiche au grand format pour une exposition de dessins genevois. Illustrations polychromes sur fond gris. (SWI)
385 Annonce de la 31e Exposition bernoise de l'artisanat, de l'agriculture, du commerce et de l'industrie en Suisse. Chapeau typiquement bernois jaune, col rouge. (SWI)
386 Pour une exposition collective d'eaux-fortes. Noir et blanc sur beige, titre rouge. (SWI)
387, 388 Illustration et affiche complète pour une exposition d'illustrations pour livres d'enfants à New York. (USA)

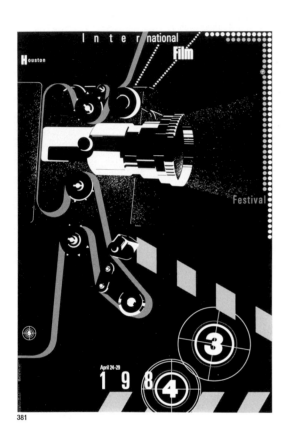

381

382

383

384

385

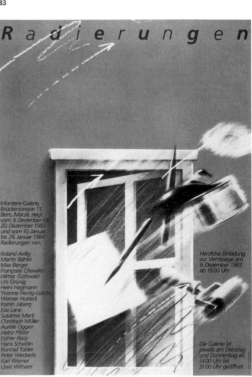

386

387

ARTIST / KÜNSTLER / ARTISTE:

381 Ken Maginnis/Mary Conrad
382, 383 Tom Eckersley
385 Kurt Wirth
386 Urs Grünig
387, 388 Friso Henstra

DESIGNER / GESTALTER / MAQUETTISTE:

384 Roger Pfund/Jean-Pierre Blanchoud
385 Kurt Wirth
386 Urs Grünig

ART DIRECTOR / DIRECTEUR ARTISTIQUE:

385 Kurt Wirth
386 Urs Grünig

AGENCY / AGENTUR / AGENCE – STUDIO:

381 Creel Morrell Inc.

388

**Exhibitions/Ausstellungen
Expositions**

389

390

391

ARTIST / KÜNSTLER / ARTISTE:

389, 390 John J. Sorbie
392 Pam Woll
393 Gert Wunderlich
394 Niko Macura
395 Joe Baraban/Arthur Meyerson

DESIGNER / GESTALTER / MAQUETTISTE:

389, 390 John J. Sorbie
391 Michael Vanderbyl
393 Gert Wunderlich
394 Zeljko Borčić
395 Alan Colvin/Woody Pirtle

389, 390 Posters for exhibitions of drawings by the American artist John J. Sorbie. Fig. 389 is in black, yellow and green-grey. (USA)
391 Screen-print poster for a lecture series on the architecture of San Francisco. (USA)
392 Small-size poster in black and blue on white for an exhibition with pictures, photography and art handicrafts. (USA)
393 For the centenary of the German Book and Lettering Museum in Leipzig. (GDR)
394 Multi-coloured poster for the 10th Biennale of Industrial Design in Ljubljana. (YUG)
395 Poster to announce an exhibition on architecture in Houston, Texas. (USA)

389, 390 Plakat für Ausstellungen von Zeichnungen des amerikanischen Künstlers John J. Sorbie. Abb. 389 in Schwarz, Gelb und grünlichem Grau. (USA)
391 Siebdruckplakat für eine Vortragsreihe über Architektur in San Francisco. (USA)
392 Kleinformatiges Plakat in Schwarz und Blau auf Weiss für eine Ausstellung mit Bildern, Photographie und Kunsthandwerk. (USA)
393 Zum 100jährigen Bestehen des Deutschen Buch- und Schriftmuseums in Leipzig veröffentlichtes Plakat. (GDR)
394 Mehrfarbiges Plakat für die 10. Biennale für Industrie-Design in Ljubljana. (YUG)
395 Plakat für die Ankündigung einer Ausstellung über Architektur in Houston. (USA)

389, 390 Affiches pour des expositions des dessins de l'artiste américain John J. Sorbie. Fig. 389 est en noir, jaune, gris vert. (USA)
391 Affiche sérigraphique pour des conférences d'architecture à San Francisco. (USA)
392 Affichette noir et bleu sur blanc pour une exposition de peinture, de photo et d'artisanat d'art. (USA)
393 Pour le centenaire du Musée allemand du Livre et de l'Ecriture de Leipzig. (GDR)
394 Pour la 10e Biennale d'esthétique industrielle de Ljubljana. Polychromie. (YUG)
395 Affiche annonçant une exposition d'architecture à Houston. (USA)

Mile High IBM Club **Arts** Thursday, October 27
thru
Photography Sunday, October 30
and at the
Crafts Plaza Hotel
Longmont
Exhibit on the
Diagonal Highway

392

3
+

100 JAHRE
DEUTSCHES BUCH-
UND
SCHRIFTMUSEUM
1884–1984

DEUTSCHE
BÜCHEREI·LEIPZIG

GEÖFFNET:
MONTAG
BIS SONNABEND
9 BIS 16 UHR

393

bio 10 / 10. bienale industrijskega oblikovanja / september/oktober 1984
Ljubljana, Jugoslavija
10. bijenale industrijskog oblikovanja / Cankarjev dom,
Likovno razstavišče
10th biennial of industrial design / Rihard Jakopič

394

Exhibitions/Ausstellungen/Expositions

395

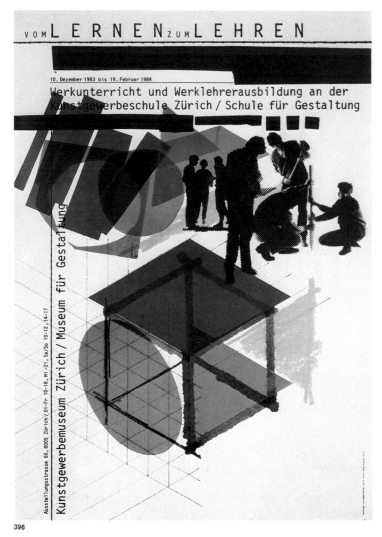

VOM LERNEN ZUM LEHREN

10. Dezember 1983 bis 19. Februar 1984

Werkunterricht und Werklehrerausbildung an der Kunstgewerbeschule Zürich / Schule für Gestaltung

Kunstgewerbemuseum Zürich / Museum für Gestaltung

Ausstellungsstrasse 60, 8005 Zürich / Di–Fr 10–18, Mi–21, Sa/So 10–12, 14–17

396

René BURRI

Fotografien und Collagen

Kunsthaus Zürich   14. Januar – 11. März 1984

397

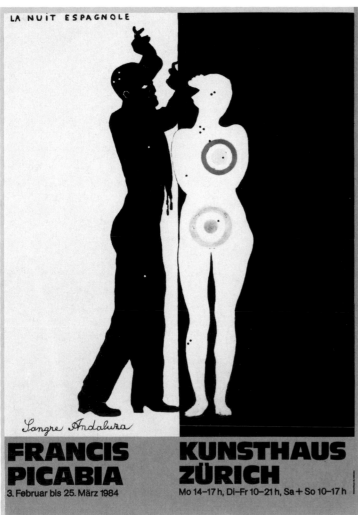

LA NUIT ESPAGNOLE

Sangre Andaluza

FRANCIS PICABIA
3. Februar bis 25. März 1984

KUNSTHAUS ZÜRICH
Mo 14–17 h, Di–Fr 10–21 h, Sa + So 10–17 h

398

1984

Kieler Woche
16.–24. Juni

399

154

ARTIST / KÜNSTLER / ARTISTE:

396 Hermann Eggmann
397, 400 René Burri
398 Francis Picabia

DESIGNER / GESTALTER / MAQUETTISTE:

397, 400 Werner Jeker
398 Kunsthaus Zürich
399 Ossi Möhr/Roland Wohler/Iris Kristofori

ART DIRECTOR / DIRECTEUR ARTISTIQUE:

399 Ernst Hiestand

396 Poster for an exhibition at the Zurich Museum of Arts and Crafts (Zürcher Kunstgewerbemuseum) about instruction and teacher-training at the School of Applied Art in Zurich (Kunstgewerbeschule Zürich). (SWI)
397, 400 Posters with black-and-white photographs for an exhibition of photography and collages by René Burri in the Zurich Kunsthaus. His main themes are the situation and living conditions throughout the world. (SWI)
398 Poster to announce an exhibition of Francis Picabia's works in the Zurich Kunsthaus. In black and white, save for the targets and border, which are in red and ochre-yellow. (SWI)
399 Poster issued in diverse sizes for the Kieler Woche—an annual summer sailing festival held in Kiel, Germany. (GER)

396 Für eine Ausstellung im Zürcher Kunstgewerbemuseum über die Werklehrerausbildung an der Kunstgewerbeschule Zürich. (SWI)
397, 400 Plakate mit Schwarzweissaufnahmen für eine Ausstellung der Photographien und Collagen von René Burri im Kunsthaus Zürich. Sein Hauptthema sind Zustände und Lebensbedingungen in der ganzen Welt. (SWI)
398 Für eine Ausstellung mit Werken von Francis Picabia im Kunsthaus Zürich. Die Umrandung der Bildwiedergabe ist rot und ockergelb, den Farben der Zielscheiben im sonst schwarzweissen Bild entsprechend. (SWI)
399 In verschiedenen Formaten erschienenes Plakat für die Kieler Woche. Das Motiv wurde für das gesamte Erscheinungsbild verwendet. (GER)

396 Affiche pour une exposition au Musée des arts et métiers de Zurich consacrée à la formation des maîtres dans les arts appliqués. (SWI)
397, 400 Affiches illustrées en noir et blanc pour une exposition des photos et collages de René Burri au Kunsthaus Zurich, surtout sur le thème des conditions de vie et des moyens d'existence dans le monde. (SWI)
398 Pour une exposition de l'œuvre de Francis Picabia au Kunsthaus Zurich. Encadrement rouge et ocre en fonction des couleurs des cibles au sein d'une affiche illustrée en noir et blanc. (SWI)
399 Affiche publiée en divers formats pour la Semaine de régate de Kiel. Motif utilisé pour l'image globale de cette manifestation. (GER)

Exhibitions
Ausstellungen
Expositions

401 Small-size poster for an exhibition of book covers. Pink, with a blue glass eye. (SPA)
402 For the announcement of an exhibition of handmade ceramic utensils. Colour photograph of a blue-painted pale-toned vase. (ITA)
403 Poster for a travelling exhibition organized by the Smithsonian Institute and dedicated to the art of Cameroon. It depicts a coloured pearl decorated mask, shown against a black ground. (USA)
404 "When the cathedrals were white". Poster for an exhibition about the cathedral of Modena after its restoration. Garments in green, brown and dark blue on a yellowish background. (ITA)
405 Announcement of a carnival exhibition and an artists' ball. (GER)

401 Kleinformatiges Plakat für eine Ausstellung von Buchumschlägen. Rosa mit blauem Glasauge, schwarze Schrift. (SPA)
402 Für die Ankündigung einer Ausstellung handgetöpferter Gebrauchskeramik. Farbaufnahme einer blaubemalten, hellen Tonvase. (ITA)
403 Für eine Wanderausstellung mit Kunstgegenständen aus Kamerun. Hier eine mit farbigen Perlenschnüren verzierte Maske. (USA)
404 «Als die Kathedralen weiss waren.» Plakat für eine Ausstellung über den Dom von Modena nach der Restaurierung. Gewänder in Grün, Braun und Dunkelblau vor vergilbtem Hintergrund. (ITA)
405 Ankündigung einer Fastnachtsausstellung und eines Künstler-Kehrausballs. (GER)

401 Affichette pour une exposition de couvertures de livres. Rose, œil de verre bleu, texte noir. (SPA)
402 Affiche annonçant une exposition de céramique utilitaire faite à la main. Photo couleur d'un vase clair peint en bleu. (ITA)
403 Pour une exposition itinérante de l'art traditionnel du Cameroun. On voit sur cette affiche un masque orné de rangées de perles multicolores, du tournant du siècle. (USA)
404 «Du temps où les cathédrales étaient blanches.» Affiche pour une exposition consacrée à la cathédrale de Modène après sa restauration. Vêtements vert, brun et bleu foncé sur fond jauni. (ITA)
405 Annonce d'une exposition de carnaval et d'un bal des artistes à Francfort. (GER)

401

402

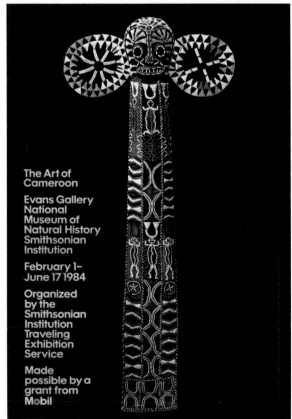

403

404

Fastnacht
Ausstellung
Frankfurter
Künstler
ab 19. Febr.
14–18 Uhr
in der
Alten Oper

Veranstaltet
vom
Berufsverband
Bildender
Künstler
Frankfurt/Main
e.V.

Unterstützt
durch die
Frankfurter
Neue Presse
und die
Stadtsparkasse
Frankfurt/M.

Künstler-
Kehraus mit
attraktivem
Programm!
Fastnachts-
Dienstag
6. März 1984
19.11 Uhr
in der
Alten Oper.

6.3. SPEKTAKULUM '84

405

406

ART DIRECTOR / DIRECTEUR ARTISTIQUE:

406 David T. Tartakover
407 Edith Freedman
408 Massimo Dolcini
410 Santiago Pol
411 Günther Kieser

AGENCY / AGENTUR / AGENCE – STUDIO:

407 Penn State University
408 Fuorischema
410 Santiago Pol

407

Exhibitions/Ausstellungen
Expositions

ARTIST / KÜNSTLER / ARTISTE:

406 David T. Tartakover
408 Massimo Dolcini
409 Witold Nowak
410 Freddy De Bari
411 Günther Kieser
412 Villu Järmut/Enn Kärmas

DESIGNER / GESTALTER / MAQUETTISTE:

406 David T. Tartakover
407 Edith Freedman
408 Massimo Dolcini
409 Marek Freudenreich
410 Sigfredo Chacon
411 Günther Kieser
412 Villu Järmut/Enn Kärmas

406 Example from a series of posters with the title "Culture Heroes from Tel Aviv". (ISR)
407*Small-format poster for a school's ceramic exhibition. Brown on beige. (USA)
408 Poster for a "small market of wonders", which was held in a piazza and was organized by the city of Pesaro. (ITA)
409 Poster for a Polish film entitled "What weather today!". In full colour. (POL)
410 Announcement of an exhibition devoted to three-dimensional art. (VEN)
411 Large-format poster for the BMW Museum. Brown engine on blue background. (GER)
412 Exhibition with pictures, sculpture and graphics by artists from Tallin, Estonia. (USR)

406 Beispiel aus einer Serie von Plakaten mit dem Titel «Kultur-Helden von Tel Aviv». (ISR)
407 Kleinformatiges Plakat für eine Schüler-Keramikausstellung. Braun auf Beige. (USA)
408 Für einen «kleinen Markt der Wunder», veranstaltet von der Stadt Pesaro. (ITA)
409 Plakat für einen Film mit dem Titel «Was für ein Wetter heute!». In Farbe. (POL)
410 Ankündigung einer Ausstellung, die Materie und Raum gewidmet ist. (VEN)
411 Grossformatiges Plakat für das BMW-Museum. Brauner Motor auf blauem Grund. (GER)
412 Plakat für eine Frühlingsausstellung mit Bildern, Skulpturen und Graphiken von Künstlern aus Tallin, Estland. (USR)

406 Exemple d'affiche dans une série intitulée «Héros de la culture à Tel-Aviv». (ISR)
407 Affichette pour une exposition de céramique d'étudiants. Brun sur beige. (USA)
408 Pour un «petit marché des merveilles» organisé par la ville de Pesaro. (ITA)
409 Affiche pour un film polonais intitulé «Quel temps aujourd'hui!». En couleur. (POL)
410 Annonce d'une exposition sur le thème de la matière et de l'espace. (VEN)
411 Affiche au grand format pour le Musée BMW. Moteur marron sur fond bleu. (GER)
412 Affiche créée pour une exposition collective des peintures, sculptures et gravures des artistes de Tallin, capitale de l'Estonie. (USR)

408

Już na ekranach kin
PROGNOZA POGODY film na motywach opowiadania
Scenariusz i reżyseria Marka Nowakowskiego
ANTONI KRAUZE Zdarzenie w miasteczku
Zdjęcia Krzysztof Pakulski Produkcja ZF TOR 1981
Już na ekranach kin!

409

SALA DE EXPOSICIONES C.A.N.T.V.   11 SETIEMBRE AL 9 OCTUBRE 1982 LA C.A.N.T.V. UNE A LA GENTE TAMBIEN...A TRAVES DE LA CULTURA

MATERIA   E S P A C I O
LA INVESTIGACION   TRIDIMENSIONAL EN LAS NUEVAS PROPOSICIONES

410

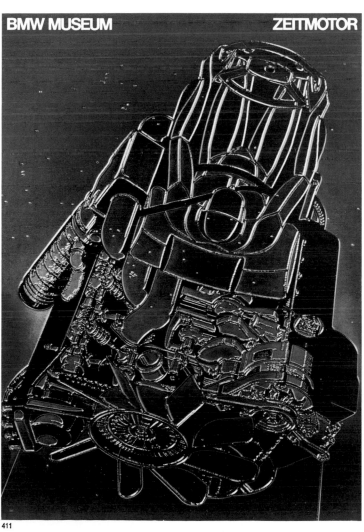

BMW MUSEUM   ZEITMOTOR

411

TALLINNA   MAAL
KUNSTNIKE   SKULPTUUR
KEVADNÄITUS   GRAAFIKA

412

159

413

Cultural Events
Veranstaltungen
Evénements culturels

ARTIST / KÜNSTLER / ARTISTE:

413 Roman Cieslewicz
414 Fritz Haase
415 Tomasz Szulecki
416 Takenobu Igarashi
417 Tadanori Yokoo
418 Seitaro Kuroda
419 Yusaku Kamekura

ART DIRECTOR / DIRECTEUR ARTISTIQUE:

413 Roman Cieslewicz
414 Fritz Haase
415 Tomasz Szulecki
416 Takenobu Igarashi
417 Tadanori Yokoo
418 Keisuke Nagatomo
419 Yusaku Kamekura

DESIGNER / GESTALTER / MAQUETTISTE:

413 Roman Cieslewicz
414 Fritz Haase
416 Takenobu Igarashi
417 Tadanori Yokoo
418 Naohisa Tsuchiya
419 Yusaku Kamekura

AGENCY / AGENTUR / AGENCE – STUDIO:

414 Haase & Knels
415 KAW
416 Takenobu Igarashi Design
418 K-two Co. Ltd.

413 For an exhibition to mark the 150th anniversary of the Polish library in Paris. (FRA)
414 Black-and-white poster for an exhibition of exemplary type design in the USA. (GER)
415 For an exhibition marking the 50th anniversary of the Frédéric Chopin School of Music. (POL)
416 Invitation to participate in an art exhibition. Blue and red on turquoise. (JPN)
417 Poster for the announcement of a Japanese film. (JPN)
418 Screen-print poster for a theatre performance. Grey, pink, red, light brown on beige. (JPN)
419 Screen-print poster for a discourse on the classical Japanese dance. Violet and white elements, "frame" and border gold-coloured, turquoise butterfly, white lettering on black. (JPN)

413 Für eine Ausstellung zum 150jährigen Bestehen der polnischen Bibliothek in Paris. (FRA)
414 Plakat in Schwarzweiss für eine Ausstellung vorbildlicher Schriftgestaltung. (GER)
415 Für eine Ausstellung zum 50jährigen Bestehen des Konservatoriums Frédéric Chopin. (POL)
416 Einladung zur Teilnahme an einer Kunstausstellung. Blau und rot auf Türkis. (JPN)
417 Plakat für die Ankündigung eines japanischen Films. (JPN)
418 Siebdruckplakat für eine Theateraufführung. Grau, rosa, rot, hellbraun auf beigem Grund. (JPN)
419 Siebdruckplakat für einen Vortrag klassischen japanischen Tanzes. Elemente violett und weiss, «Einrahmung» und Umrandung goldfarben, Schmetterling türkis, schwarzer Grund, weisse Schrift. (JPN)

413 Pour une exposition commémorant les 150 ans de la Librairie polonaise de Paris. (FRA)
414 Affiche noir et blanc pour une exposition de typo exemplaire venue des Etats-Unis. (GER)
415 Pour une exposition à l'occasion du cinquantenaire du Conservatoire Frédéric Chopin. (POL)
416 Invitation à participer à une exposition d'art. Bleu et rouge sur turquoise. (JPN)
417 Affiche annonçant la projection d'un film japonais. (JPN)
418 Affiche sérigraphique pour une représentation de théâtre. Gris, rose, rouge, brun sur beige. (JPN)
419 Affiche sérigraphique pour un spectacle de danse classique japonaise. Eléments violets et blancs, coins et encadrement or, papillon turquoise, fond noir, texte blanc. (JPN)

414

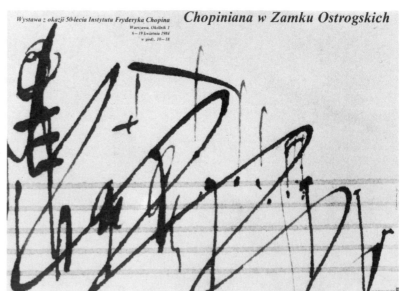

415

416

417

418

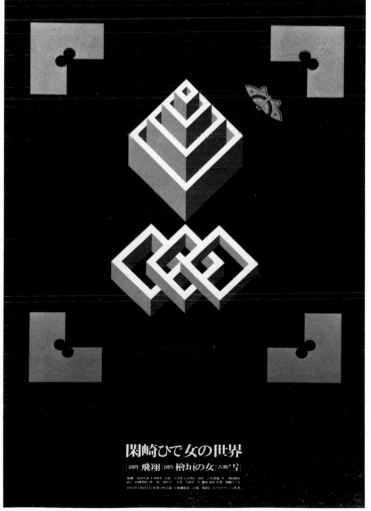

419

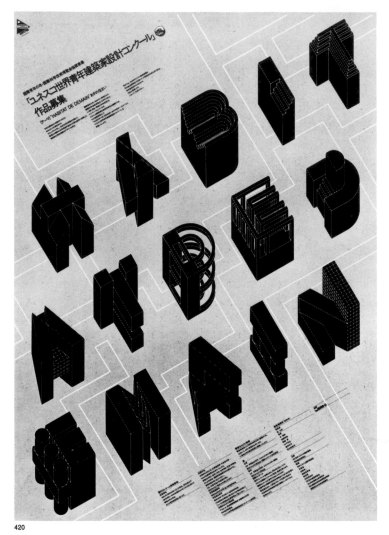

420

EXHIBITION OF WORKS BY YUSAKU KAMEKURA
曲線と直線の宇宙
亀倉雄策デザイン展
会期／10月7日(金)—12日(水) 会場／松屋銀座8階大催場 午前10時6時30分 入場無料
主催／朝日新聞社
Matsuya Ginza

421

424

425

422

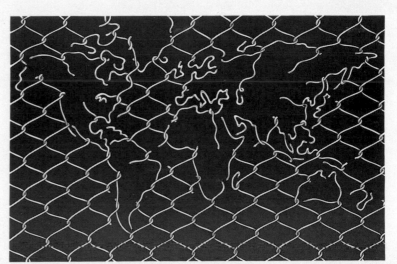

"The Fence Series" by U.G. SATO. January 23–February 4, 1984, Gallery Olive, Ginza, Tōkyō.

423

426

ARTIST/KÜNSTLER/ARTISTE:

420 Takenobu Igarashi
421 Yusaku Kamekura
422, 423 U. G. Sato
424–426 Masakazu Tanabe/Toshiyuki Ohashi

DESIGNER/GESTALTER/MAQUETTISTE:

420 Takenobu Igarashi
421 Yusaku Kamekura
422, 423 U. G. Sato
424 Masakazu Tanabe

ART DIRECTOR/DIRECTEUR ARTISTIQUE:

420 Takenobu Igarashi
421 Yusaku Kamekura
422, 423 U. G. Sato
424–426 Shinichiro Tora

AGENCY/AGENTUR/AGENCE – STUDIO:

420 Dentsu Inc.
422, 423 Design Farm

420 Poster as a call for entries for an architectural competition. Black and white on light brown. (JPN)
421 For an exhibition of works by the Japanese artist Yusaku Kamekura. Rings in green and yellow tones, background and three-dimensional elements in various shades of pink. (JPN)
422, 423 Wire interlock-fencing is featured in the posters by U. G. Sato at an exhibition in Tokyo. (JPN)
424–426 Three from a total of eleven posters for a two-men exhibition with illustrations by Masakazu Tanabe and photography by Toshiyuki Ohashi. Fig. 426 is in tones of blue-grey. (USA)

420 Plakat als Aufruf zur Teilnahme an einem Architektur-Wettbewerb. Schwarzweiss auf Hellbraun. (JPN)
421 Für eine Ausstellung des Japaners Yusaku Kamekura. Ringe in Grün- und Gelbtönen, Hintergrund und dreidimensionale Elemente in verschiedenen Abstufungen von Rosa. (JPN)
422, 423 Ankündigung einer Ausstellung der «Zaun-Serie» von U. G. Sato in Tokio. (JPN)
424–426 Drei von insgesamt elf Plakaten für eine Zwei-Mann-Ausstellung mit Illustrationen von Masakazu Tanabe und Photographien von Toshiyuki Ohashi. Abb. 426 in Blaugrautönen. (USA)

420 Affiche pour un appel d'envois à un concours d'architecture. Noir-blanc sur brun clair. (JPN)
421 Pour une exposition de l'œuvre du Japonais Yusaku Kamekura. Anneaux en nuances de vert et de jaune, fond et éléments tridimensionnels en divers degrés de rose. (JPN)
422, 423 Annonce d'une exposition des créations d'U. G. Sato de Tōkyō, série des «Clôtures». (JPN)
424–426 Trois des onze affiches réalisées pour une exposition réunissant les illustrations de Masakazu Tanabe et les photographies de Toshiyuki Ohashi. Fig. 426: nuances de gris bleu. (USA)

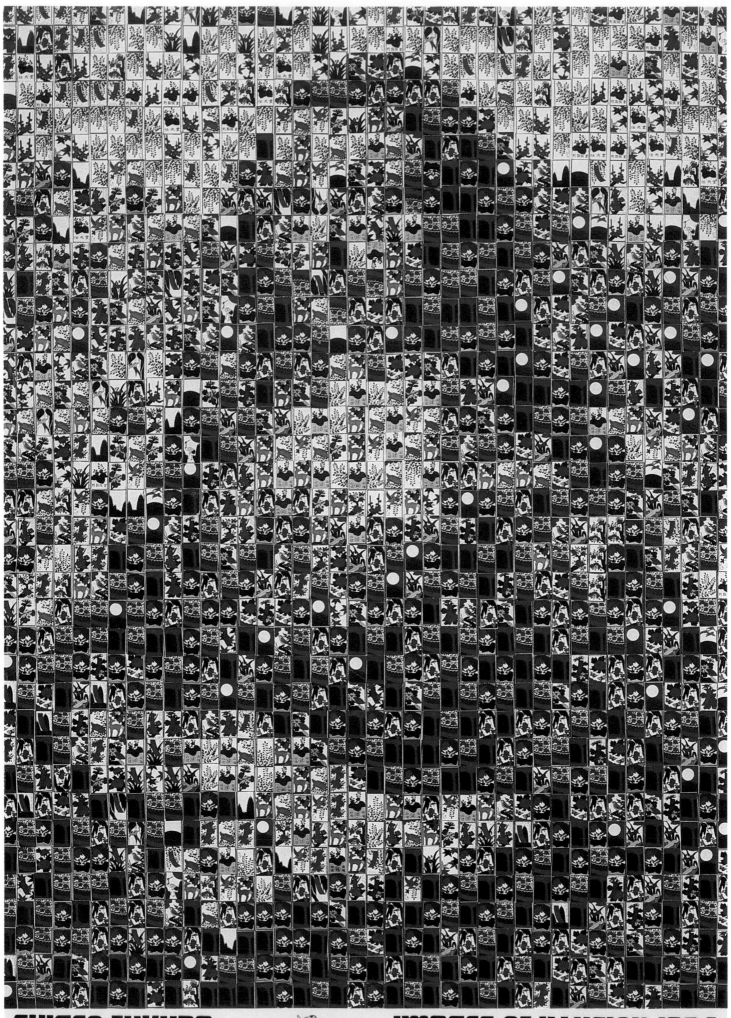

SHIGEO FUKUDA IMAGES OF ILLUSION 1984

427

ARTIST / KÜNSTLER / ARTISTE:
427–430 Shigeo Fukuda

DESIGNER / GESTALTER / MAQUETTISTE:
427–430 Shigeo Fukuda

ART DIRECTOR / DIRECTEUR ARTISTIQUE:
427–430 Shigeo Fukuda

427, 428 Examples from a series of posters with the title "Images of Illusion". The illustration in Fig. 428 is in black and white. (JPN)
429, 430 Posters in black and white with lettering in various colours, for a performance of *Madame Butterfly* and an operetta medley. (JPN)

427, 428 Beispiele aus einer Serie von Plakaten unter dem Titel «Bilder der Illusion». Die Illustration in Abb. 428 ist schwarzweiss. (JPN)
429, 430 Plakate in Schwarzweiss mit mehrfarbiger Beschriftung für eine Aufführung von *Madame Butterfly* und ein Operetten-Potpourri. (JPN)

427, 428 Exemples des affiches créées dans une série intitulée «Images d'illusion». L'illustration de la fig. 428 est en noir et blanc. (JPN)
429, 430 Affiches noir et blanc, au texte polychrome, pour une représentation de *Madame Butterfly* et un pot-pourri d'opérettes. (JPN)

428

429

430

165

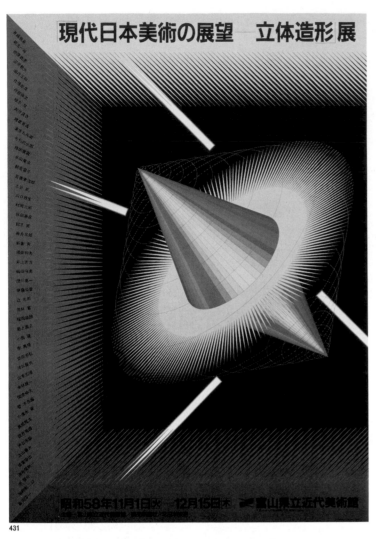

431

432

433

434

ARTIST / KÜNSTLER / ARTISTE:
431–435 Kazumasa Nagai

DESIGNER / GESTALTER / MAQUETTISTE:
431–435 Kazumasa Nagai

ART DIRECTOR / DIRECTEUR ARTISTIQUE:
431–435 Kazumasa Nagai

AGENCY / AGENTUR / AGENCE – STUDIO:
431–435 Nippon Design Center

431–434 Examples of exhibition posters issued by the Museum of Modern Art in Toyama. Fig. 431: Announcement of an exhibition; bright colours on black background. Fig. 432 is for an exhibition of works by a hundred artists to mark the centenary of the Toyama prefecture; background black and gold-toned with silver crescent, red, yellow and blue vertical stripes. Fig. 433: Announcement of a travelling exhibition; bright colours on black. Fig. 434: Poster for an exhibition of Georges Rouault prints; red cross, golden rays and lettering, multi-coloured ring on a black background. (JPN)
435 For a trade fair on shop fittings. (JPN)

431–434 Beispiele von Ausstellungsplakaten des Museum of Modern Art in Toyama. Abb. 431: Ankündigung einer Ausstellung; leuchtende Farben auf schwarzem Hintergrund. Abb. 432: für eine Ausstellung mit Bildern von hundert Malern zum hundertjährigen Bestehen der Präfektur Toyama; Hintergrund schwarz und goldfarben mit silbriger Sichel, Beschriftungsfelder rot, gelb und blau. Abb. 433: Ankündigung einer Wanderausstellung; leuchtende Farben auf Schwarz. Abb. 434: Für eine Georges-Rouault-Ausstellung; rotes Kreuz vor schwarzem Hintergrund. (JPN)
435 Für eine Ladenausstattungs-Messe. (JPN)

431–434 Exemples des affiches d'exposition créées pour le Musée d'art moderne de Toyama. Fig. 431: annonce d'exposition; couleurs vives sur fond noir. Fig. 432: pour une exposition réunissant les tableaux de cent peintres à l'occasion du centenaire de la préfecture de Toyama; fond noir, or, faucille argent, cases de texte rouge, jaune, bleu. Fig. 433: annonce d'une exposition itinérante; couleurs vives sur noir. Fig. 434: affiche pour une exposition Georges Rouault; croix rouge sur fond noir. (JPN)
435 Affiche réalisée pour une foire axée sur les équipements de magasins. (JPN)

435

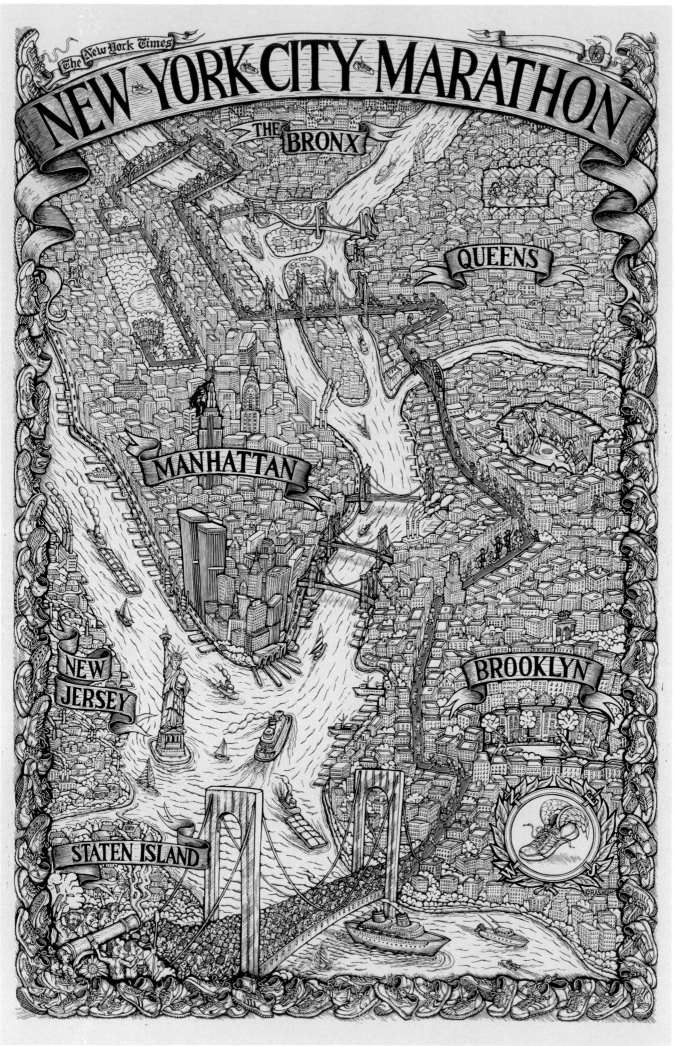

Cultural Events
Veranstaltungen
Evénements culturels

ARTIST / KÜNSTLER / ARTISTE:

436 James Grashow
437 Alan Fletcher
438 Frances Jetter
439 John J. Sorbie

DESIGNER / GESTALTER / MAQUETTISTE:

436 Emil Micha
437 Alan Fletcher
438 Frances Jetter
439 John J. Sorbie

ART DIRECTOR / DIRECTEUR ARTISTIQUE:

436 Emil Micha/Andrew Kner
437 Alan Fletcher
438 Frances Jetter
439 Peter Szollosi

AGENCY / AGENTUR / AGENCE – STUDIO:

437 Pentagram
439 Sorbie Roche

436 Poster issued by the *New York Times* with the plan of the New York marathon race shown. Mighty King Kong surveys the whole scene below from his vantage point on the Empire State Building. (USA)
437 Poster as invitation to a "Coming of Age" birthday party. (GBR)
438 Invitation to an exhibition of linocuts by the artist Frances Jetter. (USA)
439 Poster for the annual polo cup-final—a benefit match for the Denver Symphony Orchestra. (USA)

436 Von der *New York Times* herausgegebenes Plakat mit dem Plan des New Yorker Stadt-Marathon-laufes. King Kong schaut vom Empire State Building auf das Geschehen herab. (USA)
437 Plakat als Einladung zur Feier eines einundzwanzigsten Geburtstages. (GBR)
438 Einladung zu einer Einzelausstellung mit Linolschnitten der Künstlerin Frances Jetter. (USA)
439 Ankündigung eines Polo-Spiels zugunsten des Sinfonie-Orchesters der Stadt Denver. (USA)

436 Affiche publiée par le *New York Times*, montrant le parcours du marathon de New York. (On voit King Kong perché au sommet de l'Empire State Building contempler la scène.) (USA)
437 Affiche invitant à fêter un 21ᵉ anniversaire. (GBR)
438 Invitation à une exposition individuelle des linogravures de l'artiste Frances Jetter. (USA)
439 Annonce d'un match de polo en faveur de l'Orchestre symphonique de la ville de Denver. (USA)

437

438

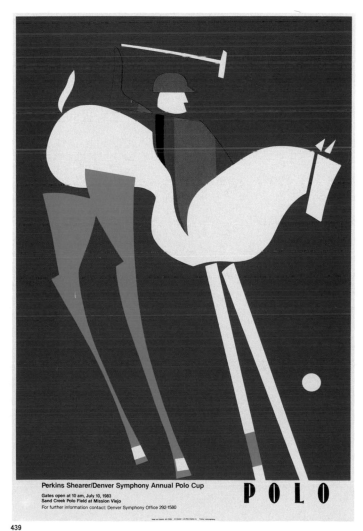

439

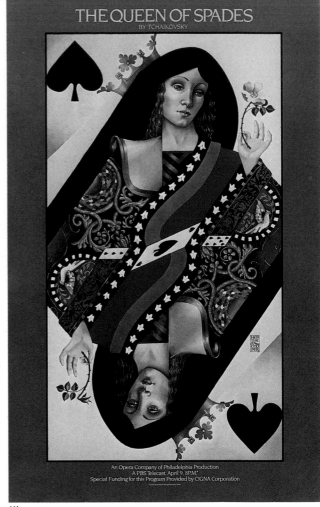

440

441

442

440 Small black-and-white poster for a charity entertainment. (USA)
441 Announcement of Tchaikovsky's opera *The Queen of Spades*. (USA)
442 "Dancing is beautiful", a poster for a dance festival in Comacchio, which included all types of dancing, from classical to Afro and aerobics. (ITA)
443 Complete poster and illustration in muted, sombre colours for a theatre in Canadian Stratford, which specializes in classical performances. (CAN)

440 Kleines Schwarzweiss-Plakat für eine Wohltätigkeitsveranstaltung. (USA)
441 Ankündigung einer Aufführung von Tschaikowskis Oper *Pique-Dame*. (USA)
442 Plakat für Tanz-Festwochen in der italienischen Stadt Comacchio, mit Ballett-aufführungen, Tanzkursen und Ballabenden. (ITA)
443 Vollständiges Plakat und Illustration in gedämpften, dunklen Farben für ein Theater in der kanadischen Stadt Stratford, das sich auf Klassiker-Aufführungen spezialisiert hat. (CAN)

440 Affichette noir et blanc pour une fête de bienfaisance. (USA)
441 Annonce d'une représentation de l'opéra *Pique-Dame* de Tchaïkovski. (USA)
442 Affiche pour le festival de danse de la ville italienne de Comacchio. Au programme: des spectacles de ballet, des cours de danse, des bals. (ITA)
443 Affiche complète et illustration aux couleurs sombres, atténuées, pour un théâtre de la ville canadienne de Stratford (Ontario) spécialisé dans les mises en scène des grands classiques. (CAN)

Cultural Events
Veranstaltungen
Evénements culturels

ARTIST / KÜNSTLER / ARTISTE:

440 Lanny Sommese
441 Heather Cooper
442 Ilde Ianigro
443, 444 John Martin

DESIGNER / GESTALTER:

440 Lanny Sommese
441 Ford, Byrne & Associates
442 Ilde Ianigro
443, 444 Gary Ludwig

ART DIRECTOR:

440 Lanny Sommese
442 Ilde Ianigro
443, 444 Gary Ludwig

AGENCY / AGENTUR / AGENCE:

440 Lanny Sommese Design
441 Ford, Byrne & Associates
442 Coopstudio
443, 444 Spencer/Francey Inc.

443

444

445

446

447

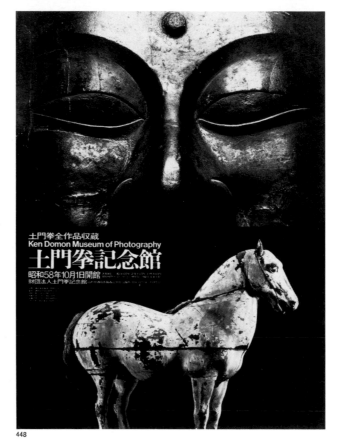

448

ARTIST / KÜNSTLER / ARTISTE:

445 Seymour Chwast
446 George Tscherny
447 Hans Erni
448 Ken Domon
449 Michael Mathias Prechtl

DESIGNER / GESTALTER:

445 Bartsch & Chariau
446 George Tscherny
447 Hans Erni
448 Yusaku Kamekura

ART DIRECTOR:

446 George Tscherny
447 Hans Erni
448 Yusaku Kamekura

AGENCY / AGENTUR / AGENCE:

446 George Tscherny, Inc.

445 Polychrome poster for the announcement of an exhibition of the American artist Seymour Chwast in the Bartsch and Chariau Gallery in Munich. (GER)
446 For the Goethe House, New York. Violet score, grey, orange lettering on black. (USA)
447 Large-size poster in full colour on the occasion of the twenty-fifth anniversary of the Radio Orchestra of Geneva. (SWI)
448 Poster with a colour photograph and polychrome lettering for the Ken Domon Museum of Photography. Ken Domon is one of Japan's most famous photographers. (JPN)
449 Poster for a Beethoven festival in Bonn, the composer's native town. (GER)

445 Mehrfarbiges Plakat für die Ankündigung einer Ausstellung des amerikanischen Künstlers Seymour Chwast in der Galerie Bartsch und Chariau, München. (GER)
446 «Deutschland im 19. Jahrhundert.» Plakat für das Goethe-Haus, New York. (USA)
447 Grossformatiges Plakat in Farbe zum fünfundzwanzigjährigen Bestehen des Genfer Radio-Orchesters. (SWI)
448 Plakat mit Farbaufnahmen und farbiger Beschriftung für das Ken-Domon-Museum für Photographie. Ken Domon ist einer der berühmtesten Photographen Japans. (JPN)
449 Plakat für ein Beethoven-Fest in der Geburtsstadt des Komponisten. (GER)

445 Affiche polychrome annonçant une exposition de l'œuvre de l'artiste américain Seymour Chwast à la galerie Bartsch & Chariau de Munich. (GER)
446 «L'Allemagne au XIXe siècle.» Affiche pour le Goethe-Haus de New York. (USA)
447 Affiche au grand format, en couleur, créée à l'occasion du 25e anniversaire de l'orchestre de la radio de Genève. (SWI)
448 Affiche illustrée de photos couleur pour le Musée de la Photo Ken Domon (ce nom appartient à l'un des photographes les plus célèbres du Japon). Textes couleur. (JPN)
449 Affiche pour le festival de Beethoven organisé à Bonn. (GER)

449

450–454 Illustration and posters shown complete from a series for college football matches. The posters are sponsored by the producers of *Budweiser* beers. The mascot of each university team is portrayed, and the colours of the particular university are incorporated in the slogan. The fur of the tiger shades from blue to violet, its eyes are bright green; the eagle is in blue shading to blue-black, with orange eyes; the rattlesnake has blazing red eyes, grey skin and a pale violet gullet; the fur of the cougar (puma) shades from brown to steel blue, the jaws are red and the eyes green. (USA)

450–454 Illustration und vollständige Plakate aus einer Serie für die Bekanntgabe der Spieltermine für die Football-Teams verschiedener Universitäten. Finanziert wurden die Plakate von dem Hersteller des *Budweiser*-Biers. Es werden jeweils die Maskottchen der Mannschaften und die Universitätsfarben gezeigt. Das Fell des Tigers ist mit leuchtenden Blau- und Violettönen durchsetzt; der Adler ist blau bis schwarzblau; die Klapperschlange hat leuchtendrote Augen, grüngraue Haut und einen violetten Schlund; das Fell des Pumas verläuft von Braun in aggressives Blau. (USA)

450–454 Illustration et affiches complètes dans une série d'affiches-programmes pour la saison de football de diverses universités américaines, offertes par la brasserie *Budweiser*. On y trouve la mascotte de chaque équipe et les couleurs de l'université en question. Le pelage du tigre est parsemé de taches de couleur violettes et bleues; l'aigle est bleu bleu noir; le serpent à sonnette a les yeux rouge vif, la peau gris vert, la gueule violette; le pelage du puma offre tout un éventail de couleurs allant du brun à des teintes bleues agressives; la gueule est rouge. (USA)

450

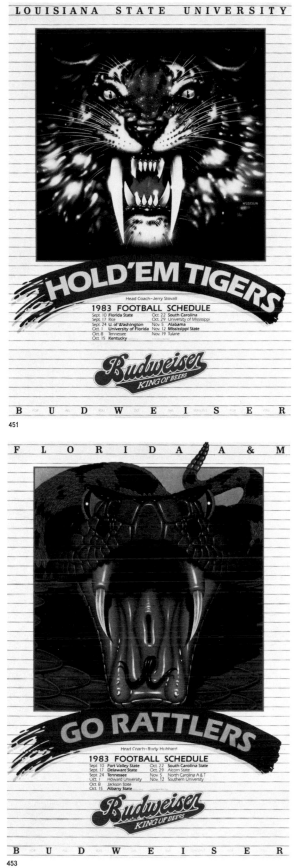

451

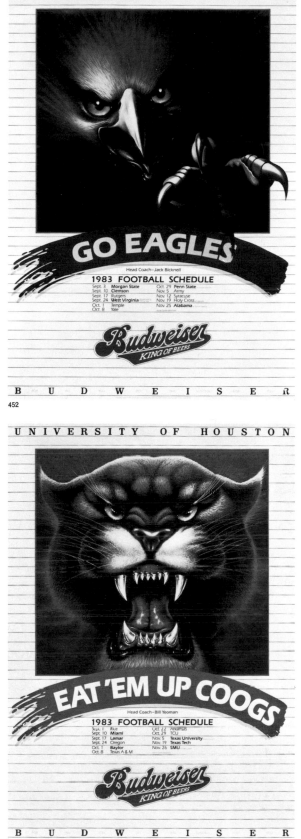

452

453

454

ARTIST / KÜNSTLER / ARTISTE:

450 Robert Giusti
451 Wayne McLoughlin
452, 454 Lonnie Busch
453 Marvin Mattelson

DESIGNER / GESTALTER / MAQUETTISTE:

450–454 Bill Kumke

ART DIRECTOR / DIRECTEUR ARTISTIQUE:

450–454 David Bartels

AGENCY / AGENTUR / AGENCE – STUDIO:

450–454 Bartels & Co.

3

Social Posters
Soziale Plakate
Affiches sociales

Consumer Posters
Dekorative Plakate
Affiches décoratives

Educative Posters
Erzieherische Plakate
Affiches éducatives

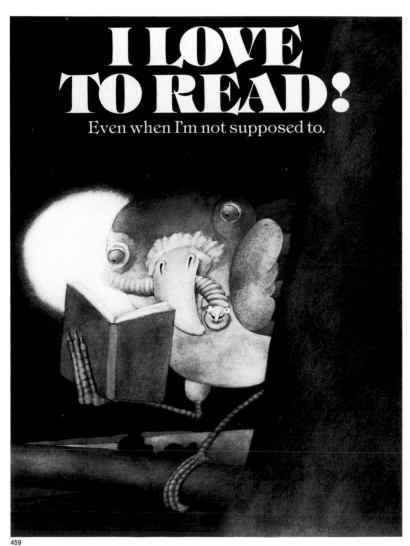

455–457 From a series of screen-print posters for a university, issued as a reminder to students of the registration deadline. The humorous text plays on the tree's characteristics. (USA)
458, 459 Multi-coloured posters from a series encouraging children to read. (USA)
460 Poster issued by the American Library Association for the promotion of public libraries. (USA)
461 Poster to aid an animal welfare rescue fund. (USA)

455–457 Aus einer Serie von Siebdruck-Plakaten für eine Universität. Mit Wortspielen, die mit den Eigenschaften der Bäume zusammenhängen, wird an den Einschreibetermin erinnert. (USA)
458, 459 «Ich hasse es zu lesen, weil es mich freundlich stimmt», «Ich liebe es zu lesen, auch wenn ich eigentlich nicht sollte». Mehrfarbige Plakate aus einer Reihe für Kinder. (USA)
460 «Wissen ist wahre Macht.» Plakat für die Förderung öffentlicher Bibliotheken. (USA)
461 «Grosse und kleine Kreaturen.» Plakat zugunsten eines Rettungsdienstes für Tiere. (USA)

455–457 Exemples d'affiches sérigraphiques publiées dans une série universitaire où l'on rappelle aux étudiants le délai d'inscription en jouant sur les qualités des arbres illustrés. (USA)
458, 459 «Je déteste la lecture, parce qu'elle me rend aimable», «J'aime la lecture même quand ce n'est pas le moment». Affiches polychromes dans une série pédagogique pour les enfants. (USA)
460 «La vraie puissance, c'est le savoir.» Affiche en faveur des bibliothèques publiques. (USA)
461 «Grandes et petites créatures.» Affiche pour un service de S.O.S. Animaux. (USA)

ARTIST / KÜNSTLER / ARTISTE:

455–457 McRay Magleby
458, 459 Etienne Delessert
460, 461 Milton Glaser

DESIGNER / GESTALTER / MAQUETTISTE:

455–457 McRay Magleby
458, 459 Rita Marshall
460, 461 Milton Glaser

ART DIRECTOR / DIRECTEUR ARTISTIQUE:

455–457 McRay Magleby
458, 459 Rita Marshall
460, 461 Milton Glaser

AGENCY / AGENTUR / AGENCE – STUDIO:

455–457 Graphic Communications
460, 461 Milton Glaser, Inc.

460

461

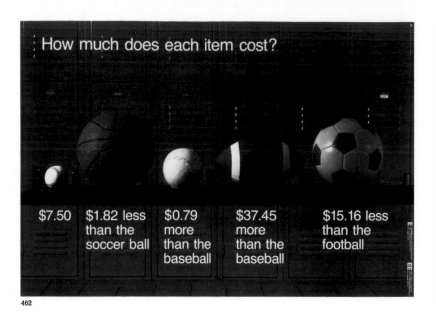

462

463

Education
Ausbildung
Education

AGENCY / AGENTUR / AGENCE – STUDIO:

462, 463 Scott, Foresman & Co.
464 Joe Scorsone Visual Design
465 April Greiman
466–468 Graphic Communications
469 Graphiti
470, 471 Arnold Schwartzman Productions Inc.

ARTIST / KÜNSTLER / ARTISTE:

462, 463 Bobbye Cochran
464 Joe Scorsone
465 April Greiman
466–468 McRay Magleby
469 Andrea Rauch
470, 471 Arnold Schwartzman

DESIGNER / GESTALTER / MAQUETTISTE:

462, 463 Jack Weiss Assoc.
464 Joe Scorsone
465 April Greiman
466–468 McRay Magleby
469 Andrea Rauch
470, 471 Arnold Schwartzman

ART DIRECTOR / DIRECTEUR ARTISTIQUE:

462, 463 Hal Kearney/John Mayahara
464 Joe Scorsone
465 April Greiman
466–468 McRay Magleby
469 Andrea Rauch
470, 471 Arnold Schwartzman

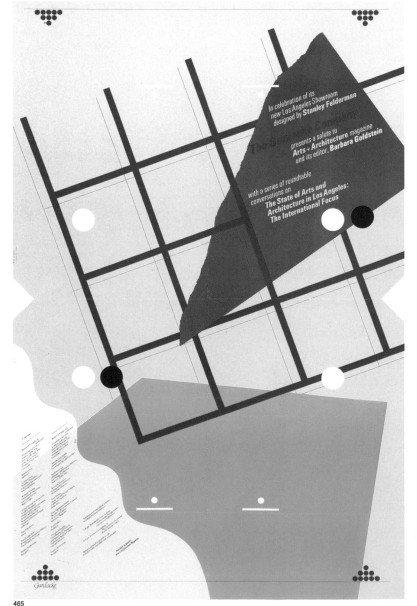

464

465

466

467

468

469

470

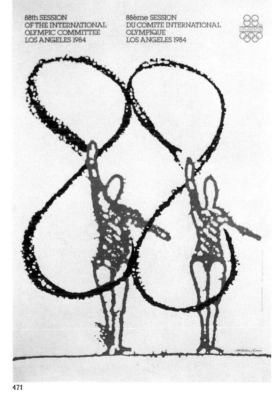

471

462, 463 Front and back of a multi-coloured poster which is intended for use in arithmetic classes in elementary schools. (USA)
464 Announcement of a lecture by the English artist Ralph Steadman at an art school. Red, blue and green on white. (USA)
465 Perforated poster for the announcement of a discussion on art and architecture in Los Angeles. (USA)
466–468 Screen-print posters for a university, humorously reminding students of the registration deadline. (USA)
469 For the International School of Theatre Anthropology, held in the Etruscan town of Volterra in Tuscany. Strong colours. (ITA)
470 Announcement of a lecture on the planned design for the Olympic "look" in Los Angeles. (USA)
471 Poster for the 88th meeting of the International Olympic Committee. The colours are grey and magenta. (USA)

462, 463 Vorder- und Rückseite eines mehrfarbigen Plakates, das für den Rechenunterricht in Grundschulen bestimmt ist. (USA)
464 Ankündigung eines Vortrags des Künstlers Ralph Steadman an einer Kunstschule. Rot, Blau und Grün auf Weiss. (USA)
465 Perforiertes Plakat für die Ankündigung einer Diskussion über Kunst und Architektur in Los Angeles. (USA)
466–468 Siebdruck-Plakate für eine Universität, die anhand von Wortspielen an den Einschreibetermin erinnert. (USA)
469 Plakat einer internationalen Schule für Theater-Anthropologie. Illustration in kräftigen Farben. (ITA)
470 Ankündigung einer Vorlesung über das geplante Design (hier «Look») für die Olympiade in Los Angeles. (USA)
471 Plakat in Grau und Magenta für die 88ste Sitzung des Internationalen Olympischen Komitees. (USA)

462, 463 Recto et verso d'une affiche polychrome destinée à l'enseignement du calcul à l'école primaire. (USA)
464 Annonce d'une conférence de l'artiste Ralph Steadman dans une école d'art. Rouge, bleu et vert sur blanc. (USA)
465 Affiche perforée annonçant un débat d'art et d'architecture à Los Angeles. (USA)
466–468 Affiches sérigraphiques pour une université. Les jeux de mots qui y figurent ont trait au délai d'inscription. (USA)
469 Affiche d'une école internationale d'anthropologie théâtrale. Illustration aux couleurs vives. (ITA)
470 Annonce d'une conférence sur le design (appelé ici «look») des Jeux Olympiques de Los Angeles. (USA)
471 Affiche gris et magenta pour la 88e session du Comité Olympique International. (USA)

472

How many dogs
will balance the pony?

472–479 Multi-coloured posters printed on both sides from a 36-part series intended for teaching in elementary classes. In Fig. 472: a circus balancing act to demonstrate equalizing weights; Fig. 473: graphics to teach addition; Fig. 474: for decimals and fractions; Fig. 475 helps to calculate volume and surface area; Fig. 476: a teaching tool for the little ones; Fig. 477 illustrates a simple method of measuring; Fig. 478 is for first-grade pupils and asks them to complete the sequence with the correct item; Fig. 479 is also with the very young pupil in mind and centres on the figure two, placing fruit in the right pairs. (USA)

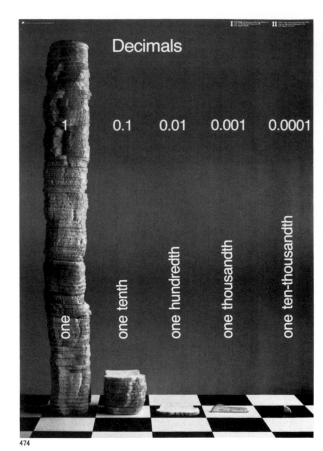

Decimals

1	0.1	0.01	0.001	0.0001
one	one tenth	one hundredth	one thousandth	one ten-thousandth

474

27 Addition **18**

$\begin{array}{r} 1\\ 27\\ +18\\ \hline 45 \end{array}$

45

473

Find the volume of the figure. Find its surface area. How many cubes have some paint on only 1 face? on only 2 faces? on only 3 faces? on only 4 faces?

All cubes are the same size.
Only the outside of the figure is painted.

1 foot

475

182

472–479 Vorder- und Rückseiten von mehrfarbigen Plakaten aus einer 36teiligen Serie für den Grundschulunterricht. In Abb. 472 wird nach der Anzahl der Hunde gefragt, die nötig sind, um das Gewicht des Ponys auszugleichen, Abb. 473 veranschaulicht eine Addition. Abb. 474 behandelt die Dezimalrechnung, Abb. 475 Volumen und Oberfläche. Abb. 476 wendet sich mit der Frage nach dem Aufenthaltsort der Hunde an die Kleinsten, Abb. 477 fragt nach der Länge der Gegenstände. Abb. 478 und 479 sind für den Kindergarten bestimmt, hier wird nach der Fortsetzung der Reihen gefragt und die Zahl Zwei veranschaulicht. (USA)

472–479 Rectos et versos d'affiches polychromes dans une série de 36 réalisée pour les classes primaires. Fig. 472: «Combien de chiens faut-il pour équilibrer le poids du poney?» Fig. 473: illustration d'une addition. Fig. 474: introduction au calcul des décimales. Fig. 475: «Trouvez le volume de la figure. Trouvez sa superficie.» Fig. 476: «Où est chaque chien?» Exercice de grammaire pour les tout-petits. La fig. 477 interroge l'enfant sur la longueur de divers objects. Les fig. 478 et 479 sont destinées aux jardins d'enfants: «Qu'est-ce qui vient après?» examine le problème des séries (fig. 478), et l'on visualise (fig. 479) le nombre deux. (USA)

476

478

477

479

ARTIST / KÜNSTLER / ARTISTE:

472, 473 John Craig
474, 475 Elwood Smith
476, 477 Linda Rothberg
478, 479 Michael Goss

DESIGNER / GESTALTER:

472, 473 George Roth
474, 475 Hayward Blake & Co.
476–479 John Mayahara

ART DIRECTOR:

472–479 Hal Kearney/John Mayahara

AGENCY / AGENTUR / AGENCE:

472–479 Scott, Foresman & Co.

Educative Posters
Erzieherische Plakate
Affiches éducatives

核兵器廃絶

AGAINST THE NUCLEAR ARMS

480

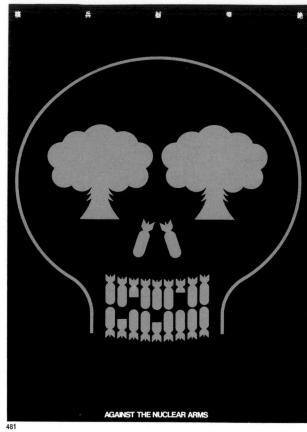

核　　兵　　器　　廃　　絶

AGAINST THE NUCLEAR ARMS

481

帰りついた時、親父はまだ少しあったかかった。

二川謙吾さんの懐中時計

当時59才の二川さんは、観音橋（爆心から1600m）で被爆。
建物疎開の作業現場に向かう途中だった。このスイス製懐中時計は、長男一夫さんが贈ったもの。
8月22日、その一夫さんが「除隊して帰郷、家にたどりつく直前に、二川さんは息をひきとった。
8時15分…被爆時刻をさしたまま二度と動かない懐中時計は、この悲劇を、人々の涙を、永遠に忘れることはない。

Kengo Futagawa's pocket watch.
The blast occurred when he was on the Kannon Bridge (1600 meters from the hypocenter).
The time was 8:15 when the pocket watch, which had been presented to
him as a gift from his eldest son, Kazuo, stopped. Kazuo was just returning home from the army
and was just in front of the house when his father died.

Father's watch never moved again.

HIROSHIMA 1945

484

ARTIST / KÜNSTLER / ARTISTE:

480, 481 Hirokatsu Hijikata
482 Kiyoshi Awazu
483 Kaj Otto Thomassen
484 Koichi Shimoda/Hiromi Tsuchida
485, 486 Stephan Bundi

DESIGNER / GESTALTER / MAQUETTISTE:

482 Kiyoshi Awazu
483 Kaj Otto Thomassen
484 Jutaro Itoh/Akihiro Hirahara
485, 486 Stephan Bundi

ART DIRECTOR / DIRECTEUR ARTISTIQUE:

480, 481 Hirokatsu Hijikata
482 Kiyoshi Awazu
483 Kaj Otto Thomassen
484 Jutaro Itoh
485, 486 Stephan Bundi

AGENCY / AGENTUR / AGENCE:

483 Kaj Otto Grafisk Design
484 Itoh Design Inc.
485, 486 Atelier Bundi

482

483

480, 481 An artist's appeal for nuclear disarmament. Fig. 480: grey and black on silver; Fig. 481: grey on glossy black ground. (JPN)
482 A poster campaign for peace which should remind people of the catastrophe of Hiroshima in 1945. (JPN)
483 A poster clearly illustrating the aims of Amnesty International. (DEN)
484 An award-winning poster, issued for the Hiroshima Peace Memorial Museum. Text and illustrations refer to the fate of some victims. (JPN)
485 Official poster for the largest peace manifestation to date in Switzerland. Green leaves, white dove, blue background. (SWI)
486 For Amnesty International "Freedom of Conscience—Civil Defence", offering an alternative in Switzerland to compulsory military service. (SWI)

480, 481 Appell eines Künstlers gegen die nukleare Rüstung. Abb. 480: Grau und Schwarz auf Silber, Abb. 481: Grau auf glänzendem Schwarz. (JPN)
482 Aus einer 1983 ins Leben gerufenen Friedenskampagne mit Plakaten, die an die Katastrophe von Hiroshima gemahnen sollen. (JPN)
483 Für die Gefangenenhilfsorganisation Amnesty International. (DEN)
484 Prämiertes Plakat für das Hiroshima Peace Memorial Museum. Anhand der Gegenstände wird die Geschichte einiger Opfer erzählt. (JPN)
485 Offizielles Plakat für die bisher grösste Friedenskundgebung in der Schweiz. Grüne Blätter, weisse Taube, blauer Hintergrund. (SWI)
486 Beitrag von Amnesty International zur Schweizer Zivildienst-Initiative, bei der es um eine Alternative zur allgemeinen Wehrpflicht geht. (SWI)

480, 481 Affiches contre les armements nucléaires. Fig 480: gris, noir sur argent, fig. 481: gris sur noir brillant. (JPN)
482 Affiche créée dans le cadre d'une campagne pour la paix démarrée en 1983 et qui veut maintenir vivace le souvenir des horreurs d'Hiroshima. (JPN)
483 Pour Amnesty International, organisation humanitaire en faveur des prisonniers. (DEN)
484 Affiche primée pour le Peace Memorial Museum d'Hiroshima. «La montre de papa n'a plus jamais marché»: en s'inspirant de tels objets, on y retrace l'histoire des victimes. (JPN)
485 Affiche officielle de la plus importante manifestation suisse en faveur de la paix à ce jour. Feuilles vertes, colombe blanche, fond bleu. (SWI)
486 Contribution d'Amnesty International à une initiative suisse pour le service civil censé se substituer au service militaire pour les objecteurs de conscience. (SWI)

485

486

185

487

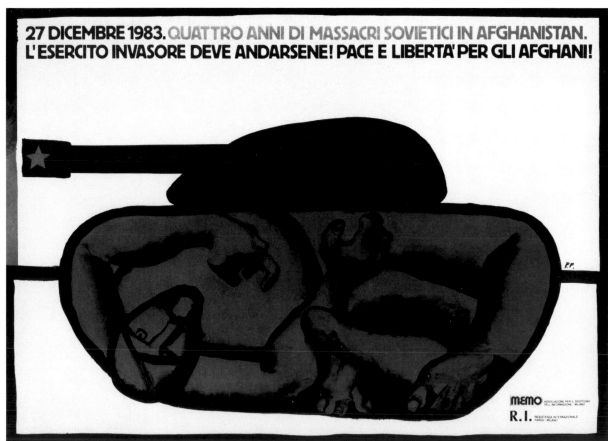

27 DICEMBRE 1983. QUATTRO ANNI DI MASSACRI SOVIETICI IN AFGHANISTAN. L'ESERCITO INVASORE DEVE ANDARSENE! PACE E LIBERTA' PER GLI AFGHANI!

488

ARTIST / KÜNSTLER / ARTISTE:

488 Ferenc Pintér
489 Klaus Staeck
490 Philippe Deltour

DESIGNER / GESTALTER / MAQUETTISTE:

491–493 Fred Bauer

ART DIRECTOR:

488 Ferenc Pintér
489 Klaus Staeck

AGENCY / AGENTUR / AGENCE:

490 Bitume
491–493 G. Tscharner AG

489

490

491

492

493

487 Poster as reminder of the insurrection in the Jewish ghetto of Warsaw forty years ago, in 1943. (POL)
488 Accusation of the soviet invasion of Afghanistan: "Four years soviet massacre in Afghanistan." Human forms red, tank khaki. (ITA)
489 "Chile fights, Nicaragua lives." Political commentary on the situation in Central and South America. Black map, olive green gun, lettering in blue and red, on white stock. (GER)
490 For the tenth anniversary of the uprising in Chile. A poster in grey tones on yellow background. (BEL)
491–493 Posters to encourage donations to a Swiss charity organization sending aid to under-developed countries. (SWI)

487 Plakat zum Gedenken an den Aufstand im jüdischen Ghetto von Warschau vor vierzig Jahren, im Jahre 1943. (POL)
488 Anklage gegen die sowjetische Besetzung Afghanistans: «Vier Jahre sowjetisches Massaker in Afghanistan.» Menschlicher Körper rot, Panzeroberteil khakifarben. (ITA)
489 Politischer Kommentar zur Lage in Mittel- und Südamerika. Schwarz und helles Olivgrün, Schrift blau und rot. (GER)
490 Zum zehnten Jahrestag des Staatsstreiches in Chile veröffentlichtes Plakat. Grautöne auf gelbem Hintergrund. (BEL)
491–493 Anlässlich einer nationalen Sammlung vom Schweizer Aufbauwerk für Entwicklungsländer veröffentlichte Plakate. (SWI)

487 Affiche rappelant la révolte du ghetto juif de Varsovie il y a quarante ans, en 1943. (POL)
488 Plaidoyer contre l'occupation soviétique en Afghanistan: «Quatre années de massacres soviétiques en Afghanistan.» Corps humain rouge; le haut du char apparaît en kaki. (ITA)
489 Commentaire politique de la situation en Amérique latine. Noir, olive clair, texte bleu et rouge. (GER)
490 Affiche publiée à l'occasion du 10e anniversaire du coup d'Etat au Chili. Divers gris sur fond jaune. (BEL)
491–493 Affiches pour la collecte nationale de l'œuvre suisse en faveur de l'aide technique aux pays sous-développés. (SWI)

494

495

498

ARTIST / KÜNSTLER / ARTISTE:

494 Roland Junker
495 Piotr Mlodozeniec
496 Inge Pape
497 Roman Cieslewicz
498 Kamen Popov
499 Klaus Staeck
500 Paul Davis

DESIGNER / GESTALTER:

494 Roland Junker
496 Inge Pape
497 Roman Cieslewicz
500 Paul Davis

ART DIRECTOR:

499 Klaus Staeck
500 Paul Davis

AGENCY / AGENTUR / AGENCE:

494 J. G. & Partner

494 For a TV discussion about journalistic sensationalism. Pencil drawing. (GER)
495 For the Polish church: 600 years of sacred pictures in Poland. (POL)
496 For a film and exhibition about Luther to mark the 500th birthday of the reformer. (GER)
497 Poster for the town of Montreuil on the occasion of the Year of the Handicapped. (FRA)
498 Poster published in Bulgaria in memory of the Russian revolution. (BUL)
499 "Europe is more than the wine glut." Polychrome poster on European politics. (GER)
500 Poster calling for participants in the march in New York to demand permission for departure for soviet Jews. Clothes in dark blue and red; blue and yellow ground. (USA)

494 Für eine TV-Diskussion über den Sensationsjournalismus. Bleistiftzeichnung. (GER)
495 Für die polnische Kirche: 600 Jahre Heiligenbilder in Polen. (POL)
496 Ankündigung einer Veranstaltung für Erwachsenenbildung im Lutherjahr. (GER)
497 Von der Stadt Montreuil im Jahr der Behinderten veröffentlichtes Plakat. (FRA)
498 Zum Gedenken an die russische Revolution herausgegebenes Plakat. (BUL)
499 Mehrfarbiges Plakat als Kommentar zur europäischen Politik. (GER)
500 Aufruf zu einem Protestmarsch in New York, mit dem die Ausreisebewilligung für sowjetische Juden gefordert wird. Kleidung dunkelblau und -rot, Hintergrund blau und gelb. (USA)

494 Pour un débat télévisé sur le journalisme à sensations. Dessin au crayon. (GER)
495 Pour l'Eglise polonaise: 600 ans de vénération hagiographique en Pologne. (POL)
496 Annonce d'une manifestation à l'occasion des célébrations Luther en 1983. (GER)
497 Affiche publiée par la ville de Montreuil pour l'Année des handicapés. (FRA)
498 Affiche publiée en souvenir de la révolution d'octobre russe. (BUL)
499 Affiche polychrome critiquant les mesquineries de la politique européenne. (GER)
500 Appel à une manifestation de protestation à New York, réclamant pour les juifs d'U. R. S. S. la liberté d'émigrer. Vêtements bleu et rouge foncés, fond bleu, jaune. (USA)

496

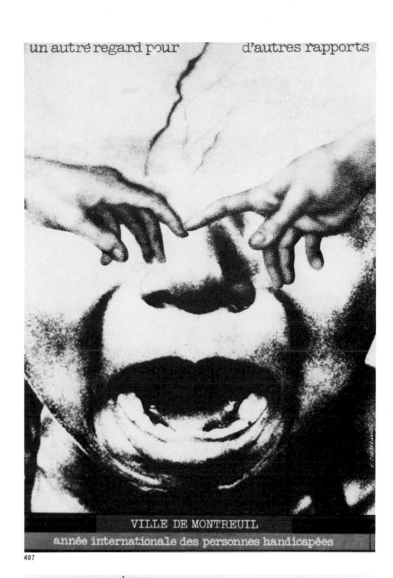

497

499

500

189

501

502

501 To announce the seventh congress of the National Cooperative of Agricultural Workers in Italy; a brilliant red apple with a green leaf. (ITA)
502 Poster issued on behalf of the Association for the Handicapped, calling for information on the integration of the handicapped. (ITA)
503 Polychrome poster for a convention by the Tourist Association in Fano concerning the local tourist amenities on offer in summer and in winter. (ITA)
504 Blue, red and yellow geometric forms on white for a poster announcing a congress of production- and work-cooperatives aimed at development in the rural areas of Italy. (ITA)
505 A plea for car-drivers to take their cars to a free-of-charge check-up for noise abatement. Beige face on a wine-red background. (ITA)
506 Polychrome screen-print poster directed at "hotrod" owners and the additional noise their engines make. (ITA)
507 For a series of natural science lectures. Green, yellow and blue. (ITA)

501 Für die Ankündigung des 7. Kongresses der nationalen landwirtschaftlichen Kooperative Italiens. Leuchtendroter Apfel mit grünem Blatt. (ITA)
502 Vom Verband der Behinderten herausgegebenes Schwarzweiss-Plakat, das zur Information über die Probleme der Behinderten aufruft. (ITA)
503 Plakat für eine Zusammenkunft des Fremdenverkehrsverbandes von Fano, deren Thema das lokale Tourismusangebot im Sommer und Winter ist. (ITA)
504 Für einen Regionalkongress der Kooperativen für Produktion und Arbeit in Ferrara. Blau, rot und gelb auf weissem Grund. (ITA)
505 An Autofahrer gerichteter Aufruf, ihre Autos zu einer unentgeltlichen Geräuschkontrolle zu bringen. Gesicht beige, Hintergrund weinrot. (ITA)
506 Mehrfarbiges Siebdruckplakat, das sich gegen die erhöhte Geräuschverursachung durch frisierte Mofas richtet. (ITA)
507 Für eine von der Stadt Pesaro veranstaltete Reihe von öffentlichen Vorträgen über die Tierwelt. Grün mit Gelb und Blau. (ITA)

504

505

503

ARTIST / KÜNSTLER / ARTISTE:

501, 504 Fabio Adranno
503 Massimo Dolcini/Jole Bortoli
505–507 Massimo Dolcini

DESIGNER / GESTALTER / MAQUETTISTE:

501 Ilde Ianigro
502 Gianni Bortolotti
503 Massimo Dolcini/Jole Bortoli
504 Marisa Rizzato
505–507 Massimo Dolcini

ART DIRECTOR / DIRECTEUR ARTISTIQUE:

501 Fabio Adranno/Marisa Rizzato
502 Maria Santi
503, 505–507 Massimo Dolcini
504 Fabio Adranno

AGENCY / AGENTUR / AGENCE – STUDIO:

501, 504 Coopstudio
502 Studio Bortolotti
503, 505–507 Fuorischema

501 Affiche annonçant le septième Congrès de la coopérative agricole nationale d'Italie. Pomme rouge vif, feuille verte. (ITA)
502 Affiche noir et blanc de l'Association des handicapés réclamant une plus
large information sur l'intégration sociale des handicapés. (ITA)
503 Affiche pour une réunion du syndicat d'initiative de Fano sur le sujet de
l'offre touristique de cette ville pour l'été et l'hiver. (ITA)
504 Pour un congrès régional des coopératives de production et de travail à
Ferrare. Bleu, rouge et jaune sur fond blanc. (ITA)
505 Appel aux automobilistes pour un contrôle antibruit gratuit de leur
voiture. Visage beige, fond bordeaux. (ITA)
506 Affiche sérigraphique polychrome protestant contre le niveau de bruit
atteint par les vélomoteurs maquillés. (ITA)
507 Pour une série de conférences publiques sur le monde animal organisées
par la municipalité de Pesaro. Vert, plus jaune et bleu. (ITA)

506

507

The 55 mph Alternative

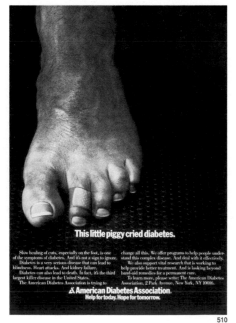

508

Educative Posters
Erzieherische Plakate
Affiches éducatives

ARTIST / KÜNSTLER / ARTISTE:
508 Jim Rohman
509, 511 James McLoughlin
510 Gary Hanlon
512 Stefan Böhle

DESIGNER / GESTALTER:
508 Dan Weeks
509–511 Dave Martin
512 Stefan Böhle

ART DIRECTOR:
508 Dan Weeks
509–511 Dave Martin
512 Stefan Böhle

AGENCY / AGENTUR / AGENCE:
508 Dan Weeks Design
509–511 Doyle Dane
          Bernbach, Inc.
512 Timmermann

508 "The 55 mph Alternative"—satirical "sick" humour in text and colour photograph to prevent fast driving. (USA)
509–511 Small-size posters in black and white for a campaign by the American Diabetes Association concerning the symptoms and causes of this disease. Fig. 509: susceptibility of overweight people; Fig. 510: slow-to-heal wounds as a symptom; Fig. 511: blurred vision is one of the symptoms of diabetes. (USA)
512 "One glass too many." A striking warning for drivers published by the League Against Alcohol in Traffic. (GER)

508 Ironische Verpackung einer ernsthaften Warnung vor zu schnellem Fahren. Plakat mit Farbaufnahme. (USA)
509–511 Kleinformatige Plakate in Schwarzweiss aus einer Kampagne der amerikanischen Diabetiker-Vereinigung, die auf die Symptome und Ursachen dieser Krankheit aufmerksam macht. Abb. 509: Anfälligkeit übergewichtiger Menschen; Abb. 510: schlecht heilende Wunden als Symptom; Abb. 511: gestörte Sehkraft als mögliches Krankheitszeichen. (USA)
512 An Autofahrer gerichtete eindrucksvolle Warnung vor dem Konsum von Alkohol. (GER)

508 Avertissement drastique aux chauffards: «l'alternative aux 90 km/h». Affiche illustrée d'une photo couleur. (USA)
509–511 Affichettes noir et blanc illustrant une campagne de l'Association des diabétiques américains sur les symptômes et les causes de cette maladie. Fig. 509: les risques qu'encourent les obèses; fig. 510: le symptôme des blessures qui ne se referment pas; fig. 511: le symptôme des troubles de la vue. (USA)
512 Mise en garde spectaculaire contre les méfaits de l'alcool au volant. (GER)

509

510

511

Das Glas zuviel

BUND
GEGEN ALKOHOL
IM STRASSENVERKEHR
E.V.

513

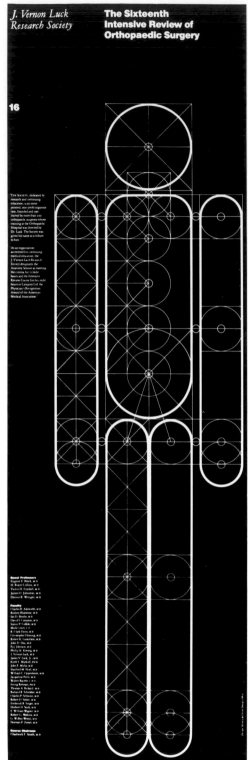

514

515

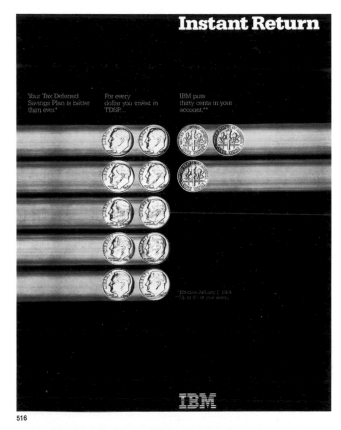

516

513 From a series of posters published annually for "World Savings Day". (GER)
514 To announce a congress on orthopaedic surgery is the purpose of this poster. (USA)
515 Screen-print poster for the "home away from home" accommodation offered at the Toledo area hospitals for parents of hospitalized children. House in pink with yellow windows, red chimney and door, on bright blue background. (USA)
516, 517 IBM's house posters informing the staff about savings programmes. (USA)
518 Poster for Goodwill Industries, a non profit-making social services organization. (USA)

513 Aus einer Serie von Plakaten, die jährlich zum Weltspartag veröffentlicht werden. (GER)
514 Orthopädische Chirurgie ist das Thema des hier angekündigten Kongresses. (USA)
515 Siebdruckplakat für «das Haus, das die Liebe baute». Es handelt sich um eine Unterkunftsmöglichkeit für Eltern von hospitalisierten Kindern. Haus in Rosa mit gelben Fenstern, roter Tür und rotem Schornstein, auf leuchtendblauem Grund. (USA)
516, 517 Interne Plakate der IBM, die das Personal über Sparprogramme informieren. (USA)
518 «Goodwill öffnet Türen.» Plakat für eine wohltätige Organisation. (USA)

513 Exemple des affiches publiées chaque année pour la Journée mondiale de l'épargne. (GER)
514 Le congrès annoncé ici traite de la chirurgie orthopédique. (USA)
515 Affiche sérigraphique pour «la maison que l'amour édifia». Il s'agit de logements pour les parents d'enfants hospitalisés. Maison rose aux fenêtres jaunes, porte et cheminée rouges, sur fond bleu lumineux. (USA)
516, 517 Affiches IBM informant le personnel des moyens propres à réaliser des économies. (USA)
518 «La bonne volonté ouvre les portes.» Affiche pour une organisation de bienfaisance. (USA)

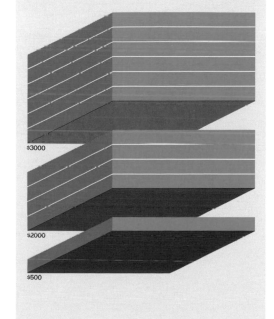

517

518

School of Visual Arts

TO BE GOOD IS NOT ENOUGH WHEN YOU DREAM OF BEING GREAT.

209 EAST 23 STREET, NEW YORK, N.Y. 10010. (212) 683-0600. DEGREE AND NON-DEGREE PROGRAMS, EVENINGS AND WEEKENDS. FINE ARTS (DRAWING, PAINTING, SCULPTURE, PRINTMAKING), MEDIA ARTS (ART DIRECTION, COPYWRITING, GRAPHIC DESIGN, COMPUTER GRAPHICS, ILLUSTRATION, GRAPHIC PRODUCTION, FASHION), ADVERTISING BUSINESS, VIDEO TAPE, FILM, PHOTOGRAPHY, CRAFTS (JEWELRY, GLASS), ART HISTORY, HUMANITIES AND SCIENCES, COMMUNICATION ARTS (PUBLIC RELATIONS, JOURNALISM), ART THERAPY, AND ART EDUCATION.

519

ARTIST / KÜNSTLER / ARTISTE:

519 James McMullan
520 Kam Mak
521 Richard Sierra
522 Tony Palladino
523 Philip Hays

DESIGNER / GESTALTER / MAQUETTISTE:

519 Bill Kobasz
520, 521 Bill Kobasz/Kathi Rota
522 Tony Palladino

ART DIRECTOR / DIRECTEUR ARTISTIQUE:

519 Silas H. Rhodes
520, 521 Bill Kobasz/Richard Wilde
522 Tony Palladino

AGENCY / AGENTUR / AGENCE – STUDIO:

519–523 School of Visual Arts Press

519, 522, 523 Posters for the New York School of Visual Arts. Fig. 519 and 522 both bear an encouraging slogan and information on the school's programme. (USA)
520, 521 Small-size posters also for the School of Visual Arts, announcing an exhibition of students' work devoted to the problem of finding accommodation in New York City. Fig. 520: door in pale yellow, locks grey and golden-yellow. Fig. 521: black and white. (USA)

519, 522, 523 Plakate für die New Yorker Kunstschule School of Visual Arts. Abb. 519: «Es reicht nicht, gut zu sein, wenn man davon träumt, grossartig zu sein.» Abb. 522: «Es ist nicht das Licht am Ende des Tunnels, es ist das Licht im Inneren.» (USA)
520, 521 Weitere Plakate für die School of Visual Arts, hier für die Ankündigung einer Ausstellung von Schülerarbeiten zum Thema der Wohnungsprobleme in New York («Wohnungen zu vermieten»). (USA)

519, 522, 523 Exemples d'affiches pour la célèbre école d'art: School of Visual Arts de New York. Fig. 519: «Etre bon ne saurait suffire à qui rêve de grandeur»; fig. 522: «Ce n'est pas la lumière au bout du tunnel, c'est la lumière intérieure.» (USA)
520, 521 Autres affiches de la School of Visual Arts. On y annonce une exposition de travaux d'élèves sur le sujet du problème du logement à New York («Appartements à louer»). (USA)

Education
Ausbildung
Education

520

521

522

523

524

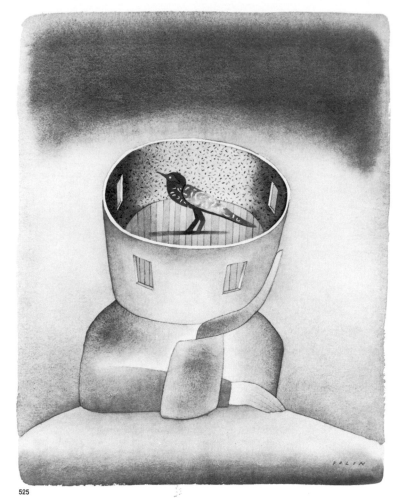

525

526

Habitat

ARTIST / KÜNSTLER / ARTISTE:

524 Yasuhiro Yomegida
525 Folon
526 Milton Glaser
527 André François

ART DIRECTOR:

524–527 Alan McDougall

AGENCY / AGENTUR / AGENCE:

524–527 Habitat Mothercare
Group Design Ltd.

PUBLISHER / VERLEGER:

524–527 Habitat Designs Ltd.

524–527 To mark its twentieth birthday *Habitat* furnishings invited five eminent artists from the five major countries where *Habitat* has stores to design five posters, four of which are shown here. The design (all with white border), format and paper are uniform. Fig. 524 shows "Mother and Children" by Japanese artist Yasuhiro Yomogida; Fig. 525 is "The Nest" by Belgian artist Folon; Fig. 526 shows Milton Glaser's "View from an English cottage into a French garden with Japanese objects, through American eyes"; Fig. 527 portrays "Good Morning", poster created by the French artist André François. (GBR)

524–527 Vier von fünf Plakaten, die von *Habitat* anlässlich des zwanzigjährigen Bestehens dieses Inneneinrichtungs-Konzerns bei Künstlern in Auftrag gegeben wurden. Sie stammen aus Ländern, in denen *Habitat* am besten vertreten ist. Die Gestaltung (alle mit weissem Rand), Format und Papier sind einheitlich. Abb. 524 zeigt «Mutter und Kinder» des Japaners Yasuhiro Yomogida, Abb. 525 «Das Nest» des Belgiers Folon, Abb. 526 Milton Glasers «Blick aus einem englischen Landhaus auf einen französischen Garten mit japanischen Objekten, durch amerikanische Augen», Abb. 527 «Guten Morgen» des Franzosen André François. (GBR)

524–527 A l'occasion de son 20e anniversaire l'entreprise de meubles et d'ameublement *Habitat* a commissionné cinq artistes internationaux, provenant chacun d'un des cinq pays principaux où *Habitat* a ses magasins, de créer cinq affiches dont quatre sont représentées ici près. Cadre blanc, format et papier identiques. Fig. 524: «Mère et enfants», du Japonais Yasuhiro Yomogida; fig. 525: «Le Nid», par le Belge Folon; fig. 526: «Vue d'un cottage anglais sur un jardin à la française parsemé d'objets japonais à travers des yeux américains», de Milton Glaser; fig. 527: «Bonjour», affiche réalisée par l'artiste français André François. (GBR)

527

528

529

528 A poster issued by AT&T, one of the 1984 Los Angeles Olympics sponsors. (USA)
529–534 Examples from a series of posters for the Olympics in Los Angeles which all bear the signature of the artist. They are of uniform size and portray athletes in various disciplines. Fig.529: discus thrower in pale grey and violet on dark ground, on grey paper; Fig.530: photograph with dark colour values; Fig.531: cycle racetrack in soft grey shades; Fig.532: javelin thrower in red vest on violet, yellow and blue background; Fig.533: in metallic red and blue tones; Fig.534: Multi- coloured flags on grey-beige background. (USA)

528 Von AT&T, einem der Sponsoren der Olympiade in Los Angeles herausgegebenes Plakat. (USA)
529–534 Beispiele aus einer Serie von Plakaten für die Olympiade in Los Angeles, die alle mit der Signatur des Künstlers versehen sind. Sie haben ein einheitliches Format und zeigen verschiedene Sportler in Bewegung. Abb.529: Diskuswerfer in Hellgrau und Violett vor dunklem Grund, auf grauem Papier; Abb.530: Aufnahme mit dunklen Farbwerten; Abb.531: Rennbahn in weichen Grautönen; Abb.532: rotes Trikot vor violett-gelb-blauem Hintergrund; Abb.533: in metallischen Rot- und Blautönen; Abb.534: bunte Fahnen auf graubeigem Grund. (USA)

528 Affiche publiée par AT&T, l'un des sponsors des Jeux Olympiques de Los Angeles. (USA)
529–534 Exemples d'affiches des Jeux Olympiques de Los Angeles dans une série signée par l'artiste. De format identique, elles présentent des athlètes en plein effort. Fig.529: Discobole gris et violet sur fond sombre, papier gris; fig.530: photo aux teintes assombries; fig.531: vélodrome aux tons adoucis; fig.532: le tricot de ce lanceur de javelot apparaît en rouge sur un fond violet, jaune et bleu; fig.533: tons métalliques rouges et bleus; fig.534: drapeaux multicolores sur fond beige gris. (USA)

ARTIST / KÜNSTLER / ARTISTE:

528 Michael David Brown
529 James Cross
530 Saul Bass
531 Arnold Schwartzman
532 John van Hammersveld
533 Charlie White/Paul Mussa
534 Marvin Rubin

ART DIRECTOR / DIRECTEUR ARTISTIQUE:

528 Michael David Brown
529 James Cross
530–532 Arnold Schwartzman/Larry Klein/Darrell Hayden
533, 534 Larry Klein/Darrell Hayden

AGENCY / AGENTUR / AGENCE – STUDIO:

528 Michael David Brown, Inc.
529 Cross Associates

PUBLISHER / VERLEGER / EDITEUR:

528 AT & T/Ewing-Robinson, Inc.
529–534 Los Angeles Olympic Organizing Committee

532

Games of the XXIIIrd Olympiad Los Angeles 1984

530

Games of the XXIIIrd Olympiad · Los Angeles 1984

531

GAMES OF THE XXIIIrd OLYMPIAD

LOS ANGELES 1984

533

GAMES OF THE XXIIIrd OLYMPIAD, LOS ANGELES, 1984

534

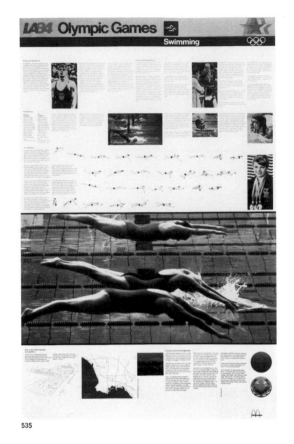

535

536

537

538

539

540

ARTIST / KÜNSTLER / ARTISTE:

537 Gjalt Van der Wyk
538–540 Brent Bear
541 Milton Glaser

DESIGNER / GESTALTER / MAQUETTISTE:

535–537 John R. Rieben
538–540 James Robie/Tony Woodward
541 Milton Glaser

ART DIRECTOR / DIRECTEUR ARTISTIQUE:

535–537 John R. Rieben
538–540 James Robie
541 Milton Glaser

AGENCY / AGENTUR / AGENCE – STUDIO:

535–537 Mobium
538–540 James Robie Design
541 Milton Glaser, Inc.

PUBLISHER / VERLEGER / EDITEUR:

535, 536 AT & T
537 Mobium Press
538–540 Los Angeles Olympic
         Organizing Committee
541 Proscenium Inc.

535, 536 Examples from a series of posters with colour and black-and-white photographs to mark the occasion of the Olympic Summer Games in Los Angeles. Each poster offers comprehensive information on a certain discipline in addition to the event's history, regulations and highlights of past games. Here: swimming and sailing. (USA)
537 Polychrome poster with illustrations of different sailing-boat types and sailing terms. (USA)
538–540 Three examples from a series of multi-coloured posters in uniform size for the Olympic Summer Games in Los Angeles, each devoted to a discipline; shown here for shooting, archery and fencing, respectively. (USA)
541 Poster published in the United States for the Olympic Winter Games in Sarajevo 1984. (USA)

535, 536 Beispiele aus einer Reihe von Plakaten mit Farb- und Schwarzweissaufnahmen (letztere für die Dokumentierung früherer Ereignisse), veröffentlicht anlässlich der Olympischen Sommerspiele in Los Angeles. Sie bieten jeweils ausführliche Informationen über eine der olympischen Disziplinen, hier Schwimmen und Segeln. (USA)
537 Mehrfarbiges Plakat mit Illustration verschiedener Segelboottypen und Fachausdrücke. (USA)
538–540 Drei Beispiele aus einer Serie von mehrfarbigen Plakaten in einheitlichem Format für die Olympiade in Los Angeles, die jeweils einer Disziplin gewidmet sind, hier dem Schiessen, Bogenschiessen und Fechten. (USA)
541 Für die olympischen Winterspiele 1984 in Sarajevo kreiertes Plakat. (USA)

535, 536 Affiches dans une série illustrée de photos couleur pour le présent, de photos noir et blanc pour les événements du passé, et qui a accompagné les Jeux Olympiques de Los Angeles. On y trouve une information détaillée sur diverses disciplines olympiques, ici la natation et la voile. (USA)
537 Affiche polychrome illustrant différents types de voiliers et termes de marine. (USA)
538–540 Exemples d'une série d'affiches polychromes au format uniforme consacrées aux disciplines olympiques lors des Jeux de Los Angeles, ici au tir, au tir à l'arc et à l'escrime. (USA)
541 Affiche créée à l'occasion des Jeux Olympiques d'hiver 1984 organisés à Sarajevo, capitale de la Bosnie-Herzégovine yougoslave. (USA)

XIV OLYMPIC WINTER GAMES ⬭⬭⬭ SARAJEVO 1984 YUGOSLAVIA

541

542–547 The Japanese artist Shigeo Fukuda has created intriguing visual illusions in his silk-screen posters. When Fig. 542 is turned the flat elliptic disc becomes three-dimensional. Fig. 543 shows that by the addition of a few simple lines the man's direction appears to have changed. Fig. 544: two figures walking with jackets upside-down over their heads—until the poster is turned 180 degrees—and there are heads where the buttocks were and the legs are walking on high. Fig. 545 is in red and grey and causes confusion with the "steps" illusion. Fig. 546 is in pink and black and half conceals a violinist and a pianist. Fig. 547 is in blue and red—16 legs drawn in one line. (JPN)
548 Illustration from a poster without text which was published by the French city of Montreuil as good wishes for the citizens. (FRA)

542–547 Visuelle Illusion ist das Thema dieser Siebdruckplakate des japanischen Künstlers Shigeo Fukuda. Wenn man Abb. 542 umdreht, ändert sich die Wirkung völlig, und aus der flachen Scheibe wird ein Oval. Abb. 543 zeigt, wie durch blosses Hineinzeichnen eines Revers und Kragens der Eindruck einer Vorderansicht entsteht. Beim Umdrehen von Abb. 544 ergeben sich zweigeteilte Gestalten mit den Köpfen in der Mitte. Abb. 545 (rot und grau) zeigt die Illusion der Treppe. Abb. 546 (rosa und schwarz) lässt einen Geiger und einen Pianisten erkennen. Abb. 547 (blau und rot) zeigt nach innen und aussen gerichtete Beine. (JPN)
548 Illustration eines Plakates, das von der französischen Stadt Montreuil für ihre Bürger veröffentlicht wurde. (FRA)

542–547 Ces affiches sérigraphiques de l'artiste japonais Shigeo Fukuda concernent des illusions d'optique. En retournant la fig. 542, on change radicalement l'effet du disque plat qui devient un ovale. La fig. 543 montre que l'insertion d'un seul détail, col et revers, transforme une vue de dos en une vue de face. En retournant la fig. 544, on obtient des figures partagées en deux, avec la tête au milieu. La fig. 545 (rouge et gris) démontre l'illusion de l'escalier. La fig. 546 (rose et noir) fait distinguer un violoniste et un pianiste. Quant à la fig. 547, exécutée en bleu et rouge, on y voit des jambes tournées vers l'intérieur et vers l'extérieur. (JPN)
548 Illustration d'une affiche publiée par la municipalité de Montreuil à l'intention de ses citoyens. (FRA)

542

543

544

545

546

547

548

ARTIST / KÜNSTLER / ARTISTE:

542–547 Shigeo Fukuda
548 Roman Cieslewicz

DESIGNER / GESTALTER / MAQUETTISTE:

542–547 Shigeo Fukuda
548 Roman Cieslewicz

ART DIRECTOR / DIRECTEUR ARTISTIQUE:

542–547 Shigeo Fukuda
548 Vincent Pachés

PUBLISHER / VERLEGER / EDITEUR:

542–547 Isetan Museum
548 Ville de Montreuil

Decorative Posters
Dekorative Plakate
Affiches décoratives

Decorative Posters
Dekorative Plakate
Affiches décoratives

ARTIST / KÜNSTLER / ARTISTE:

549, 553, 554 Richard Avedon
550–552 Tom Eckersley

DESIGNER / GESTALTER / MAQUETTISTE:

549, 553, 554 Marvin Israel
550–552 Tom Eckersley

PUBLISHER / VERLEGER / EDITEUR:

549, 553, 554 Andrew Grenshaw Ltd.
550–552 MDC Prints Ltd.

549, 553, 554 Examples from a series of posters available to the general public, in which Marilyn Monroe is posed in the guise of various famous filmstars. Fig. 553: Red dress, with white, red and pink balloons, background in shades of grey; Fig. 554: predominantly blue and grey tones. (USA)
550–552 Posters by MDC Prints Ltd. characterizing famous filmstars. Fig. 550 and 552 are mainly in black and white and Fig. 551 in two brown tones, orange and black on white stock. (GBR)

549, 553, 554 Beispiele aus einer im Handel erhältlichen Serie von Plakaten, auf denen Marilyn Monroe andere Schauspielerinnen verkörpert. Abb. 553 mit rotem Kleid und weissen, roten und rosa Luftballons, Hintergrund in Grautönen. Abb. 554 vorwiegend in Blau- und Grautönen. (USA)
550–552 Bei MDC Prints Ltd. erhältliche Plakate mit Porträts berühmter Schauspieler. Abb. 551 in zwei Brauntönen, Orange und Schwarz auf weissem Papier. (GBR)

549, 553, 554 Exemples d'affiches dans une série commercialisée où Marilyn Monroe incarne d'autres actrices. Fig. 553: robe rouge, ballons blancs, rouges et roses, fond en diverses nuances de gris. Les bleus et les gris prédominent dans la fig. 554. (USA)
550–552 Posters d'acteurs célèbres commercialisés par MDC Prints Ltd. Fig. 551: deux nuances de brun, orange et noir sur papier blanc. (GBR)

MARILYN MONROE AS THEDA BARA BY RICHARD AVEDON 1958

549

DIETRICH

550

GROUCHO

551

KEATON

552

MARILYN MONROE AS
CLARA BOW
BY RICHARD AVEDON 1958

553

MARILYN MONROE AS
LILLIAN RUSSELL
BY RICHARD AVEDON 1958

554

Paper / Papier: Papierfabrik Biberist–Biber GS SK3, blade coated, pure white, 150 gm² and
Biber Offset SK3, pure white, machine-finished, 140 gm² /
Biber-GS SK3, hochweiss, satiniert, 150 gm²
und Biber-Offset SK3, hochweiss, maschinenglatt, 140 gm²

Printed by / gedruckt von: Offset + Buchdruck AG, 8021 Zürich
(Colour pages and dust jacket / Farbseiten und Schutzumschlag),
Merkur AG, Langenthal (black and white / schwarzweiss)

Typesetting / Lichtsatz: Sauerländer AG, Aarau
(Univers, MONOTYPE-Lasercomp)

Binding / Einband: Maurice Busenhart SA, Lausanne

Glossy lamination / Glanzfoliierung: Durolit AG, Pfäffikon SZ